D1691345

Obbligato
1939–1979

Obbligato

1939–1979

Notes on a Foreign Service Career

BY

William H. Sullivan

W · W · Norton & Company

NEW YORK · LONDON

Copyright © 1984 by William H. Sullivan. *All rights reserved.* Published simultaneously in Canada by Stoddart, a subsidiary of General Publishing Co. Ltd, Don Mills, Ontario. Printed in the United States of America.
First Edition

THE TEXT OF THIS BOOK *is composed in photocomposition Baskerville, with display type set in Garamond Old Style. Composition and manufacturing by The Maple-Vail Book Manufacturing Group. Book design by Marjorie J. Flock.*

Library of Congress Cataloging in Publication Data
Sullivan, William H. (William Healy), 1922–
   Obbligato : notes on a foreign service career.
   1. Sullivan, William H. (William Healy), 1922–
   2. United States—Foreign relations—1945–
   3. Ambassadors—United States—Biography. I. Title.
E840.8.S84A36   1984   327.2′092′4 [B]   83–19502

ISBN 0-393-01809-1

W. W. Norton & Company, Inc., 500 Fifth Avenue, New York, N.Y. 10110
W. W. Norton & Company Ltd., 37 Great Russell Street, London WC1B 3NU
1 2 3 4 5 6 7 8 9 0

obbligato: *n.* a subordinate part to a solo in music

—*Webster's Seventh New Collegiate Dictionary*

Contents

	Introduction	9
One	The Storm Clouds 1939–1942	17
Two	Navy Days 1943–1946	22
Three	The Ends of Empires 1947–1949	78
Four	Occupying Japan 1950–1952	118
Five	Nurturing NATO 1953–1958	138
Six	Foggy Bottom 1959–1963	153
Seven	War in Indochina 1964–1968	196
Eight	The Indochina Peace Treaty 1969–1972	236
Nine	The Philippines 1973–1976	248
Ten	The Iranian Revolution 1977–1979	261

Obbligato
1939–1979

Introduction

WE ALL KNOW THAT EVENTS shape people and that people, in turn, shape events. This truism is best observed in a time of significant change. The four decades from 1939 to 1979 were such a time for the United States. During their span, the American people were spun through a series of material and emotional changes of greater intensity than any our society had known since the years of the Civil War. Those of us who have lived through that period can describe the various revolutions we have experienced in technology, in social mores, in family life, and in our perceptions of the world around us. We can also attempt to describe the way in which the international position of the United States has changed.

We know that, in the first few years of the 1940s, our nation was transported from the doubts and despair of the Great Depression to the self-confident euphoria of military victory and to the status of superpower. Our leaders, who, in the 1930s, had been reluctant to engage in foreign affairs, soon found themselves making choices and decisions affecting the lives of every human being on earth. The United States was the great winner in World War II. We emerged from that conflict as the paramount nation in the world. We had a monopoly on the atomic weapon, the most powerful conventional military forces, the most productive economy, and the most resilient political system. Harry Luce told us that we were entering "The American Century."

And yet, at the end of the 1970s, many of the old doubts and uncertainties had reasserted themselves in the American public mind. Most of the superlatives seemed ephemeral, and much of the splendor that followed from World War II seemed tarnished. Our frustration over Vietnam, our faltering economy, our restless society, and our listless political leadership were all troubling. Pundits had difficulty in describing our international stature.

One of the reasons for this difficulty has been the vast gap between public perceptions of the international scene and the more human dimensions of reality. As a people, we have, through most of our history, been intoxicated by some rather jingoistic exaggerations of the international context in which our nation exists. Perceiving through these distortions, most of the American public failed to understand that much of our postwar paramountcy was artificial and was due to the enormous destruction that other nations had suffered. Our apparent hegemony in the world was destined to be of short duration unless our leaders sought to perpetuate it unrealistically.

It is to the credit of our presidents, beginning with Roosevelt, that they understood this fact and resisted the temptation to try for a Pax Americana. Instead, they settled on a policy which would seek a world order balanced on a number of cooperating centers of power. But, when the most aggressive of these power centers—the Soviet Union—refused to cooperate, the tenor of our foreign policy pronouncements had to change. The language of leadership shifted from the rhapsody of the Four Freedoms to the rhetoric of the Cold War.

Introduction

From Truman through Nixon, our international actions were justified by statements that catered to the traditional jingoism of the American imperium. In order to command the support of Congress and the votes of the great American public, presidents had to stress American national security and American hegemony more than the facts would warrant. Even while their actions were deliberately reducing our international imperium, some leaders felt compelled, for reasons of domestic policy, to rationalize them in Cold War terms.

The alliances we have fostered, the wars we have fought, and the international confrontations we have faced all contributed to the perception of the United States as an expanding empire. And yet, I would argue, from Truman through Nixon, the facts were just the opposite. We were, as a nation, deliberately reducing our hegemony and shrinking our international responsibilities to a scope more commensurate with our national capabilities.

The situation that obtained under Carter is more difficult to assess. It is not clear that Carter personally had a concept for global policy. His Secretary of State, Cyrus Vance, clearly favored continuity of actions that would tailor our obligations to our capabilities. But his assistant for national security, Zbigniew Brzezinski, introduced a more primitive reliance on power politics that seemed to tempt Carter's sympathy to the detriment of the quiet professionalism of Vance. Hence, the confusion surrounding our foreign policy at the end of the 1970s was enough to confound our enemies, distress our friends, and trouble the great American public. The voters wanted our positions stated in simpler, less sophistic terms. They were tired of the obvious disparity between the rhetoric of our leadership and the objective facts that they could perceive in the world press. They were, in effect, the victims of their own delusions.

When an objective history of American international performance in the middle decades of this century is written from the perspectives of the next century, I believe that the pattern which will emerge will be more straightforward than the current record would suggest. It will be seen not as an effort to grasp for greater power but rather as a sustained attempt to devolve unwanted responsibilities on others worthy of our national respect. There has often been confusion between our attachment to those we could control and those we could respect. It was the sort of thing that refracted our relations with Charles de Gaulle at one end of the scale and Tacho Somoza at the other. But objective circumstances usually caused us eventually to opt for respect rather than control.

Our foreign policy during the four decades considered in this interpretation will ultimately be seen not as a series of rearguard actions by cohorts defending against assaults upon a jealously guarded empire, but rather as a constant struggle to find and develop worthy heirs to handle those elements of our hegemony we no longer wished to dominate. The problem was always to try to do this in a responsible way, so that the devolution would be constructive rather than chaotic.

Such a policy did not lend itself to great sweeping gestures or grandiloquent description. It was not a policy politically profitable for national leaders nor easily encompassed in the quick capsules of the television newscasters or the pundit columnists. It was messy and needed constant care and attention. It therefore did not especially attract the politically ambitious except when something went wrong and created a crisis. By and large, it was left to a collection of specialists and professionals to muddle through. These people became the centurions of a far different American Century than Harry Luce had envisaged.

At most, there were never more than a few thousand in this cohort. Most of us had been junior officers in World War II and chose to stay in government service out of some vague sense of responsibility for avoiding a repetition of that catas-

Introduction 13

trophe. Since we had been actively involved in winning most of the battles of that war, we knew how narrow were the margins of victory and at what great cost it had been achieved. We didn't see the world in sharp contrasting shades of black and white, but rather in the murky shades of grey that color most human endeavors.

We were deployed in the Cabinet and Congress, in the Armed Forces, in the Foreign Service, and occasionally in such private areas as the press; and we knew each other through mutual association or by reputation. We had an unspoken assumption that we all shared the same civilized objectives and that the only questions at issue concerned means rather than ends. Although many of us had been educated at Eastern universities, we were drawn from a broad geographic and social spectrum, and it would be inaccurate to suggest that we were an "Eastern Establishment." But there is no doubt that we dominated the execution of our country's international affairs during those four middle decades of this century.

My purpose in writing about some of the events of that period is not to extoll our cadre of centurions or even to try to explain our cult. It is rather to provide some anecdotal terms of reference which may help to illuminate the atmosphere within which we lived and worked. The anecdotes are arranged chronologically, but do not pretend to constitute an autobiography. They are, instead, subjective fragments of a career in the field of foreign policy.

I entered that career shortly after the United States was drawn into World War II. As a young naval officer, I served in destroyers in the Atlantic, Mediterranean, and Pacific theaters of the war. My squadron was nearly wiped out during the battles we fought. Only two of our original twelve ships remained when Japan surrendered. From the navy, I returned to the United States, took an advanced degree in graduate school, and married a classmate who had served as a woman marine and who, like myself, felt that something could be done better in the field of foreign policy to prevent the recurrence of global war. Marie became not only my wife and the mother of our four children, but a valuable, active partner in my foreign service career. When I took the examinations and became a Foreign Service officer of the United States in 1947, I brought our government two professionals for the price of one.

My service took us to Bangkok, to Calcutta, to Tokyo, to Naples, to Rome, and to The Hague before we returned to the United States in 1958. By that time, we had accumulated a family of two boys and two girls, a world of experience, and a certain seniority in the service. After three years in the Department of State dealing with Southeast Asia, I was assigned to Geneva to participate in the international conference on Laos. That assignment involved me with Indochina and eventually Vietnam. By 1964, I found myself in Saigon and, later that year, as ambassador to Laos.

After four-and-one-half years of attempting to stem the tide of North Vietnamese aggression in Laos, I returned to Washington and went on to Paris for the tedious negotiations that ended American involvement in the Vietnam war. After that, I went to the Philippines as ambassador for four years, and then, in 1977, to Tehran as ambassador to Iran. I arrived there just as the revolution against the Shah began to take form, and I stayed until the Ayatollah Khomeini succeeded in overthrowing the old regime. Because of sharp disagreements with the Carter administration's handling of events in Iran, I resigned from the Foreign Service in June of 1979, as the decade drew to an end.

In retrospect, it is apparent that I enjoyed some unusual opportunities for insight into events that have shaped our current world. Some of the people who will be encountered in these pages had much to do with shaping those events. However, I am not attempting to usurp the function of future historians, who will assess the main themes of those events and the roles of those personalities. Instead, I am recording some of the obbligato that was subordinate to the more spectacular performances. It is hoped that when played against the background of that obbligato, the main themes and personalities may be more subtly appreciated, and as Wordsworth once wrote, "the still, sad music of humanity" may once again assume "ample power to chasten and subdue."

Chapter One

The Storm Clouds
1939–1942

In 1939, I entered Brown University as a freshman. As our class assembled on campus, the German army was pounding across Poland and World War II had begun. In retrospect, it is strange to realize how far that European conflict seemed from our New England college scene. Most of the students shared the general national feeling that our country should remain neutral and let the governments on the other side of the Atlantic settle their differences without American involvement. The "phoney war" period of American opinion which followed the blitzkrieg in Poland reinforced this sense of isolationism.

Brown was then quite a small college, with a student body of about 2,000, and a New England regional character. Most of the students came from Rhode Island and the adjacent states. A few came from "the West," which was usually described as any place across the Mississippi. Many of these were from New England families who had migrated with the frontier and wished their sons to have the benefit of an Eastern education.

A number of my ancestors had gone to Brown, and I was naturally expected to follow in their footsteps. It was tacitly assumed that I would graduate, go on to law school, and join the family law firm. When I matriculated, I really had no other intention.

Gradually, the war in Europe began to impinge upon the serenity of our college life. Our new president, Henry Wriston, despite being from the isolationist heartland of the Middle West, was an internationalist. Distinguished members of the faculty, such as Leland Goodrich in political science and James Hedges in history, spoke openly in their classrooms of the need for American involvement in the enveloping tragedy of Europe. Our dean, Samuel Arnold, who was a chemist, spent most of his time away from campus recruiting scientists for some mysterious enterprise called "The Manhattan Project."

Well into 1941, however, the focus of political attention on campus remained with domestic politics. The campaign of 1940, which pitted Wendell Willkie against Franklin Roosevelt (who was running for an unprecedented third term), brought out a surprising burst of partisan activity among students and faculty alike. There was active recruiting on campus by a whole spectrum of youth organizations, ranging from the most conservative to the communists.

As might be imagined from its origins, Brown was quite a conservative institution. It had been founded, in the colonial period, as a Baptist seminary, and it had taken nearly two centuries for the college to lose its sectarian character. Many of its old traditions survived. For example, there was compulsory chapel every Thursday noon, when the entire student body was assembled in Sayles Hall for services more or less of a religious character. During my years on campus, these services tended to become politicized. Speakers were imported to argue domestic or foreign policy issues, and often President Wriston used the pulpit to express his own partisan views.

The Storm Clouds

Sometimes, these views concerned the war in Europe, but more, they were directed against That Man in the White House. Wriston did not care for Roosevelt and seemed to get a great pleasure out of making that fact known in fairly harsh rhetoric.

Although it didn't much matter in the mores of those years, Wriston's views were offensive to a large portion of the student body, who, despite their conservative origins, admired Roosevelt and the New Deal. A good portion of the faculty also took issue with their university president, some more vocally than others. I remember one occasion when Professor Hedges came back fuming from one of Wriston's more flamboyant chapel orations, and devoted his lecture to a vigorous rebuttal of the speech. He was interrupted in the full flight of his emotions by an activist conservative student who, in effect, told him he was out of order in criticizing the leader of the university. Hedges was so outraged at being provoked in such fashion that he ran off the lecture platform, seized one of the long poles used to lower the great Palladian windows of Manning Hall, and used it as a lance to run the student out of the hall. The next session of the class was preceded by a little ceremony in which both professor and student apologized to a tolerantly amused class for their indecorous behavior.

In the meantime, however, the war was becoming more intrusive. By the time France and the Low Countries were overrun and the Japanese attacked Southeast Asia, Brown "accelerated" its academic program by eliminating summer vacations so that we would graduate earlier and be prepared to enter military service at the time the newly established national conscription would overtake us. When the Japanese attacked Pearl Harbor, we were well into this accelerated curriculum. On that particular Sunday, I happened to be at Yale University, attending a student conference on Latin America. One of my fellow students from Brown, who was attending with me, was a Peruvian named Cesar Graña. At the time the

Japanese attack was announced to our gathering, Cesar and I were seated together. He was astonished by the way in which the news was imparted and received.

As I recall it, a stuffy old professor from Columbia, who was the presiding dignitary at the conference, and who wore a blue serge suit and a high starched collar, stood up at an appropriate interlude in the conference proceedings. He said he had an important announcement to make, but he did not wish it to interrupt the work for which we were assembled. He then told us of the attack in Hawaii and the Philippines, gave us five minutes to discuss this development among ourselves, and immediately reconvened us for a continuing pursuit of our agenda. Cesar was flabbergasted by the fact that this student gathering, made up almost entirely of young men for whom the news meant military service in a world war, accepted the old professor's stern injunctions and returned diligently to a discussion of esoteric events in Argentina. He told me later that in Peru, the gathering would have burst into a frenzy, adopted a number of patriotic resolutions, formed itself into a line of march, and paraded to the nearest government building to demonstrate its martial resolve. The behavior of the American student representatives at Yale on December 7, 1941, reflected a culture and a tradition that most of the rest of the world would have found hard to explain.

That day, however, ended once and for all whatever neutralist, isolationist sentiments remained on the campus at Brown. Our purpose after that was to finish our curriculum as rapidly as possible, join the military, and help defend the "Free World." We were made all the more impatient for that task by the continuing series of military disasters that struck our forces, especially our Navy, in the Southwest Pacific. It was therefore with some sense of liberation that I joined the procession in the following winter and marched down College Hill to the Old Baptist Meeting House for the traditional Brown Commencement. I had done well at the university and

The Storm Clouds

was graduated summa cum laude. I was also designated to deliver the Class Oration.

The subject I chose for my speech was Harry Luce's editorial "The American Century." Rather than giving it bombastic support, I took the line that the days of empire and hegemony were over, that America's destiny was not to dominate the world but rather to live with and cope with other people, other cultures, and other powers that were alien to our values and occasionally anathema to our ideals. According to the *Providence Journal* the following day, I said, "We must aid in repairing not only the damage suffered by our Allies, but also that sustained by our enemies—damage which we ourselves have inflicted. We must treat these people whom we shall have conquered not as a captive horde, but as nations of men, each similar to ourselves. It will be no easy task to view with dispassion those who have killed our brothers and our sons." I had no way of knowing it at the time, but it was a theme which would become the leitmotif of my professional life.

Chapter Two

Navy Days
1943–1946

I<small>N 1942, I ENLISTED</small> in the navy. After a mandatory period of service as an apprentice seaman, I took midshipman training and was commissioned as an ensign. My first assignment was as assistant gunnery officer aboard a destroyer on duty in the North Atlantic. Because I also became the junior officer aboard, tradition decreed that I should be assigned additional duties as wardroom mess treasurer. The mess treasurer was responsible for stocking the officers' galley with those foods and condiments which made wardroom fare superior to that of the enlisted men. He then divided the costs of those provisions equally among the ship's officers and collected the shares on a monthly basis.

When I joined, the ship was in Boston Navy Yard for repairs, and, therefore, reprovisioning became my first responsibility. In those days, ships chandlers representatives roamed the docks with order books in hand and were delighted to encounter a neophyte mess treasurer, who could be wheedled into large purchases from their gourmet catalogues. I was soon beseiged by these gregarious hucksters. The executive officer made clear to me that the ship's captain came out of the old China service and rigidly maintained the tradition of curry tiffin every Sunday, no matter what the weather or sea conditions. He also specified that it had to be curry with thirteen side dishes and that I should assure that we never ran out of the means to serve them.

My first priority with my chosen chandler was to lay in an adequate store of side dishes, and I relied on the salesman to tell me what I needed. He was used to the China fleet rituals and ticked off the chutney, the shredded cocoanut, the chives, and all the other condiments with aplomb. At the end of the list, we came to something called Bombay duck. By this time, I felt pretty cocky about my competence in this new routine, and didn't deign even to ask what Bombay duck was. I casually ordered a gross, one hundred and forty-four boxes of it, signed the order, and paid for it with a check on the wardroom mess fund.

A few days later, when the order was delivered alongside, and the mess stewards were busy storing it below decks, the chief mess steward came to see me and asked whether there was some error with the Bombay duck order. He said there were 144 one-pound boxes of the stuff, and we usually consumed only about two pounds a year. It was only then that I discovered that Bombay duck was a British colonial name for a heavily salted dried fish, which was broken up into small chips and served very sparingly with the curry. We were sailing the next day, and there would have been no time to track down the chandler, convince him to take back 120 or so of his boxes, and get a check from his company in credit; so I decided to chalk this folly up to experience, store the boxes, and hope my colleagues in the mess wouldn't ask why their shares were so high that month.

Over a year later, we were docked once again in Boston, and I was sought out by that same crafty chandler, who slyly asked whether we happened to have any Bombay duck remaining in our stores. It seemed that the captain of a newly commissioned aircraft carrier, with an officer complement nearly fifty times greater than our destroyer, was from the old China service and wanted curry tiffin with thirteen side dishes every Sunday. We were quite happy to unload most of the 142 boxes remaining, but our captain, as president of the wardroom mess, refused to let the incumbent mess treasurer make any profit on my providential trove.

The other aspect of my wardroom mess duties was to supervise the mess stewards. In those days, the navy was segregated, and the only blacks aboard were the officers' mess stewards. They cooked, served meals, cleaned staterooms, took our soiled clothing to the ship's laundry, returned it carefully to our wardrobes, and otherwise acted as batmen to the officers. There were ten of them and only twenty officers. We were, in other words, very well taken care of, with one steward serving each two officers. For their sleeping quarters, the stewards had a small compartment of their own, and at battle stations, they were assigned to handle powder charges for the main battery, down in the lowest handling rooms of the barbettes. They were, in short, about as thoroughly segregated as was possible on a 300 foot ship with a 300 man crew.

In matters of administration and discipline, this little band was also treated differently than other members of the crew. They were the sole responsibility of the wardroom mess treasurer, who approved their duty schedule, checked on the tidiness of their quarters, supervised their personal hygiene, and controlled their leave and liberty privileges. When I became mess treasurer for what turned out to be a four-month stint until a more junior officer came aboard, I was given, along with the inventory of stores, the check book, and the record of accounts, the liberty cards of all the stewards. Without those liberty cards, they could not go ashore when we were in port. In order to get their cards for that purpose, they had to come to me, convince me that their chores were all done, their bunks were made, their uniforms were clean, their shoes were shined, and their fingernails cut. Only then could they go ashore. The navy, in the interwar years, had been run very largely by Southern gentlemen.

In those first few days in Boston, I realized that one liberty card had never been used. It belonged to a very quiet, but very efficient, young black man whom we shall call Jefferson. He was from Mississippi, an abandoned child who had been raised in an orphanage run by nuns and who had received a good education, not only in the three Rs, but also in the piano, which he played with great style and talent. He had also been quite effectively instructed in the place which a young black man occupied in a society run by white gentry. He had joined the ship in Boston, only a few days before I had.

On the day before we were to sail, I found Jefferson in the galley when I was inspecting it before lunch. He stood at attention when I entered and stared straight ahead. I told him that I had noticed his liberty card had never been used and asked whether he disliked Boston as a liberty port. After much hemming and hawing he explained to me that his pay card had not yet caught up with him and that he had no money to spend if he went ashore. He had concluded that, without money, it was better to stay aboard. I checked in the ship's office and disovered that the yeoman in charge had sent for the pay card, but that it had not arrived, and that Navy regulations strictly forbade the advancement of any official funds to enlisted men, especially to black mess stewards.

I had grown up in a small town in Rhode Island and had had very little experience with blacks. In fact, I had never met a black until my mother took me to New York as a boy of about four. I remember the occasion well because I caused some embarrassment when I did. My mother, whose family was from New York, took my brother and me down to visit our relatives on what was considered, in the twenties, to be a considerable journey. We sailed on a vessel of the Old Fall River Line from Providence to Manhattan. That, in itself, was quite an adventure. My brother, who was not much more than a year older, shared a cabin with me while my mother had the adjoining cabin.

We sailed from Providence at about eight in the evening, after everyone in New England had already had dinner. Nevertheless, dinner was served in the rather elegant dining salon as we moved slowly down Narragansett Bay. The ship was a side-wheeler, and the chunk-a-chunk of the huge, glistening piston and travelling rods gave a sort of stately rhythm to the passage. At about ten, we rounded Point Judith and headed out to the Sound. When we reached the three-mile limit, a bell was rung, and a great cheer arose. Prohibition was surpassed! Padlocks were unlocked, panels were slid back, and the bar was opened in the grand salon. Attractive young ladies, whom my mother probably never realized were prostitutes, appeared from nowhere, and my brother and I were shuffled off to bed. My mother, I suspect, lay sleepless in the next cabin guarding against the possibility that we might decide to wander into the iniquity of that grand salon and be lost forever to perdition.

But, we survived and slept soundly through the revels, which apparently ended only when the vessel entered the narrows, where the waters were less than six miles wide and the rules of Prohibition once again came into force. (Later, when I studied international law, I came to the conclusion that the waters of Long Island Sound hardly qualified as international waters, but I suspect these refinements were overlooked by the Volstead Act enforcers in those years.) The bell, which announced the restoration of padlocks and which wags said also signalled the time for all businessmen to return to their own cabins, woke my brother and me (but not our mother) in time for us to get dressed and out on deck as we sailed by Throg's Neck and down the busy waters of the East

River. I remember, on that and other similar trips, the thrill of slipping under the great bridges and seeing the skyscrapers of Manhattan. The Woolworth Building was the paramount structure in those days, and the Brooklyn Bridge our favorite.

We docked, with much tooting of whistles and throwing of lines, on the Manhattan side, just south of Brooklyn Bridge, at about eight in the morning. In theory, the businessman from New England had made a restful voyage and was landed close to Wall Street before the New York business day began. In practice, most of them lay abed for a couple of hours and the breakfast service in the dining salon lasted until midday. We three were off the ship, however, as soon as the gangplank was secured and our baggage could be brought to join us. And there, I met my first black man. He was large and rather resplendent, in a brown uniform with jodhpurs and gleaming brown riding boots. He held his cap in his hand and his glistening white teeth were fixed in a smile of welcome. He was my uncle's chauffeur and he was there to greet us and drive us to the home of my mother's sister. But I was practically paralyzed by his appearance. His black skin shone in the bright morning sunlight, and he spoke with a voice that resonated in baritone contrast to the reedy New England twang I had known all my life. Bags were stowed, doors opened, jump seats pulled down, and we were settled in the posh back seat of the car before I could recover my tongue.

Stunned by the chauffeur and his black skin, the first question I asked was "Does it hurt?" Fortunately, the car was one of those stately old cabriolets with a solid glass partition between the driver's seat and the passengers. Communication was through a system with carved horns and a flexible tube. Consequently, my mother was able to admonish me for my rude, open-mouthed staring and, at the same time, gently answer my question. In retrospect, I have always considered her answer ingeniously inspired. She assured me that black skin was not the result of burns, accident, or deformity, and did not cause physical pain. But, she said, there was a lot of pain associated with being black because many white people didn't like the color and were unpleasantly mean to those who carried it. She suggested that my staring had been hurtful to the chauffeur and that I should be careful to avoid such indiscretions in the future. In general, she advised both my brother and me to be especially kind to black people, because life was hard for them. I recall that my brother and I both took this counsel so seriously in the next few days that the chauffeur must have found us curiously provincial.

A few years later, I had another, even more interesting introduction to blacks. My father's younger brother, John, was the junior partner in the family law firm and a bachelor. He lived in the old family home, doted upon and taken care of by two older maiden sisters, who never really shared his libertarian intellectual interests or his hobbies. He was a linguist, a leader in prison reform, a geneticist who experimented with breeding chickens and dahlias, and, withal, the head of the Rhode Island Board of Canvassers, which tried to keep the election systems honest.

In one of his more quixotic undertakings, Uncle John sought to get the state prison system to introduce a more liberal parole regime. As a test case, he sponsored an old black man, descendant of slaves, who had been condemned to life in prison in the accidental murder of his wife. He and his wife had lived in a sort of cabin on the Dean Estates, a huge plantationlike apple orchard near our home. Dan Hawkins and his wife both worked in the Dean home (locally it was called the John M. Dean Mansion), and both enjoyed tippling from the liquor stock that was abundant there, before Prohibition. One evening, they both had had too much to drink, got into an argument, and eventually into a fight during which their kerosene lamp was upset and exploded. Dan managed to get out of the cabin but collapsed outside. His wife died in the ruins and he, incompetently defended, was sentenced to life imprisonment without parole.

He was a model prisoner and became a trusty, working in the chaplain's office. He learned to read and write and eventually came to my uncle's attention. By this time, Dan had spent more than twenty years in contrite imprisonment and was a perfect example of the potential parolee. However, he had no relatives or others who could vouch for his status if he were released. And, so, Uncle John became his guarantor.

As he soon discovered, this guarantee meant more than just a legal obligation. Dan was a born dependent. He had descended from household slaves and he had worked as a household servant. He knew no other life or profession. He was over 60 when he was paroled and was unlikely to learn another livelihood at that age. It soon became clear that he was my uncle's charge, not only legally, but economically as well.

However, with two maiden sisters taking care of the household, Uncle John hardly had need of a manservant. With great discretion, he decided he could use someone to assist him with his chickens and his dahlias. This, in itself, caused some problems, since my brother and I earned pin money from these two hobbies. My brother assisted on the chickens largely by grinding shells to mix with corn so that gizzards were exercised, while I trimmed and sprayed stalks, sanded and boxed bulbs, and tagged experimental cross breeds during the growing season. But this matter was easily resolved when it was arranged that we should continue to receive the same money for less work, while Dan took over some of our more demanding chores.

His housing arrangements were provided by a rather simple expedient. The chicken coop assigned to the Rhode Island Reds was expropriated—they were overly inbred anyway. A wooden floor was laid on top of the cement foundation. Insulation was added. Heating and plumbing were installed. Dan became a permanent feature. He declined to eat in the house, but came to the kitchen and took away enormous servings from Aunt Deed when she rang a cowbell and handed him a huge platter to take back to his rooms. The plates always returned empty, and I assume from Dan's slender figure that the chickens enjoyed a far richer diet than my uncle ever knew.

In the summer, he mowed the lawns, raked under the trees, and trimmed the hedges. In the winter, he shovelled the walks and chipped the ice away. And, at Thanksgiving, Christmas, and at rare times in between, he donned his black suit, white shirt, black tie and white gloves to do what he loved best. He was an excellent butler and would have preferred that role every day of his life if it hadn't encroached on the jealous prerogatives of my maiden aunts.

So, he contented himself, in the spring, summer, and early fall, in learning to breed dahlias. Uncle John had gone a long way in crossing single, double, and even quadruple dahlia strains in a complicated formula that required careful control over stray stamens for periods ranging up to eight years. Although I was permitted to assist in some minor functions of this program, I was carefully isolated from the more sensitive features of pollination and record keeping that required meticulous controls. Dan, however, began to work his way into my uncle's confidence in these matters. He was a man who had gone into prison semiliterate, with a very limited vocabulary and a rudimentary sense of mathematics. In those twenty years, he had realized the value of a better education and had applied himself to gain one. In mathematics, he had become a quick and accurate calculator, with a fairly sophisticated knowledge of algebra as well.

In reading, his scope had been limited. The chaplain had given him a full set of Gibbon's *Decline and Fall of the Roman Empire*, which he read every night in his cell. Apparently, no one ever told him that he had the right of access to the prison library, because he confined his reading to a repetitive study of Gibbon. How many times he reread it in those twenty years is hard to imagine, but the fact is that he must have become one of the world's foremost scholars of Gibbon, if not of that period in Roman history. Here was a man who knew precious little of anything else that had happened in the world, but who knew, in detail, all the complex turns and twists of Roman politics, from the time of the early Caesars through the glories of the Byzantine empire, to the collapse of Constantine, and the triumph of the barbarians.

As we worked our way among the dahlias, I used to listen to Dan and Uncle John discussing in great animation the characters of various Roman leaders, their foibles, their mistakes, the speculation on what might have been if Scipio Africanus or Claudius had done otherwise than they did, and the fate of the various Roman military campaigns. For Dan it was the only reality that he knew. He didn't bother to read the daily newspapers on events in the United States as we spiralled into a great depression. His world was two thousand years away, and the people around him lived lives that did not interest him.

These esoteric relations with a tiny segment of blacks prepared me very poorly to deal with the young black mess stewards who became my charges in my first serious responsibility as a naval officer. They were particularly irrelevant in dealing with the plight of poor Jefferson, who had lost his pay card and had no money. But the prospect of a young sailor heading off into the North Atlantic in the fall of the year with no liberty in beautiful Boston seemed hard to bear. I had two twenty-dollar bills in my pocket and I gave one to Jefferson along with his liberty card, and insisted he go ashore.

That effect of that gesture on Jefferson was something I never expected. Apparently, I was the first white man who had ever shown trust in this Mississippi waif. Twenty dollars was a rather princely sum for a young black sailor in the days when they earned a little over thirty dollars a month, but I had not made him sign or otherwise pledge for it. In actuality, since I controlled all his affairs, including his pay account, it was no risk whatsoever to me. But, for him, it was a radical departure from his past and one which I understood only years later when the civil rights movement made me more conscious of the station of blacks in the South.

This simple action resulted in a relationship that was extraordinary. Jefferson, in effect, became my personal batman and I became his surrogate family. Had I been a proper Annapolis product, I probably would have cut his attentions sharply and resisted the subtle seductions they entailed. But he made life too comfortable for that. He saw to it that he was always assigned to my stateroom, which was visibly more polished than even the captain's cabin. My laundry was always the first back, always impeccable. On midwatches, in the dark of night, he would show up on the bridge, with a milkshake or a hot chocolate, depending on the season. My dessert servings were always palpably larger than others in the wardroom. I was consistently pampered.

In return, I was given confidences about the problems of the messboys that I was expected to resolve. Jefferson became their collective conduit to me, because I was considered to have some responsible liege line toward him, and, by association, toward all of them. It was my first introduction to the dependent, paternalistic pattern of the South, inconsistent with the fiercely independent Yankee-Irish habits of redoubtable privacy in New England. In effect, I became their channel to whoever was acting as mess treasurer for the next two years until Jefferson was transferred.

Well before he was transferred, a minor transformation began. I had somewhere along the line accumulated the additional duty of ship's welfare officer and discovered there was a rather healthy kitty of funds that had been contributed to the ship by the shipyard workers at the time of her commissioning. I took some of these funds on one occasion when we were in port at Norfolk and bought a number of musical instruments, including a small upright piano. In no time at all, the crew had organized a ship's orchestra and made Jefferson the piano player. His talent and ability soon made him the orchestra leader and one of the most popular men aboard ship. He could play anything and gladly obliged, whenever he was available, up to the moment of evening tatoo.

Shortly after the Normandy landings, Jefferson was promoted and transferred to another ship in the Atlantic fleet. This time he took his pay card with him, and he was a far more confident young man than the day he first crossed our gangplank. A few months later, I saw him in Marseilles.

We had gone down to the Mediterranean after Normandy to take part in the invasion of Southern France, which proved to be a piece of cake. We had put ashore a force of U.S., French, and Senegalese forces at St. Tropez, and moved down the coast to take over Toulon. Then we had been summoned urgently back to Marseilles on a bizarre mission—to accept the surrender of a German force at the Chateau d'If, scene of the tales of the Count of Monte Cristo. It seems that the small German garrison, looking through their field glasses, realized they were to be attacked by Senegalese forces and panicked. They envisaged all sorts of atrocities and offered to surrender on the condition they could be taken into custody by Americans. We took a barge load of them in tow and bestowed them on a large prisoner camp established to house a column, composed very largely of Austrians, that had marched over from Toulouse looking for a place to lay down their arms.

As a matter of fact, the German fears of the Senegalese were groundless. They were superbly disciplined troops, trained and officered by the French Foreign Legion. They were also most impressive physical specimens, obviously handpicked for their appearance. All of them were over six feet, trim, well muscled, and strong. With the tribal warrior slashes on their cheeks, they were splendid looking soldiers.

But the French Foreign Legion martinets had made them so conscious of the respect due an officer that they were rather awesome. I remember walking along a sidewalk in Oran with another U.S. naval officer when we were spotted by four Senegalese soldiers in the process of crossing the street. They spontaneously snapped to attention and held their freeze until we could return the salute. In the meantime, the frenetic auto traffic of the French *colons* cut perilously close to them on both sides while we watched in horror with the sickening feeling they would all be killed merely for the sake of French military etiquette.

My fleeting encounter with Jefferson in Marseilles came about because of these same Senegalese. Marseilles is an old seafaring city with the usual amenities for sailors, including a thriving red-light district. As soon as the invading French forces established order in the city, they turned their attention to a careful regulation of the oldest profession, and provided one street of houses exclusively for the use of their Senegalese mercenaries. The American naval units in port had been advised of these arrangements, and the traditional reply from our Senior Officer Present was that the entire red-light district would be off limits to the American fleet.

A canvass of U.S. ships in port soon established that I was the only French-speaking officer available, and I was inevitably put in charge of the shore patrol, with the primary responsibility of returning drunken sailors to their ships and arresting any found in the bordellos. My first quick run through the city indicated that our sailors, with cigarette cartons in the ample trousers of their uniforms, were doing far better outside the bordellos than they would have done within them. But, I made the mandatory inspection of the red-light district anyway. All was routine until I reached the farthest street, which was the one reserved for the Senegalese.

There, a carnival was in progress. The whores there were probably among the coarsest in the enclave. They wore short red dresses with nothing under them, and, in the brief intervals when they were sitting down, they splayed their legs to leave nothing to the imaginations of their clients. Drinks were served at the bars, phonograph music blared, and sporadic dancing went on. There was a parade of the lusty young Senegalese troops, each whetting his courage on a couple of beers or a cognac, strutting across the floor to choose his whore, and then standing in rather glowing pride as she fished inside his trousers, produced his generous masculine member for the other whores to admire with whistles and applause, and finally following her with docile lope up the stairs to the business part of the establishment. I decided there was no possibility American sailors would choose to compete in this milieu.

My surprise was considerable, therefore, when I came out of the most raucous bordello and, looking across the street, spied Jefferson and a fellow messboy from his new ship. Jefferson nearly collapsed when he saw me and whipped to attention in a sharp salute. He and his companion stumbled over each other in explaining that they had become lost while returning to their ship, and they hustled away toward the port. My paternalistic feelings toward Jefferson and his obvious walk on the wild side surprised and amused me. In almost any other circumstance, this chance encounter would have provided grist for the preprandial chatter in the wardroom before the captain descended for dinner; but somehow, I couldn't bring myself to violate Jefferson's confidence through indiscreet gossip. I decided in my own mind that he had been led astray by a raffish companion and that, at bottom, he was still that shy little orphan who would one day make the nuns proud of his purity.

The sequel came several months later in Panama, when we were crossing through the canal with a number of other ships from the Atlantic fleet to join the war against the Japanese. Once again, because I spoke some Spanish, I was assigned as head of the shore patrol. Panama City was a pretty raunchy place in those days, and famous spots such as Ma Kelly's Bar attracted talent from all over the world.

I had made the tour of the big night spots on the main street and found most things in good order. In some of the louder ones, I left a petty officer behind, to stand conspicuously near the bar with his arms folded over his billy club and his .45 caliber automatic ominous in its white holster. That sort of presence always had a calming effect. On the second street, in some of the more discreet bordellos, things seemed to be busy, but in a quiet, efficient way. I decided not even to enter them, but halfway down the street, something caught my ear. The music of a barrelhouse piano sounded somehow familiar. So, I sidled up on the porch and pressed my nose against the window. There, in a lush Victorian parlor was a touching scene. Two or three chief petty officers sat quietly drinking with strikingly beautiful girls, dressed in handsome evening gowns and coiffed in the latest style. At the piano, relaxed and cool, sat Jefferson, playing his blues, and beside him on the piano bench was an elegant blonde, her dress off one shoulder to reveal her tawny white skin, with one hand gently stroking the back of Jefferson's neck. I tiptoed off the porch and down the street, thinking how the war and the navy had changed that young man's life.

— 2 —

In the early years of the war, naval operations in the North Atlantic followed a pattern that had been developed during the period of American neutrality. Convoys from "the arsenal of democracy" formed up on the east coast, from Norfolk, Baltimore, Philadelphia, and New York, sailing under the protection of the Coast Guard until they passed through the Cape Cod canal and were joined by the ships from Boston. Then, from Boston, Portsmouth, and Portland, Maine, the scrappy grey destroyers of the Navy took over, whipped them into formation, and herded them east to the "chop line," a meridian off Iceland where they were met by the British Royal Navy and escorted to their destinations in the United Kingdom or the Soviet Union.

The enemies to this movement were the stormy seas and the German U-boat wolfpacks in the western reaches as well as the ice floes and Stuka dive bombers in the North Sea and the Channel. Other impediments were the mechanical breakdowns of the freighters, tramps, and tankers in the convoy as well as the general indiscipline and occasional incompetence of the merchant crews. For the destroyers of the U.S. Atlantic fleet, each convoy was a new battle in the relentless effort to keep the sea lanes open. Sometimes, convoys would consist largely of well-built, well-maintained, and well-operated merchantmen that could maintain a steady steaming speed, control their boiler rooms to prevent easily detectable plumes of jet black smoke, enforce blackouts, execute changes of course correctly, and keep proper intervals of space and distance. Sometimes they were composed of a motley collection of tramps sailing under different flags, operating erratically at various speeds, spewing smoke, flashing lights at night, inept in their station-keeping, and unpredictable in their execution of changes in course and speed.

Whatever the character of the convoy, it was the navy's task to shepherd it safely to the point of exchange with the British. Depending on the size of the convoy, we sometimes used as many as two squadrons of twelve destroyers each to perform this task, and, on rare crossings, were joined by a cruiser, presumably to guard against surface raiders. We operated in the conventional V-shaped pattern, sweeping ahead of the main body of ships, but sometimes broke into more innovative search procedures when German submarines seemed to be trying solitary raids. When the U-boats struck, the destroyers were a frenzy of activity, dropping depth charges, criss-crossing the areas of contact, firing their main batteries when a submarine was flushed to the surface, and desperately dodging the bubbling wakes of the torpedoes that were fired into their midst. Then, with the sickening explosions and the smoky fires from the ships in the convoy that were hit, eventually doubling back through the oil and debris on the surface of the sea to look for survivors.

The encounters with the wolfpacks grew less frequent as the awful attrition of German submarines reduced the numbers that could be sent on long-range patrols. By 1943, we were more likely to encounter the single U-boat on lonely patrol, hoping by its cunning to penetrate our screen and spray a spread of torpedoes into the hapless hulls of the convoy. Therefore, our pattern became one of constant vigil against the single raider that would attempt to move undetected on our flanks, or even to overtake our charges from the stern. This meant a routine of dawn and evening twilight alerts that robbed us of our sleep and made the daily work schedule of a navy ship almost impossible to complete. Every morning at about 4:30 a.m., the ship would be sent to general quarters, with all battle stations manned, damage control plans, including the shutting down of all ventilation, in effect, and the period of watchful waiting would begin. It was the operating assumption that the lone raiders approached the conveys at night and took position so that their periscopes could function against the silhouettes in the morning twilight; or conversely, that they closed from the flanks or from astern during the daytime and planned to fire their weapons in the evening twilight and steal away under cover of darkness. Hence, evening alerts covered the long hours of sundown.

A whole generation of North Atlantic destroyer sailors must have nauseous memories of those interminable twilight alerts, when all the ship's machinery was still except for the main turbines, when the eerie red lights in the passageways and ammunition rooms gave every face a deadly pallor and when the stale, warm air of the compartments made breathing a clumsy chore.

Navy Days

Fortunately, during my first few months in the North Atlantic, my battle station was on deck with the 40 millimeter batteries and the torpedoes. This meant that I at least could breathe, even if sometimes the air was saturated with noxious diesel fumes. But, it also meant that, in foul weather, I had no place to shelter from the wrath of the North Atlantic.

When I chose the navy, I conceived of it as far preferable to the mud and misery of the army. It seemed a relatively civilized way to go about the essential incivility of war. But, when I got my baptism in the North Atlantic, I was sure I had made a mistake. The biting cold, the relentless heaving and pitching of the wind-wrestled sea, and the great green-grey masses of water that swept over the decks of the ship were more than I had bargained for. In those little Bristol class destroyers, wave after wave of heavy seas swept the decks from stem to stern. On some days, they broke over the bridge and flooded the deck of the pilothouse.

The Bristol class had been designed before the war, and their construction had been largely completed by the time we entered the war. On the basis of British experience, they were hastily refitted to provide more protection against aircraft and to accommodate more radar. This meant the installation of significant antennae on an extended mast and the mounting of antiaircraft weapons on the upper decks. Despite a certain amount of ballast and calculated weight reduction by eliminating a great deal of armor, there was no way to compensate for the destabilizing topside weight. These ships were therefore always top-heavy, and their roll and pitch in a heavy sea was an awesome thing to behold. It was even worse to live through. The ship was never at peace with the ocean. It was almost impossible to stand without holding on to some support for balance. We could sleep only by tilting our bunks and wedging our mattresses against the bulkheads. Our bodies never had a second of repose. Fortunately, we were young and healthy.

Our captain, from the professional Naval Academy elite, and surrounded by young amateurs, would never relax his standards. No matter what the weather or the sea conditions, we were required to dress for lunch and dinner in our dress blues, with white shirts and stiff collars, and eat a proper meal at the ward room table. In order to preserve decorum at the worst of times, we had the "monkey cage" and the "fiddle board." The monkey cage consisted of a series of steel stanchions, which were screwed into the deck and the overhead, to form a cage around the wardroom table. Each stanchion was a little more than a chair's width from the next and was equipped with a steel ring at seat level. Each chair, in turn, was equipped on either side with catches, of the type found on a dog's leash; and, by means of these devices, the chairs were lashed against sliding away from the table with the roll and pitch of the ship. The table itself was fitted with the fiddle board. This was a mahogany-stained plywood sheet, mounted about two inches above the surface of the table itself with cutouts in front of each seat. One cutout accommodated a plate, another a cup, another the silver forks, still another the knives and spoons, and so on. Hence, when our plates were placed before us and served, they would be kept in place with a minimum number of hands.

The poor wardroom stewards had to serve the food to this outlandish arrangement as if they were in a posh restaurant or a private club. They would emerge from the pantry with a tray balanced on one hand and the other grasping for a stanchion to steady themselves before they made their rounds. I remember one unfortunate lad who thought he could round the far end of the table on the starboard side without holding on to the cage. We were beam-ended just as he made his move and he, his tray, and its contents all took off through the air for the port bulkhead. Fortunately for him, a leather transom, or sofa, broke his fall, but the food and the silver service splattered all over the port end of the wardroom. The captain, seated at the port end of the table, never changed facial expression or the rhythm of his conversation. No one at the table dared take notice of the mishap. We were all officers and gentlemen, and the dignity of the service had to be preserved.

On the bridge, in weather such as that, it was impossible to keep warm and dry. We had "foul weather gear," consisting of fleece-lined waterproof overalls and parkas, as well as heavy lined boots and thermal underwear. On our faces we wore British Red Cross knitted masks with goggles over our eyes. But, after four hours in the weather, we were walking icicles and had constantly to beat the layers of ice and caked salt off our clothing so that we could bend our arms and legs.

One vicious early morning, when we were returning a convoy of empty cargo ships westward from the chop line, I completed my midwatch and swung onto the inside ladder in order to go below and warm up for 20 minutes before general quarters would be sounded for morning twilight. As soon as I stepped on the first step of the ladder, I realized that I had failed to remove the caked ice from the instep of my boot. And then, as I started to fall and grasped for the chains with both hands, I discovered that I had also failed to crack the ice off the palms of my gloves. Down I went, with nothing to break my fall until I hit the deck below. Unhappily, at the same time my feet hit the deck, the underside of my left jaw hit one of the lower steps on the ladder. Although I was momentarily stunned, I picked myself up in the grateful realization that nothing was broken and that my bulky clothes had prevented me from any more serious damage than a bruised jaw.

By breakfast, however, the jaw had begun to swell and by that evening, it had ballooned to enormous size. The ship's doctor opined that I had done some damage to my submaxillary glands and thought it wise to take me off watch. When we arrived in Boston two days later, I still could not swallow solid food or open my mouth far enough to brush my teeth. There was no acute pain, but enough contusion to cause the doctor concern that I might have broken the jaw bone. Since he planned to leave ship shortly after we docked in order to visit his wife, he drew up the papers to admit me for hospitalization and examination at Chelsea Naval Hospital and consigned me there in care of a hospital corpsman, who was also anxious to be gone on liberty. In order not to prejudge my examination at the hospital, he had me admitted under the catchall category of "D.U."—diagnosis unknown.

The nurse lieutenant in admissions, busily efficient with paperwork, took one look at me and consigned me to an isolation room in the ward reserved for officers with contagious diseases. In order to get to my room, I had to pass through a ward filled with young Marine Corps officers just back from Guadalcanal and suffering from malaria. As they saw me enter, they shouted in unison "Mumps! Get him out of here!" I was hustled through them and into the luxury of a private room.

A weekend intervened, and I discovered that the shore-based hospital had not altered its peace-time routine of making it a holiday. Exhausted by the ordeals at sea, I slept like a baby and by Sunday evening, the swelling of my jaw had subsided to the point that I could eat solid foods—in large quantity. My dishes were brought specially from the kitchen and returned separately from those delivered to the Marines in the ward. I noticed that they were all marked "A.C." By Sunday evening, I had enough interest in things to ask the young Wave who brought my food and took away the dishes what those initials meant. She blushed as she stammered "active case," and it was only from the nurse that I realized that the Wave assumed I had venereal disease.

By Monday, the papers had caught up with the doctors and my medical history began to have some effect on my treatment. From X-rays, it was determined that there was no fracture of the jawbone. By probing and prodding, it was

Navy Days

decided there was no permanent damage to the swollen glands. But, in true navy fashion, the doctors decided I should stay a few more days for observation.

By Tuesday, the swelling had subsided completely and I was obviously fit for duty. But the doctor had not scheduled another visit until Thursday and there was no way I could be discharged without a doctor's certificate. In fact, I discovered, there was no way I could even get by the front desk and out of the hospital for an evening on the town without that formal certificate. However, in examining my premises, I discovered that my room, which was obviously designed for flag rank occupants, had French doors opening onto a terrace, which, in turn, had steps leading into the garden. A little reconnoiter on Tuesday afternoon disclosed that the garden led into the parking lot and to the outer gate, through which passage was arranged merely by returning a Marine's salute.

That evening, after the day's routine had finished, I slipped out the French doors, through the garden, out the gate, and took a taxi to the Officer's Club at the Boston Navy Yard. As I entered the bar, the first people I saw, and who saw me, were two nurses from the hospital. Rather than retreat, I decided to bluff it out with them. They had no reason to know that I had not been formally discharged. While we were having a drink, we were joined by an officer from my ship and the four of us decided on impromptu dinner in the Club's restaurant. As we were tucking into the first course, a group arrived to take the adjacent reserved table. It included our captain and his wife, whom we greeted with polite reserve.

Before the evening was over, I had to confess to my shipmate that I was absent from the hospital without leave and would probably not be released until Thursday afternoon. He confided to me that our ship's squadron had orders to sail Thursday morning for the Mediterranean. If I didn't join, I might be left behind and transferred to another ship on the North Atlantic. Thus began a desperate effort to frustrate the naval medical bureaucracy. With the help of our ship's executive officer and our ship's doctor, a way was eventually found. The duty doctor at the hospital agreed, late Wednesday afternoon, to transfer me to the care of our ship's doctor, and the papers were duly executed, once again pronouncing that I was "D.U.," diagnosis unknown. In that condition, I sailed with my ship, on our way to join the Mediterranean fleet. The North Atlantic was calm as we rounded Cape Cod and set our course for the southeast.

— 3 —

Destroyer sailors are a special breed. They are apt to be smaller than battleship men and more cocky in appearance. They walk with an "eight-second roll," a swagger that combines the need to compensate for the motion of their ships and, at the same time, to indicate their general readiness for action. They consider themselves "the real navy." In the winter of 1943–44, when our ship was operating in the Mediterranean, its happy company of destroyer sailors was disrupted by the arrival of two young petty officers who hardly qualified as real Navy. They were electronic specialists, and one of them actually had a college degree in engineering. They arrived aboard with a large bundle of complex electronic gear, because our ship had been chosen to conduct an experiment.

We were operating out of the Algerian port of Mers-el-Kebir at the time, engaged once again in the protection of convoys and working very largely against submarines. We had participated in the landings in Italy and were now busily occupied with assuring the movement of supplies to build up the armies we had landed there. These came in ships that moved across the South Atlantic, through the Straits of Gibraltar, and along the north coast of Africa until they reached the passage which was called the Sicilian War Channel. We had been pulled back from Anzio for this service because there had been two devastating attacks on the convoys in the Mediterranean. In

Navy Days

one, a submarine had scored with a short range salvo of torpedoes that had sunk several ships, including an ammunition ship which had exploded with the loss of all aboard. In another, a German long range bomber had come down from France and had sunk two ships with "smart bombs," which were equipped with gliding fins and guided to their targets by radio direction.

Mers-el-Kebir was an old French colonial naval station near the city of Oran. It was from this port that a small Vichy-controlled French fleet sallied forth in 1942 to engage the British and to be sunk rather than surrender during the Allied landings in North Africa. It had certain rather primitive naval installations and was close to a very pleasant beach resort called Ain-el-Turk. Before the U.S. Army had moved on to Sicily and the Italian mainland, several of its units had been located in this vicinity, resting up from the North African campaign and training for the tougher Italian terrain.

Also in the vicinity were a number of prisoner-of-war camps, principally housing Italians who had been wrapped up in the Allied sweep across the desert. For them the war was over. They were content to await the capitulation of their homeland in the rather pleasant Algerian sun. They had very little motivation to escape the lax controls and plentiful rations of their American captors. A number of them had been given special status as cooks, waiters, gardeners, and general servitors in the various facilities our army had established in their brief stay at Ain-el-Turk. Three of them had been "assigned" to care for Villa 13, a gracious French beach house that had been "requisitioned" by a group of American army officers as their living quarters. When these officers departed for Italy, they gave the key and the control of their villa to some nurses from the mobile field hospital that remained temporarily behind. When the field hospital eventually followed the troops, I inherited the key. This good luck resulted from carefully cultivated acquaintance with a couple of the nurses, who occasionally appreciated the pleasure of dressing up and dining in our wardroom from real silver off white linen tablecloths.

While we were in port between convoys, I made some effort to determine how we could manage a villa, a staff of three Italian household servants, and a jeep that went with it from the meager resources of our small company of officers, no more than seven of whom could be ashore at any time. We finally concluded that we would have to share our bounty with the other five ships in our division and arranged a party to let them view the premises. In the middle of this event, I was summoned back to the ship and told I had an urgent mission.

It turned out that the mission was to take responsibility for the two electronic technicians who had come aboard with their equipment for the experiment. I learned from the executive officer that the experiment concerned the German "smart bombs." Since the bombers that carried them stayed out of the range of our naval batteries, we were unable to shoot at them. However, because the bombs were radio-controlled, Washington had decided that we could jam the radio signals and neutralize their menace. Our ship had been chosen for the jamming mission. We were to sail north of the convoy after it passed Gibraltar, decoy the bombers and frustrate their bombs. Since I was at that point the assistant communications officer, the project was put in my care.

The petty officer with the college degree was tall and slim, with a very effete manner and a slight lisp. His companion was short, fat, rather unkempt, and seemed to sweat a lot. The captain had taken one look at the two of them and retreated to his sea cabin. It must have shaken him to realize that the fate of his command was in the hands of these two youngsters. In talking to the two of them, I decided that, despite their unorthodox appearance and unmilitary bearing, they were intelligent and responsible. Their equipment was relatively simple. It consisted of a scanning receiver, operated by the short, fat one, which was supposed to detect the wavelength of the German transmissions, and a variable-frequency transmitter, which could be adjusted to the German signals and jam them with conflicting signals.

In conjunction with the engineering officer, we worked out space for their gear and installed it. The scanner with its sweaty operator would be in the engineering deck house, and the jammer with its willowy technician would be on the deck immediately above it, just aft of the torpedo tubes. A voice-powered, self-contained telecommunications circuit was installed so that the two could talk to each other, and we were in business. In order to test the system, we arranged with one of our sister ships for a quick run to sea. The other ship stood off about ten miles and transmitted on various frequencies. Our two technicians went through their paces under the watchful eye of the executive officer and myself, and in the curious gaze of a good portion of the crew. Their performance approached hysteria.

As the scanner detected a frequency, he screamed into his phone set, his voice rising with his excitement. His companion with the jamming antenna on the deck above became agitated as he tried to adjust his signals to the scanner, and, when he found it difficult, stamped his feet in frustration. The executive officer and I exchanged glances, and we could hear dark muttering among the spectators from the crew. Nevertheless, after a couple of hours of practice, the technicians seemed to get their act together and managed to detect and jam signals within acceptable time limits. We decided that the practice session could end and returned to port.

That evening, as I walked out on deck, I was accosted by one of the ships's carpenter's mates, a tough, swarthy little Italian from New Jersey whose claim to fame rested on the fact that he had been a handler for heavyweight boxer Two Ton Tony Galento. He said that some of the crew had gathered on the fantail and would like to talk with me. The navy was very touchy about anything that might be considered a group action, since that definition bordered very closely on mutiny. Nevertheless, I went back to meet with about twenty very worried crewmen, who offered as their collective judgment the conviction that "these two queers" would panic when they faced a real German bomber and that we should train some real sailors to operate the electronic gear. It took a couple of hours of gentle persuasion to jolly them into accepting the realities of the situation as it was, but none of them was comforted or converted.

It was, as a result, a rather moody crew who stood out to sea on a quiet calm morning when the next convoy came through the Straits. We steamed toward Cartagena, then turned northeast about thirty miles north of the convoy, slowing our speed to conform with theirs, and fixing our search radars toward the coast of France. Early that afternoon, we detected a lone intruder and went to general quarters. Fifteen minutes later, a Heinkel bomber came into sight at about 10,000 feet, moving slowly in our direction. We were soon spotted and the plane began to circle in the sky.

After a wait that seemed longer than it was, we could see a large object detach from the belly of the plane on a long umbilical, and we watched as the pilot lined up his bearings on our hull. Although our fire control director and main battery were tracking throughout this maneuver, the plane stayed carefully just beyond our effective range. The tension among our crew was palpable, and we silently waited for the inevitable. Only in the after deck house was there action. There, the scanner was frantically twirling his dials and screaming into his microphone. On the deck above, the jammer was jumping around, and screaming just as loudly into his microphone. They did not inspire great confidence in their fellow crew members, waiting at battle stations in helmets and lifebelt-jackets.

Then, suddenly, the bomb detached from its cable and the plane began a slow turn to the east. We lost sight of the falling missile for awhile, then picked it up again, gliding in a deadly ballistic sweep toward our ship. All was silent, except for the frenzy of our two technicians. Suddenly, their clamor took on meaning, as they locked onto the German signal and began their jamming. Those who were following the bomb could see it falter and dip, and then suddenly begin a long spiral down into the sea. A cheer began from the bridge, where the best binoculars were located and swept back along the gun mounts and the damage control crew. By the time the bomb hit the water, five miles away, throwing up a large geyser followed by the muffled sound of its explosion, the ship was rocking with joy. The Heinkel turned and headed back north. The electronics technicians were vindicated.

I never knew what happened to them, their equipment, or their experiment. We offloaded them that evening at Oran, and the next morning were back at sea with the rest of our squadron, steaming at flank speed toward a bay near the Tunisian border. The convoy we had protected from air attack had been hit during the night by a pair of submarines, and one of the subs was trapped in the bay by two destroyer escorts detached from the convoy screen. Our ships were being summoned to relieve the escorts and try to kill the submarine.

By the time we arrived on the scene, however, a new player had intervened. A French destroyer-escort, built in the United States and newly commissioned for the forces of Free France, had been in port at Algiers when word of the submarine attack had been flashed on the radio network. The young captain of the ship saw a chance for glory and, despite the fact that half his crew was on shore leave, steamed off into the night and arrived at the bay in the early morning. He scorned the two American vessels blocking the exit from the bay and began a sonar run against the U-boat in the shallow waters where it was trapped. It was not difficult to find his target and to straddle it with depth charges. There was great elation when the submarine surfaced and raised a white flag.

But then the young Frenchman got careless. Instead of closing immediately on his prey, he and his crew watched as the Germans began to get into life rafts and abandon their boat. He didn't notice the fact that the submarine's engines were still turning over and that its bow was slowly swinging toward his ship. Suddenly, the clap and hiss of two torpedoes being fired snapped him too late from his distraction. Before he could maneuver, they slammed into his stern, blowing the entire after portion of the ship out of the water, doubling the fantail back onto the main deck, and snapping his propeller shaft. It took him half an hour to get the fire out, stop the exploding ammunition, drop an anchor against drift, and recover his dead and wounded. In the meantime, the Germans had headed their small rafts toward the beach and attempted to escape ashore. Fortunately, they were immediately captured by a small detachment of British soldiers stationed at the little port settlement of Dji-jelli. The fact that their captors were British probably saved their lives, since the treachery of a false surrender would not have been excused by French troops or partisans.

By the time we arrived on the scene, the submarine, scuttled by its crew, had sunk to the bottom of the bay. The two American ships had gone to the aid of the French destroyer-escort, and the worst wounded had been evacuated to a small British field hospital ashore. There was no task left for our squadron except to salvage the French destroyer-escort and tidy up the consequences of its intervention. Accordingly, all but two of our ships returned to Oran, taking with them the surly German prisoners and those wounded Frenchmen who could be released for travel. Our ship and one other were left behind, awaiting orders on the action to be taken with the French ship. It was supposed that one of us would take her in tow and the other would act as escort back to Algiers. But, because she flew the French flag, we had to await instructions from the French command.

Navy Days

When the instructions had not arrived by late afternoon, our captain began to fidget. Our ship had once been hit by a spent German torpedo while anchored in an open bay and had nearly sunk. The captain had an understandable aversion to anchoring overnight or to leaving the helpless French vessel at anchor. Therefore, on his own initiative, he decided to take the immobilized destroyer-escort in tow and move both our ships into the postage-stamp sized harbor of Dji-jelli, safely behind a sturdy seawall. Our sister ship would remain on patrol at the mouth of the bay. The maneuver was accomplished just before sundown, and we moored outboard and alongside the crippled French ship.

Shortly after we moored, we became aware that acid from our neighbor's smoke-screen generators, which had been doubled back by the torpedo attack, was dripping down onto the depth charges located on the ship's after deck. We felt this could cause an accidental explosion in which we would all be blown apart. Therefore, the captain instructed me to seek out the French captain, explain the situation in my fractured French, and offer to dismantle the generators by cutting their cradles with an acetylene torch and to remove them to the dock. I found the young skipper in the wardroom of his disabled command, with a half empty bottle of cognac on the table in front of him and a rather wild look in his bloodshot eyes. Before I could finish my pitch, he interrupted with an emotional tirade about American tyranny, and accused us of treating the French as inferiors. As he grew more frenzied, he drew a revolver from a side holster, cocked it, pointed it at me, and ordered me off his ship. I left in a hurry, considerably shaken by the experience.

When I reported this development to our captain, he told me to arm myself, take two torpedomen with submachine guns and go back to force our neighbor's compliance. While it seemed a rather irregular thing to do, I saw no alternative but to follow instructions. When I entered the French wardroom the second time, I was flanked by my two burly assistants, their tommy guns trained on the young captain's belly. This time, he threw his revolver on the table and broke down in hysterical sobs. With the cooperation of his own junior officers, we had our ship's doctor give him a shot of tranquilizer and led him off to bed. The smoke screen generators were dismantled and removed. The night passed uneventfully and, with the dawn, came orders from the French command. We were asked to leave the French ship at Dji-jelli and steam back to Oran. I have often wondered what happened to that young captain.

— 4 —

We lost the first ship in our squadron during the invasion of Normandy. The squadron had been widely dispersed after we arrived in England from the Mediterranean in preparation for the channel crossing. Our ship and one other from our same division had, for example, been sent over to the west to form the destroyer nucleus of the screening forces for the troop convoy that embarked in the tidy little harbor of Falmouth. Other ships were assigned to other duties and sailed from other ports. We didn't all reassemble until we had delivered our charges to the beachhead and assumed our new duties on the screen deployed to protect the Mulberries, as the artificial harbor works were called.

Functioning in these scattered assignments was a new experience for us and, since Normandy was such a massive undertaking, all its maneuvers seemed a little less disciplined than the destroyer formations we had been used to in the North Atlantic and the Mediterranean. In our crossing, the screening forces were British, French, and even contained one U.S. Coast Guard vessel. The convoy consisted of LSTs, which moved slowly, wallowed badly in the Channel seas, and crabbed constantly out of formation. Shore bombardment elements, which had left England long after our departure, sped by our scattered flock with cavalier contempt, and arrived off the beaches well before the break of dawn. We didn't get our infantry units into position until daybreak.

When the ungainly LSTs left our charge, spread out in line of advance, and surged forward to discharge their troops on the beachhead, we reported our availability to the screen commander and turned for our next assignment. The beaches were by this time a turbulent battlefront with air attacks, naval bombardment, infantry charges, and artillery fire all taking place simultaneously. The waters off the beaches were oily and scattered with flotsam as a number of naval units sank or drifted helplessly, disabled by mines and coast artillery fire. Near us, the large troopship Susan B. Anthony burned out of control and billowed great columns of oily black smoke before she sank.

In the midst of all this turmoil, radio commands were being issued in a crisp, clear female British voice from the maritime headquarters in Portsmouth. There, in their bunker, the Allied sea lords controlled the invading forces, plotted all our positions as we reported them, and instructed us what to do. How to do it was left to the harried seaborne commanders on the spot. Hence, when we reported that we had discharged our LSTs and had given our navigational position, the cheery female voice told us to replace a sister ship in the Dixie Line, and gave us coordinates of the position. The significance of the word "replace" did not quite become clear until we neared the designated spot and could see the masthead and the top of the fire-control tower of a Bristol class destroyer sticking out of the water ahead of us. The ship had hit a mine and gone straight to the bottom. The explosion must have opened all her compartments along the keel so that she flooded evenly, and she must have wedged into rock formations on the ocean floor so that she remained vertically positioned where she sank.

We didn't have much time to contemplate this strange phenomenon because we were soon busily engaged in an artillery duel with German shore batteries which had just hit a British cruiser close aboard and had begun to straddle our position. The Germans were well emplaced and hard to damage. They were assisted by a large radar with apparently effective ranging capability, since their salvoes were distressingly accurate. U.S. aircraft made several passes at the radar, but the huge screen emerged intact after the smoke and debris cleared from each bombing run. Finally, a U.S. heavy cruiser, relatively far out at sea, swung her main battery in the direction of the radar screen and with one broadside salvo, blew it away.

After that, it was only a matter of hours before our troops cleared the beaches, mounted the cliffs, and began the battle of the hedgerows across the fields of Normandy. Our attention then turned towards our patrol assignment on the Dixie Line and the protection of the landing areas from sea raids. Our sector of responsibility was relatively limited and position keeping became a matter of ranging regularly on the mast of the sunken sister ship. Visually by day, though radar by night, we kept that reminder of our frailty always with us, and made our turns in a figure eight patrol by marking on that steadfast mast.

We endured nearly two weeks of this activity, survived one encounter with torpedo boats, rode out a storm, and eventually returned to Plymouth for resupply. There was one curious interlude in this period. It came in late June, after we had returned to Plymouth from the landings at Normandy and from the partially botched operation at Cherbourg, which history has nevertheless recorded as a brilliant success. Plymouth had been all but destroyed by German bombing raids, and those residents who remained there lived very austere lives indeed. It was a depressing place for shore leave by the standards of young men just back from the active front across the channel.

Somehow, we learned that there was a very pleasant oasis

at Torquay, which had escaped the ravages of the war. One sunny morning, three of us took a train to that old resort and found that the rumors were correct. There, by the sea, we discovered that the old prewar England that all of us had known only through the drawing room comedies of Noel Coward and his ilk was still impeccably intact. Lanquid British gentry and their overdressed ladies engaged in cocktail chatter, enjoyed a tea dance, and behaved as though they had never heard of the war. There was an occasional uniform among them, but the three of us in our naval officers' blues were definitely out of place. Liquor and canapes were plentiful, and the contrast with the rationed scarcities in Plymouth struck us as bizarre. We returned that same evening to our ship, not entirely certain whether the whole experience had been a hallucination.

 We had little time to think about it, however, since we were soon underway again. We moved up to Belfast, picked up a convoy, and headed back to the Mediterranean to take part in the landings of Allied forces in Southern France. Two days after our duties in the St. Tropez sector were complete, and we were on leisurely patrol along the perimeter of the sea lanes, we received an urgent order to proceed at top speed to Toulon. There we were to replace a destroyer-escort on duty station at the entrance to the harbor of Toulon. It seems that this ship, under command of a young officer who had made a great name for himself as a P.T. boat skipper in the Philippines, had disabled her main battery. The disability occurred when the ship opened fire against a vessel attempting to emerge from the harbor in the middle of the night. The main battery had been fired with such intensity and at such length that the barrels became overheated, the rifled linings expanded against the barrel casings, and the guns all warped. The ship, in effect, was useless except for depth charges and anti-aircraft weapons. The irony of it all was that its target, a German tug, had escaped unharmed in order to fulfill its purpose, which was to surrender to the destroyer-escort itself rather than face the French colonial troops from Africa who were massing on the outskirts of Toulon.

We arrived on station in the early afternoon, exchanged signals with the destroyer-escort, which sailed off with its German prize in tow, and settled into our new task. Our orders were rather vague, and we seemed to have no specific assignment except to prevent German naval units from escaping into the Mediterranean from the Toulon harbor. However, since the German tug crew avowed that theirs was the only German vessel in the harbor, the task seemed less than demanding.

Our captain, while generally accepting the German claim, decided it would be prudent to enter the harbor in order to make certain there were no other elements of the German fleet located there. The next morning, at first light, we passed through the narrow harbor entrance into the large bay known as the outer *rade*. It was a warm, hazy day in late August, and the surface of the bay was glassy calm. Our charts showed shipping channels clearly defined and we had no trouble picking out the buoys that marked the way towards the inner *rade*, where the piers and moorings of France's main naval port were located.

As we trained our glasses through the morning mist, we suddenly became aware of an awesome sight. There throughout the harbor, like some sort of ghost fleet, were the masts and superstructures of ship after ship of the old French fleet, all protruding from the surface of the bay and glinting through the fog, but all resting serenely in the mud bottoms of their moorings. We had forgotten the fact that the French Navy had scuttled its ships when France surrendered, rather than turn them over to the Vichy government and eventual German control. Four years after the scuttling, they were still there where they had gone down, silent mementoes of a tragic defiance.

Navy Days

We moved very slowly through the ship channels towards the piers, hardly rippling the surface of the waters. We passed close aboard many of the larger fleet units, and in some instances could read their names as their superstructures cleared the surface of the bay. The drifting patches of mist, as the morning sun began to break it up, gave the whole scene an eerie cast, with the silence broken only by an occasional screech from a wheeling gull. Our crew lined the railings, looking in awe at this unexpected vision and talking to each other in subdued whispers. It took us nearly half an hour to pass all the vessels in this nautical graveyard and to find an unoccupied pier alongside a German supply depot, where sacks of flour, in white gunny bags, each marked with the eagle and swastika of the German armed forces, were guarded by two young Frenchmen, with machine guns, bandoliers of ammunition, and the arm bands of the FFI maquis.

As the first Allied ship to enter the naval port, and, indeed, the first Allied forces the former French shipyard workers had seen, we were given a riotous welcome. However, we were somewhat disconcerted to discover that Allied ground forces, which should have moved in from St. Tropez, had not yet established control over the naval base, even though we had been assured that all the Germans had left. We radioed back to the fleet to report our situation and received a somewhat flustered order to stay where we were until the base had been officially invested and the channels had been swept for mines. For the next three days, until these formalities had been completed, we lived among the ghosts of the former French fleet, the only living ship in a vast, dead armada of the past.

Once the Toulon harbor had been swept and the naval base formally invested, we returned to Marseilles. Moving into that harbor immediately after the city had been liberated proved an interesting experience. The old port was a fascinating relic of earlier years, entered by passing under a narrow drawbridge. Our division of six destroyers occupied all its available berths and were oddly out of place among the sleek yachts and other pleasure craft that had been immobilized there by the war. We lay at our piers at the foot of Rue des Cannibieres, looking uphill into the center of the old city, facing the cobbled esplanade that fronted on the port. The fence that separated us from the commerce of the street was made of wrought iron grillwork, and it was strange that it had survived the cannibalistic search for scrap that had stripped most of Europe of its ironwork.

At that stage, control over the city was being disputed between the Free French military units of General de Gaulle, whom we had landed at St. Tropez and other points along the Riviera, and the FFI, the communist dominated guerrilla forces from the underground, which had moved in rapidly behind the departing Germans. These latter soldiers were young, most of them in their early teens, with a motley lot of equipment captured from the Germans, or which the Germans had abandoned in their flight. They wore red armbands and made themselves conspicuous by taking up positions at main traffic intersections and directing the sparse vehicular movement in the city. They were often draped with bandoliers of machine gun ammunition of an obviously different caliber than the rifles and automatic weapons they handled so recklessly.

After a quick look at the situation, the captains of the six destroyers decided that it would be imprudent to permit our crews to have liberty ashore. Hence, they were confined to the cobbled esplanade area within the iron fence, where they could pursue only limited recreational activity. Most ships carried athletic equipment to be used on shore parties in deserted places, and so, in very short order, baseball gear and footballs were broken out and in use on the cobblestones. The good citizens of Marseilles had obviously never before seen a round ball thrown and caught in leather mitts, or an oblong ball tossed in arching spirals. They came by the thousands to stand outside the fence, gawk for hours at *les matelots americains,* and applaud at some spectacular catch. Our sailors became great hams and deliberately exaggerated their athletic feats, especially when comely young girls joined the spectators. They were the greatest show in town and probably served constructively to divert attention from the friction that developed between the French troops and the FFI.

However entertaining it may have been for the Marseillais, it was definitely not enough for red-blooded young destroyer men, who felt very strongly that real liberty should consist of booze and broads. Accordingly, the skippers decided that we should seek to establish a club in town, where our men could go, but from which they could not stray into occasions of darker vice or deeper danger. I was assigned the task of finding such a place.

It proved quite simple. An inquiry directed to the French military police gleaned the fact that there were a number of rather ornate nightclubs along the Rue de Cannibieres that had been run by collaborators for the benefit of the German occupation forces. Their proprietors had prudently departed with the German troops. We could have our pick of them. I looked over a half dozen and chose two. One was a large, chromed and mirrored place with a big dance floor and a long bar. This was my choice for the crews. The other was a small, plush-lined club with a bar below and a dining room above. This I chose for the officers. Both had been partially sacked and were in need of clean-up and repairs. I proposed having a working party from the ships come up the street to do the job. My French hosts suggested that a better source of hard labor was the German prisoner of war camp on the edge of town. It was filled with troops who had marched all the way from Toulouse to surrender. Most were Austrians.

I went to the camp and recruited a work party of twenty men who spoke some degree of English. They came with reluctance, since they weren't sure what would become of them.

I put them to work in the larger club under the supervision of a boatswain's mate who had sandwiches and beer sent up from one of the ships. (Although our navy was always "dry," we carried hundreds of cases of beer in locked compartments for recreation parties ashore.) The Austrians cleaned things up in four hours while I was at the smaller club arranging that establishment. At the end of those four hours, the bos'n fed them. Then, since I had not returned, he had them clean up the place all over again. Our clubs were to be ready for business the next day, so I went back to the P.O.W. camp that morning to pick up my Austrian work party again. When the inmates saw me coming, there was a vast stampede in my direction. The word of our enterprise had gotten around, and I had a difficult time retrieving our original twenty-man work party. However, I did pick up two highly qualified cooks for the officers' club in the bargain. Both places proved a great success.

Nevertheless, as the days moved on, there was great pressure to have the entire city opened for liberty parties. In order to investigate the feasibility of this, I was sent out with an armed shore patrol detachment to reconnoiter the state of affairs. As we set off on foot up the main street and along the areas we had picked out on an old tourist map of the city, we rapidly accumulated an entourage. All the young street urchins, who abounded in that area, fell into line behind us, so that I soon felt like the Pied Piper of Hamlin marching along at the head of a queue that must have numbered a couple of hundred. We were greeted everywhere with applause and shouts of welcome, with most cafe and restaurant owners inviting us to their tables. Because it was a hot, sticky day, I did halt our little patrol at one sidewalk cafe and accepted one beer all around. Before setting off again, I asked the proprietor if we could use his plumbing facilities to relieve the calls of nature. With a great flourish, he led me around the corner toward a little square that was dominated by a large, green-metalled pissoir of semicircular design. It was built with a chest-high metal barrier facing the square, and those using it performed their duties while gazing serenely out over this barrier and sheltering under the overhang of a corrugated roof.

Those brought up in the culture of Marseilles would presumably have had no hangups about these accommodations, even in the face of an audience that filled the little square. Our gaggle of gamins had by now been joined by about one hundred *citoyens du quartier*, who had paused to watch as we were led into the municipal facility. Whatever our feelings, nature overcame them and there we stood, one khaki officer's cap and four white seaman's caps perched on crimson faces, as the whole packed square burst into sustained and sincere applause for this tangible gesture of Franco-American friendship.

— 5 —

By September of 1944, naval activity in the European theater had all but ended, and our squadron was redeployed to the Pacific. That winter was spent around the atolls and in the phosphorescent waters of the South Pacific, tidying up in the wake of our ground forces. By spring, we were prepared for the massive assault against Okinawa. It was an effort in which our squadron was to lose nine more ships, all to kamikaze attacks. My own ship was hit twice, but suffered only minor damage. The four months we spent in that campaign were a devastating experience.

It all began when we became part of a small task force sent to the Okinawa region at the end of March, 1945, in order to prepare the landing areas for the April 1, 1945, invasion. Our force included mine-sweepers to clear operating areas off the beaches, underwater demolition teams to open passages through the coral reefs, and frogmen to remove obstacles from the beaches themselves. Despite a heavy deployment of crack Japanese troops on the island, the short distance to airfields on the Japanese home islands, and a formidable artillery concentration available to the defenders, we were undisturbed as we went about our business with a minimum of air cover from the carrier fleet, which stood off a considerable distance to the east.

We moved close enough to Japanese defenses to observe that they had built dummy airplanes of bamboo on their airfields and seemed to have very flimsy defensive positions along the principal invasion routes. As the first three days of our operation went by without significant resistance, we began to feel uneasy, sensing that something was wrong. Just as we were finishing the preparatory work, three days before the scheduled invasion, the captain assembled the ship's officers and explained the situation to us.

The United States had broken the Japanese military codes and therefore knew that our unhindered operations were part of a complex entrapment. It was the Japanese plan to let our invasion forces land on the Okinawan beaches without serious resistance. But, before they could be supplied with anything more than they carried ashore, our supply ships would be sunk in a massive suicide assault, to be carried out by a fleet of three hundred plywood boats, each carrying a large lethal explosive charge in its bow. Then, with our troops ashore but without resupply, the Japanese forces would sweep out of their bunkers and annihilate the invaders.

The suicide boats and their boatmen were sequestered in a heavily forested atoll, called Kerama Retto, about twenty miles west of Okinawa. They were scheduled to slip out to sea on the night of Sunday, April 1, and sink as many as possible of the huge naval armada we were amassing for the invasion taking place that Easter morning. Our assignment was to join with a cruiser, some fast attack transports, and a marine assault force at the crack of dawn on March 30, neutralize the atoll defenses by a rolling barrage from our main batteries, land the marines, capture the suicide boats and frustrate the Japanese plans. At the same time, we would capture and hold a deep-water anchorage facility that could serve as a staging area in support of the invasion.

It all went according to the book. The Japanese were stunned by the surprise attack, and marine casualties were very light. The boats were quickly rounded up and disabled. Their explosive charges were removed and detonated, their hulls stove in and their carcasses left lying around the atoll in mute testimony to the plan's frustration. The Okinawa invasion went off like clockwork. The flotilla discharged its cargo without incident, and the bloody, grinding battle of Okinawa began.

It took the Japanese a few days to recover from the shock of losing their fleet of suicide boats and the failure of the clever strategy of ambush they had devised for our navy. When they did recover, their next weapon was the kamikaze plane. Their attacks usually took place in the late afternoon, and their planes came in swarms. Over the next few months, they were to strike over three hundred of our naval craft and eliminate most of them from the war.

This unexpected toll among our naval vessels was more than our limited repair and refit facilities could handle. Although we eventually acquired a small floating drydock and increased contingents of Seabees, badly damaged ships were moored by the score in Kerama Retto, where the shoulders of the surrounding hills provided shelter from kamikazes. The place soon became known as "Cripple Creek," and was the temporary home of a great many crews waiting to get minor repairs completed so that their ships could get back on the line.

Shore facilities were soon developed on the largest island in the atoll, and a primitive recreation field was laid out. Since the atoll was of volcanic origin, the baseball diamond was rolled flat out of grey volcanic ash, and marked with white lime. It had, unfortunately, been the location of one of the suicide boat drivers' camps, most of whom had been killed in our shore bombardment. As a result, small pieces of human anatomy occasionally turned up in the course of a vigorous softball game. A dismembered foot emerged from the ash once at second base and was gently buried again behind the coach's box on the first base line.

These anomalies made for some unusual softball games, but were not really a match for the phenomenon of the unseen audience. This audience consisted of a fairly intact Japanese marine company, which had been part of the atoll garrison force. They had well dug in positions up on the hill that dominated the level playing field and were protected from observation by a thick tropical growth of vegetation. During the U.S. Marine assault, they had withdrawn into those positions and stalled for time. Our marines, realizing that it would be very expensive to dig them out, and moreover, that it would be a distraction from the main event over on Okinawa, entered into negotiations with the Japanese. The result of those talks was an agreement under which the Japanese could keep their weapons, but agreed not to use them so long as a truce was maintained. They would withdraw above a well-marked position on the hill and stay there undisturbed while the battle on Okinawa took place. They maintained their communications equipment and the ability to stay in close touch with their parent command on Okinawa. If the parent command surrendered, they would do the same. But, so long as the parent command remained intact, they would be safeguarded from surrender by a cease-fire regime on the atoll.

Under this remarkable agreement, the Japanese stayed silently in the hills, out of sight of the American invaders. However, when softball was in progress on the recreation field, their discipline was breached. Whenever there was a particularly good play, applause would drift out of the jungle; and, eventually, there were wags who tipped their hats to the unseen audience in acknowledgement of the cheers. It was a far cry from what was happening on the destroyer picket line, fifteen miles away.

There, the reaction to the sustained wave of suicide attacks took different forms among different people. But, it was all summed up in the grim realization that a human torch, encased in a plane load of high-octane aviation fuel, was an impossible weapon for a ship to counter. We devised various methods of improved damage control, as well as tactics to evade the deadly planes, but the fact that we could produce no sure defense was attested by the large number of casualties we incurred.

One evening, rather late in the campaign, our ship was patrolling off the eastern cliffs of Okinawa, and I had the senior watch as officer-of-the-deck. We had witnessed an extraordinary event that day, and were a very sobered crew as we stood down from evening general quarters without incident. All the hushed talk concerned the mass suicide of Japanese troops that we had seen through our binoculars. They were an element that our marines had pushed back from their positions, and they now found themselves with their backs to the sea, and apparently very low on ammunition. We watched with awe as they stacked their rifles, removed their uniforms down to their breech cloths, and then, in close formation, marched to the edge of the cliff and threw themselves over, rank upon rank, one hundred and fifty feet to the crashing surf and jagged rocks below. There must have been two hundred who committed suicide this way, while Japanese-speaking U.S. Marines pleaded with them through bull horns to stop the madness and surrender with honor. When it was all over, an awful stillness settled over every one of us who had seen this happen, and that mood prevailed all during the evening twilight.

As we moved quietly through a sea that was speckled with phosphorous and bathed in the light of a full moon, I received a constant stream of reports about aircraft in our vicinity, and had them all tested by use of a high frequency directional radar that triggered an "IFF" transponder on the planes. If they made the automatic signal, we knew they were friendly and made a mental note of their positions and course on our radar display. Most of them were patrol planes whose nightly courses we knew well and whose activities were part of the enormous amount of scattered information about our operational environment we managed to store in our precomputerized memories.

One of the patrols was called the "Jack" patrol, and was flown nightly by a single torpedo bomber, presumably against the rare possibility that our picket screen might be attacked by a surface raider or a submarine susceptible to torpedo attack. As I watched the radar screen that evening, I followed the progress of one aircraft tentatively identified as the Jack patrol, a plane that responded positively to an IFF challenge. Yet, there seemed to be something unusual about the plane's course, much closer to the island's beaches than normally. In fact, the flight was so close to shore that it's course would take it between us and those cliffs where we had seen the mass suicides that afternoon. Out of curiosity, I stepped back towards the after wing of the bridge, leaned against the starboard 20 mm antiaircraft gun and scanned the sky with my binoculars while my "talker" kept calling out the range and bearing that the radar operator reported on the plane's progress. Visibility was somewhat hampered by the glow of the full, bright moon, and I was having difficulty picking out my target even as the plane closed to only two miles range.

Suddenly, there it was, much lower than I had been looking, closing swiftly on our starboard quarter. It was a torpedo bomber, all right, but not one of ours. Instead, it was a Japanese "Betty," with fixed landing gear and a large, nasty looking torpedo carried externally. I shouted the command to set general quarters and lunged at the 20 mm weapon in front of me. Breaking it out of locked position, and sweeping it down to the level of the target, I squeezed off two or three bursts from the magazine just as the plane came alongside. At about the time I began firing, the pilot, apparently previously distracted by the moonlight, suddenly realized he had nearly run into a destroyer, and swung his plane wildly up and away.

The roar of his engine and the chatter of my anti-aircraft gun startled the crew who were tumbling out on deck to take their battle stations. I locked the gun back in position and sprang into the wheelhouse. By this time the main battery was swinging into action and taking "feed" from the search radar, which continued to track our intruder. The plane swept off on our starboard bow several thousand yards and then began a wide turn back, apparently to cross ahead of us and come back on the other side, so that we would be silhouetted against the moon for his torpedo run. But, before he could complete his maneuver, the main battery scored a direct hit on him, and he blew up in a violent explosion in the warm summer sky.

The next day, there was much sly allusion to the duty section that invited Japanese planes to land on our quarterdeck and a number of comments about the benefit for some people to check on the need for eyeglasses. It all came to a climax when the executive officer announced a special Captain's Mast for noon. Such events are usually an occasion for summary punishment or special awards to be handed out. At this one, I was summoned front and center and, much to the amusement of all, given a leather medal with a collar cut from a jute gunny sack, and read a citation allegedly from Emperor Hirohito for my assistance to the kamikaze corps.

Within two days, this comic relief was shattered tragically. We were once again on the western side of the island, near the city of Naha. Word came on the intercept network that the Japanese had prepared a last, desperate plunge to destroy our supply fleet. A large task force, composed of almost everything they could scrape together in the home islands, was gathering at Kagoshima for a wild dash south. It was built around their new, untested battleship *Yamato,* the largest and most powerful ship ever built in Japan. She was to be accompanied by at least three cruisers and a bevy of destroyers. They were to come straight down the western side of the Nansei Shoto, the string of small islands north of Okinawa, swing around Ie Shima and rake the anchored American transports with their heavy guns.

Our navy intended to turn this foray into a major Japanese fiasco. Carriers were assembled east of the Nansei Shoto, and an enormous air armada, with wave after wave of attack planes, was prepared to sink the fleet in midpassage. But, in classic navy manner, a stopgap secondary force was prepared to be interposed between Okinawa and the attacking task force in the event they somehow slipped past the carrier aircraft. This secondary force was to be composed of our ship and the three remaining sister ships from our division, the *Ellison, Emmons,* and *Rodman.* We refueled and assembled off Ie Shima. Our captain, as senior officer present, took command of the unit.

He spread us out, four ships abreast, and began the sweep northward along the western side of the island chain in the early afternoon. He reported the unit's movement to the admiral in charge, who was embarked on one of the carriers to the east. He routinely asked for instructions concerning action to be taken in case we actually encountered the Japanese fleet. He got back a message that soon became known as the "Farragut Signal." It read something like, "Engage the enemy and destroy him!" The idea of four small destroyer types sinking the *Yamato* and her escorts caused wry mirth in our division. But we had full confidence the fleet air arm would save us from that embarrassment.

What we failed to anticipate was the advance umbrella of kamikazes. Just as the sun began to set, they came over the northern horizon in a drove. Our four ships turned to bring the greatest number of guns to bear and filled the sky with flak. A few went down, but the rest came relentlessly on, and two whole packs of them concentrated on the *Emmons* and the *Rodman*, the two ships furthest east in our formation. Within minutes, both were in deep trouble.

The *Rodman* took a plane directly on her No. 1 mount, and the forward magazine exploded, ripping off all her forecastle forward of that point. She was dead in the water and burning badly. The *Emmons* took one after another of the attackers all along her superstructure and began to burn and explode overall. Within a short time, she listed heavily to starboard and the crew abandoned ship. Once we had succeeded in swatting off the remaining Zeros, Bettys, and biplane trainers, we closed rapidly on the still exploding *Emmons* and began picking up her crew from the oily waters. By sunset, we had completed that task and found that there were remarkably few casualties. *Ellison* stood by *Rodman* until her fires were out and it was determined she would not capsize. Ironically, her losses were greater than those on the *Emmons*, because her bow section sank so rapidly.

As night fell, the decision was made that the *Ellison* would sink the abandoned and red-hot *Emmons*, which was drifting towards the beaches of a Japanese held island. (It took over ninety five-inch shells near her waterline to capsize her.) We, in the meantime, would act as escort to get the *Rodman* to "Cripple Creek" in Kerama Retto. She would undertake the voyage in reverse because her forward bulkheads were gaping to the sea. In the course of all this activity came the word that our fleet aircraft had sunk the entire Japanese fleet, including the *Yamato*, in one of the biggest air to sea assaults of the war.

Threading our way through the Okinawa traffic that long night was a wearisome task, and I drew the midwatch without any prior sleep. When we got to the designated area, we discovered that the remainder of the kamikaze swarm that had passed over us descended for the first time on the ships anchored in the atoll. The flagship to which we were bringing the *Rodman* had taken a plane in her wardroom, which had wiped out over half the officers. When we got the *Rodman* finally moored alongside the flagship, we discovered her loss of officers had also been disproportionately high.

The chief engineer and I, in an effort to be of some assistance to the shell-shocked survivors on both ships, went aboard the flagship to work out some logical disposition for our sister ship, which would obviously never sail again in that war. As we were talking with one of the flag-staff officers, another cripple came alongside, a medium-sized mine-sweeper that had taken a hit in the deck house. Her skipper was a raffish character with a beard and a battered cap. From the top yardarm of his mast, he had suspended the mangled body of the kamikaze pilot who had been thrown from his plane when he hit. The staff officer began to quake with anger and disgust when he saw the sight and screamed for the mine-sweeper to cast off and go elsewhere. The cocky young skipper was bewildered by this reaction and could only be talked into reason when the chief engineer and I went aboard and persuaded him to lower his macabre pennant and stow it in a plastic body bag. The reactions of young men at war to the vagrant brutalities of combat were always impossible to predict.

— 6 —

On August 14, 1945, we had assembled a strike force off Okinawa and set sail toward Shanghai. Our purpose was to intercept a convoy of Japanese vessels scheduled to sail from Shanghai to Japan. The intelligence on this movement, obviously gained from penetration of Japanese communications, indicated that the ships would be mostly merchant vessels, empty of cargo and sailing in ballast, escorted by a handful of destroyers. We had a task group built around a cruiser, with the equivalent of a destroyer squadron. It promised to be a turkey shoot in the Yellow Sea.

On that same evening, while we were still in radar range of Okinawa, word reached our strike force that Japan had decided to surrender. Within minutes after we got that word, the sky lighted up in the east with the tracery of fireworks. It was some time before the sound reached us, and we realized that our forces on Okinawa were celebrating by firing tracer rounds into the air. The fusillade lasted for a good fifteen minutes. On our ship, despite the fact that we were on the midwatch, the word spread rapidly through the crew and soon more than half of them were out wandering around the darkened decks, leaning against the rails, talking in loud tones and joking with each other. Those on watch were soon surrounded by their off-duty companions.

I had the senior watch on the bridge and, because we were the senior escort vessel, I was also in charge of the screening forces. My task was therefore not only to maintain command and control of our own ship, but also to monitor and control all the destroyers in the screening force. By constant attention to the radar screen, I could observe the positions of all ships in the task group and their diligence in maintaining their formation.

Within ten minutes, it was clear that formation discipline was disintegrating and that position keeping, especially by the destroyers, was growing ragged. Two ships were so close to each other that a minor error in course or speed might cause a collision. It seemed to me useless to expect all the ebullient young men on all the bridges and in all the engine rooms to keep tight control over their emotions at such a dramatic time. Therefore, instead of attempting to hector them all into position, I decided to change formation and open up the interval among ships. This would, in theory, give any lurking submarines a greater prospect of a clear torpedo shot at the cruiser, but, in practice, it rendered far less likely the chances of a collision among the destroyers.

After I had given the order and observed its execution on the radar screen, I called our captain on the intercom system, informed him briefly of our new disposition, and continued to steam westward. I had hardly released the button on the intercom when the communications watch officer brought me a message. It was a copy of an order to the admiral commanding our task group aborting our intercept mission and assigning us to a rendezvous point northwest of Okinawa for midday on August 15. Within half an hour, our strike force had reversed direction and was steaming for the rendezvous. It seemed certain the war was near its end.

That afternoon, as we assembled with a great number of other vessels just a few miles off the northern tip of Okinawa, we began to hear reports on the air defense network concerning the approach of a very special aircraft. It was a white-painted transport, bearing a green cross and carrying the Japanese delegation flying to Manila to negotiate the terms of surrender with General MacArthur. We watched as the plane came into sight from the north and dropped slowly down for the approach to Ie Shima airstrip just north of the main island, where she was to refuel before continuing her voyage south.

The feelings aboard ship were a remarkable mixture of emotions. Some had been so hyped to undertake the invasion and final defeat of Japan that the prospect of surrender seemed a frustration. Others had learned so well to inure themselves against good news that they steadfastly believed the surrender story was a hoax. Very few could accept the information as straight fact and begin to calculate its consequences. All were enormously relieved to be given an assignment and to use the distraction of duty to divert thought away from the contemplation of victory.

The assignment was an odd one even for such an experienced crew as ours. We were designated, along with a great many other ships, to provide a number of able-bodied seamen to form a "bluejackets landing force." This was a rather

Navy Days

anachronistic term which most of us had seen only in navy manuals to describe an armed militia drawn from a ship's company to do shore duty. Somewhere in its hold, each ship carried the accoutrements for such a militia. They consisted of canvas puttees, web belts, canteens, knapsacks, bayonets, and Springfield 30-06 single shot rifles. As we steamed northeast toward a second rendezvous south of Japan, all the ships disgorged these musty items from their lockers, selected the young men who were to constitute the force, and drilled them in their duties. The pop-pop of rifle fire could be heard in the wakes of all ships of the fleet as we moved toward our destination. Once there, in "Area Badger," named for Admiral Oscar Badger, who commanded the operation and was embarked in the light cruiser *San Diego*, we steamed in large circles while waiting for each ship contributing "bluejackets" to transfer its contingent to one of two transport vessels by breeches buoy. This required winching each sailor on a small wooden seat across a steel cable slung between ships while we continued to steam in formation.

Within a few days, we were ready for our move on Japan, and set course northward for Honshu. During this passage, there was only one untoward incident in which a maverick kamikaze made a futile attempt to reach our task force, and one somewhat confusing event when a large Japanese submarine surfaced and surrendered nearby. By the end of the third week in August, the Japanese had been given time to comply with the terms of the surrender, and the fleet moved into the approaches to Tokyo Bay. As we came abreast of the island of O Shima at the mouth of the sea channel, each ship paused briefly to pick up a Japanese pilot. By this time, we had taken up the formation under which we would enter the bay. Two small wooden minesweepers were in the lead, each streaming shallow-water sweeps to clear a path ahead of the screen. Then came our sister ship the *Ellison* and ourselves, each streaming deep paravanes to sweep the entire breadth of the channel. Then followed the other destroyers, the cruiser, and the transports in single file, moving slowly up the bay.

We had been given a general synopsis of the surrender terms and could look out to shore to see how some of them were being observed. For example, the Japanese corvette which delivered our pilot to us had its guns all locked in their maximum vertical position so that they could be seen not to threaten us. Similarly, the coastal batteries were marked with white strips of cloth and their barrels elevated. Other shipping in the bay was out of sight or out of motion. I had the senior watch as we picked up our pilot and rounded into the bay. The task force commander signaled general quarters and all ships were put on alert. Our captain, however, had the quirky notion that he and his crew would rather savor their passage as spectators than be shut up at duty stations. He therefore ordered me to set only a modified alert, to retain conning command, and to continue to navigate the ship up the bay. About one thing, he was absolutely adamant. I was to have nothing to do with the Japanese pilot who had been placed aboard. He could stay on the bridge—and he did, clinging to the starboard pelorus stand—but I was to pay no attention to him or the treacherous charts rolled under his arm. U.S. Navy charts were good enough for our captain!

This, then, was the way we made our way into the enemy's homeland to accept his surrender. I generally followed in the wake of the wooden minesweepers, steering a course verified for me by the executive officer, who acted as navigator. I kept on enough way to be sure my paravanes streamed straight. As I moved back and forth from one wing of the bridge to another, I occasionally heard a small hiss escape from our Japanese pilot. But, otherwise, in accord with my captain's instructions, I had nothing to do with him. None of us really knew if the surrender was some sort of elaborate trap, or the real thing. All of us could conceive of it being a massive ambush, in which our task force would be baited into the bay and then destroyed.

Navy Days

Indeed, the carrier task forces just over the horizon and the bombers on Saipan and Tinian had contingency preparations to retaliate in such an event.

As it happened, the whole naval passage went very smoothly. We arrived as a task group in the anchorage area between the naval base at Yokosuka and the commercial docks at Yokohama in the middle of the afternoon. By prearrangement, we anchored Conestoga fashion, with the transports and cruiser at the center, the destroyers in a circle outboard, and we launched motor whaleboats to picket against the possibility of saboteurs trying to place "limpets," or explosive charges, against our hulls during the hours of darkness. The Japanese population was nowhere to be seen. The only activity was from a large warehouse in Yokohama where P.O.W.'s had strung banners of welcome to the U.S. Navy and where signalers sought to get our attention.

It had been a long day for me and, after the ship had been anchored and the whaleboat launched, I still faced the task of writing my log before I could go below deck for some rest. I turned over the watch to my successor and began to record the day's events in the ship's log. One of the early items to be recorded was the arrival on board of the Japanese pilot, who was still quietly waiting on the bridge deck, near the flag bags. I sent a quartermaster to fetch him and asked him his name. With great courtesy, a toothy smile, and much bowing of his head, he introduced himself in quite respectable English and carefully spelled out his name for me. He also gave me his rank and serial number, all of which I dutifully entered in the log. I then asked about the charts he carried under his arm. He produced them with great pride, spreading them on our chart table to show me their merit. They were, indeed, somewhat more detailed than our own, especially with regard to soundings at the channel edges and obstructions on the floor of the bay. But what made them especially useful was that they clearly showed the location of all the minefields in the bay and the disposition of all military installations on the bayshore. In their usual meticulous way, the Japanese had been quite anxious to be helpful to their enemy's navigators as we entered their heartland.

"We come ber-r-ry crose to minefiers," the pilot said with a giggle as he pointed to a couple of places where our paravanes had reached the outer limits of the channel. I supposed that this explained some of the hissing sounds that had marked his reaction to our stately passage of the narrows below Yokosuka. He then began to explain himself somewhat more than my log writing required. He was, he said, a former merchant marine officer who had spent a great deal of time in American ports, particularly in California and Oregon. Because of his great admiration and affection for the United States, he had learned to speak English. The war was a matter of great distress to him and he was pleased it was over. He hoped he could be of service to us and would one day again visit the United States.

Although I gave all this rendition a rather frosty reception, he was not at all deterred from his continued efforts at ingratiation. Rather shyly, he asked whether I was regular navy or reserve. When I assured him I was reserve, he beamed, grasped my right hand in both of his and chortled, "Me, too!" I couldn't resist such chutzpah and shook my head with laughter.

It was clear that our pilot had become my responsibility, but I had not quite figured what to do with him. Since he was not a prisoner, I wouldn't put him in the brig. As he was an officer, I wouldn't send him into enlisted country. But I was clearly not going to let him wander freely around the ship, and I was not going to put him in an officer's stateroom. My final decision was to call the master-at-arms, have him bring a folding army cot and a blanket to the wardroom, and post a guard at the passageway while our guest slept. He was to be allowed, when accompanied, to use the officer's head. I then showered and went to my stateroom for a long night's sleep.

When I awoke, dressed, and emerged into the wardroom the next morning, I was surprised to see the cot neatly folded up in a corner and the blanket carefully rolled up on the leather transom. The pilot was nowhere to be seen. I asked the wardroom mess steward where he had gone. He said the officer of the deck had authorized him to go out, under guard. Curious as to his whereabouts, I opened the hatch to the starboard deck. There, where the crew's mess line might normally be at that hour, I found a line of sailors leading up the ladder to the bridge deck, all carrying letters in their hands. I swung back in and up the inner passage to the bridge. The quartermaster on duty, seeing me arrive, and assuming I was looking for the pilot, merely jerked a thumb in the direction of the flag bags.

There I found our pilot, armed with an ivory chop and an ink pad, which must have been in his chart kit, placing a kanji cachet as a souvenir on each sailor's letter as it was presented to him. I watched as he practiced a little ceremony for each man. He would bow from the waist, state his name, and ask the sailor his. He would then repeat the name, carefully preceded by a loud "Mister," and shake the right hand. He would then take the letter or letters, pronounce the name of the city of destination, breathe on his chop, dip it into the ink pad, painstakingly affix the cachet, hand back the letters with a deep bow, and move on to his next client. Before breakfast, he had succeeded in meeting nearly every enlisted member of the ship's crew, and, I discovered, a few of the officers as well. Fortunately, our captain was unaware of all this. Later that afternoon, we briefly docked at the main pier in Yokosuka to test it for booby-traps before letting the cruiser moor there. I put our pilot ashore, and the crew gave him a fond farewell. Had he been able to appreciate it, he would have discovered that vengeance was a rather fleeting sentiment among that generation of Americans.

Chapter Three

The Ends of Empires
1947–1949

IN 1947, I WAS ASSIGNED as third secretary and vice consul in the American legation to Siam. Bangkok, in those days, was a rather squalid tropical city sprawled along a bend in the Chao Phya river, laced with canals and shaded with flame trees. The houses were either in traditional Chinese style with tile roofs and inner court yards or in the British colonial style, built on pilings with spacious wooden verandahs. There were perhaps three hundred "Europeans" in the city, among whom were numbered the sixteen Americans who served in our legation.

The legation was housed in three ramshackle wooden buildings in the British colonial style located in a rather spacious compound on Sathorn Road. In the aftermath of World War II, our relations with the Siamese were friendly, but not yet intimate. The country had been vaguely aligned with the

Japanese and the Axis Powers in the war and was still somewhat tainted with enemy status. This issue had been obscured in the immediate postwar period because the government had been headed by a man who had cooperated with the Allies in an amateurish sort of underground movement during the latter part of the war.

However, my arrival in Bangkok coincided with a coup d'etat mounted by a military officer whose record had been decidedly pro-Japanese. Diplomatic relations were therefore in a state of limbo when I joined the legation. For reasons not entirely clear to me, our compound affected an attitude of siege. Although we were open to what precious little official business we conducted, we practiced a posture of defense.

Since this was before the days when marine guards were assigned to all our diplomatic missions, it was not easy to be convincing about our defense. Our only guard was an arthritic old Indian, who wore a khaki jacket over a dirty dhoti and lounged on a rope charpoy at the principal entrance to the compound. He had been much honored by our government for the act of cradling our flag and preventing it from touching the ground when the Japanese lowered it from the flagpole in December 1941. But he was patently useless as a defender of the compound against invasion or depredation.

Accordingly, someone on the staff had devised a more conspicuous and presumably more effective form of defense. Junior officers, on a rotating basis, were designated as "duty officers," and stationed in a defensive post on the verandah outside the Minister's office. So it was that on my second night in Bangkok, I found myself attempting to sleep on an army cot under a mosquito net with a loaded M-1 rifle on the verandah floor and several clips of ammunition nearby. I was never quite certain what I was guarding against nor what my plan of action entailed. The whole scene did not exactly fulfill my fantasies of the diplomatic lifestyle.

Before these questions had to be answered and before I

had to spend another night under the mosquito net, the United States government chose to recognize the government installed by the coup, which changed the name of the country to Thailand, and full diplomatic relations were resumed. In fact, within a short time, our representation was elevated to the rank of embassy, albeit we were still the same small group of slightly bewildered bureaucrats in the same tacky compound. Thus, I began my diplomatic career.

I was told that my task was to take over the commercial and economic section of the embassy because the man who had been rather grandly called economic counselor and commercial attaché had left, having reached the mandatory retirement age, and his successor had not yet been named. This information pleased me because it meant that I would be acting head of an embassy section and would be able to practice the economic knowledge in which I had recently acquired a master's degree. It came therefore as quite a surprise to me to discover that reports of the commercial attaché's departure were not entirely accurate. He had lodged an official appeal for an extension of his tenure beyond the mandatory retirement age, and despite the fact that it had not been acted upon and that he had been separated from the embassy's payroll, he continued to occupy his office, use the official vehicle assigned to him, and behave as if he were still on active duty. His only concession of consequence was to cut off all contact with the ambassador, whose office was in the large building in the center of the compound. The economic and commercial section, which occupied a smaller building in the western end of the compound and was reached by a separate gate, became, to all effects, an autonomous entity, practicing its own measure of diplomatic relations quite apart from the embassy.

The attaché himself was a rather crusty old man who always wore a tropical white suit and incessantly smoked cigarettes in a long ivory cigarette holder which he clenched in stained, uneven teeth. Because he talked with the holder in his mouth, the cigarettes constantly quivered in their perch, spilling ashes down the bosom of the white suits and, by midday, leaving them splotched with humid grey stains. He spoke airily of powerful friends in Washington who would correct the injustice of his forced retirement and restore him to authority within the premise of the embassy. The ambassador, who was about to go on home leave, chose not to confront the unpleasantness inherent in enforcing his authority over the economic and commercial section. Instead, he procrastinated until he could quietly leave the country and dump the problem in the lap of his timid deputy, who became chargé d'affaires on the ambassador's departure. The deputy had no stomach to confront the old rebel attaché, and thus the anomalous impasse continued.

I had, in the meantime, moved into my office in the economic and commercial section. The old rebel received me warmly and with great courtesy as his assistant. He assured me that his status would be resolved favorably in a few days and that we would be a great team. He would concentrate on commercial representation and I could do economic reporting and analysis. In the meantime, because of his awkward situation, I could initial all the cables and restore some communication with the rest of the embassy. A modus vivendi was thus established which enabled all of those concerned to avoid confrontation with reality.

In about ten days time, however, a message arrived from Washington saying that the old man's appeal had been denied and that he was officially and inexorably retired. By this time, I had adequately established myself with the one American secretary and the several Thai employees of the section to bring our ordeal to a conclusion. On the day after the message from Washington arrived, we cleared out the old man's desk, packed his few personal possessions into cardboard boxes for delivery to his bachelor's quarters at a local hotel, and spread a small buffet on the bare surface of his former desk. When he came to the office that day, we gave him a modest farewell party and had him driven to the hotel in a defeated daze, using for the last time the official automobile, which thereafter called at my house rather than at his hotel in the mornings. I was finally able to turn my attention to running the section I had temporarily inherited.

The first thing I discovered was that reports requested by the Departments of State and Commerce had been long neglected. A whole stack of requests had merely been assigned to a "hold" basket. I flicked through them with dismay, but soon realized that they constituted a framework that I could use in order to develop some systematic economic knowledge about my first country of assignment. The problem was to decide where to begin. More or less at random, I chose a request for a report on "Crude Drugs and Medicinal Herbs." The choice was dictated by the fact that the subject matter contained in the request seemed quite straightforward and factual. The drug and herb industry seemed rather small and well defined. It would provide a useful test case for me to learn how one went about acquiring information in Bangkok and how reliable statistics might prove to be. I devised a brief outline in questionnaire form to assist in developing a systematic compilation of information and arranged to sally forth on my first quest for economic facts.

One of my Thai assistants assured me that the crude drug and medicinal herb industry in Bangkok was divided into two sectors. One was the traditional sector controlled by the Chinese, who handled all their commerce exclusively in Chinese channels. The other, which engaged in export commerce with the western world, was dominated by the French-Siam Drug Company, a Parisian-owned concern of some vintage doing business from a rather formidable concrete building I had often passed in the commercial district along New Road. Since the telephone system in Bangkok had not yet been repaired from wartime neglect, it was not possible to telephone for appointments in those days. A European seeking a business appointment merely presented himself at an office and asked to meet with the person he sought. Those of our complexion were so rare that we were usually not kept waiting more than a few minutes before being ushered into a fan-cooled inner sanctum to conduct our business.

On the morning I set out for the French-Siam Drug Company, I dressed, as usual, in the accepted European manner. I wore a white shirt open at the neck, white duck trousers, white sox and sandals. I carried a small leather portfolio. I was driven in our drab official car through the trolley cars, samlors, bullock carts, and teeming human traffic on New Road. Because I had been warned that the personnel of the company spoke only French and Thai, I rehearsed in my mind some of the French phrases that would be useful to my inquiry.

When I edged past the inevitable Indian guard at the door of the building and bounded up the stairs to a reception desk in the lobby, I found a beautiful young French métisse with lustrous black hair and a lissome figure whom I greeted in effusive French and from whom I asked directions to the office of Monsieur le Directeur. With great charm and grace, she rounded her desk and led me down a dark corridor to a massive door. She gently knocked and then pushed open the door in response to a muffled answer from within. When the door opened, it precipitated amazement on both sides of the threshhold. I was halfway into the room before I comprehended the scene on which I had intruded. There, around a large conference table in the director's room were nearly a dozen men, who gazed up at me with startled looks. They were men who had the sunburned faces, the short-cropped hair, and the muscled bodies of military men. They sat at a table which was spread with maps and papers. They seemed to be engaged in a council of war.

As soon as the director, whom I recognized as someone I

had seen at the Sports Club, could recover his composure, he leaped up from the table and led me gently but urgently from his office into another smaller adjoining room. With much apology for having barged in on his meeting, I innocently explained the purpose of my call and produced my questionnaire as evidence of my bona fides. In short order, it was agreed that I would leave the questionnaire with the director, who would undertake to have all my questions answered in writing and would send the documents to my office. Nervously but pleasantly, he then escorted me out past the charming métisse to where my car was waiting at the front door.

What I had obviously invaded was a top-level meeting of French intelligence agents. I recognized the man seated alongside the director at the head of the table as the chief of military intelligence for the French Republic because his picture had appeared rather often in the world press those days as attention had begun to focus on the intensified warfare taking place in Indochina. What I had also uncovered was the fact that the French-Siam Drug Company had become a front for French Intelligence and that its newly arrived director was the senior French Intelligence officer in Bangkok. The French worry was about the weapons and other supplies being infiltrated through Thai territory into Laos and Cambodia. Their meeting, given all the maps, apparently concerned itself with infiltration routes that could be subject to ambush. My penetration of it was quite simply attributable to the fact that I was a "European," spoke French, and could be mistaken by any young métisse for a military officer.

But, to the subtle mind of a French Intelligence officer, nothing so innocent was possible. The French knew that we had recently organized the Central Intelligence Agency. They also knew that an officer of that agency had recently been assigned to Bangkok. (He was, in fact, under cover as an assistant naval attaché.) They logically assumed that I was the CIA man and that I was aggressively making my presence

The Ends of Empires

known. They decided to seduce me. My bride had just joined me, and we soon found ourselves overwhelmed with French hospitality. The French legation, located on the banks of the river, housed a fascinating ménage-à-trois. The French minister, a rather elegant intellectual who later shot himself in a "hunting accident," was married to the ribald daughter of a Greek cavalry officer, and she, in turn, was infatuated with a virile first secretary of legation, whom she had established in residence at the legation. Dinners and soirées in that establishment were, to say the least, titilating for a young American couple from our nation's mainstream.

Other French attention similarly attracted us away from the English-speaking circles largely influenced by the considerable British community and the Thai alumni of American universities. I found myself, for example, in the cast of a theatrical farce staged by the Alliance Francaise. Conversational interest invariably centered on the fighting in Indochina, something which was only of marginal concern to the English speakers. It was generally assumed by our French hosts that I knew more about the subject than I admitted, and, in due course, I did become, by osmosis, more knowledgeable than any other American in our embassy about events to our east.

But, in due course, bureaucratic intelligence triumphed. One muggy evening, my wife and I were invited to dinner in the home of a colonel from the French security services, who was assigned as an attaché to the French legation. The only other guests were our assistant naval attaché, who was actually the CIA representative, and his wife. After dinner, the colonel took his two American male guests into the garden, leaving the three women to swelter in the house. In austere, accusing tones, he informed me that I was *not* the CIA representative and, in similar cartesian rhetoric, informed the assistant naval attaché that he *was*. Both of us readily confirmed the good colonel's conclusions and presumably cut him off from whatever lengthy proof he had assembled to buttress his case. Our reaction deflated him and the evening ended after a single snifter of cognac. My seduction by the French community ended just as swiftly. It was clearly a major social affront to frustrate the presumptive conclusions of gallic logic.

— 2 —

Shortly before our first child was born, we moved into a new house, in a tree-shaded part of Bangkok close to the embassy and immediately adjacent to the Silom Tennis Club. On the next street was a small Buddhist temple, with a large community of monks, whose low, droning chants could be faintly heard from dawn to dusk. One morning, we were startled awake by the thrumming of their prayers just below our windows. I threw on a bathrobe and went out on a balcony to see what was going on. Our whole front garden was filled with saffron-robed monks, their shaven heads glinting in the first rays of the morning sun. They squatted on their heels with their hands clasped above their foreheads and their eyes fixed on the ridgepole of our roof, over my head. Looking up, I was astonished to see a magnificent peacock perched there, spreading his tail and preening his feathers. He seemed to revel in the attention being paid to him.

I soon learned from our servants that the bird had been presented to the monks by a devout worshipper and had been a very special prize for the temple. They had been very distressed when the bird disappeared during the previous night, especially since they thought its plumage made him too heavy to fly. When he was spotted on our roof at dawn, they had come to persuade him gently to return home. In the meantime, we were informed, the fact that he had chosen our house as his perch conferred much merit on us, and the abbot of the temple offered his prayers for our well-being.

We exhausted our supply of rice by distributing it to the monks and invited them, somewhat redundantly, to make themselves at home in our garden. When I returned from work that evening, the bird was still there, but the monk population had been reduced to three young men who had been left behind to retrieve their peacock, should he decide to descend. The next morning, all were gone and I discovered that our wash amah had captured the bird by clucking to him as if he were a rooster, placing some food in the noose of a clothesline, and then yanking the line taut around his legs when he came down to eat. The monks departed jubilantly with their trophy.

That evening was the annual American Alumni Association dinner and ball. The Association was a rather potent force in Bangkok, since its members were drawn from the elite merit scholars who had been chosen by examinations to be educated in American universities and to return to senior positions in the Thai civil service. For at least three generations, since the times of Kings Mongkut and Chulalongkhorn, the Thai government had followed the practice of sending its brightest young scholars abroad to France, England, Germany, Japan, and the United States for such training. Consequently, Thailand had one of the most effective and powerful bureaucracies in Asia.

During the war, those who had been trained in Germany and Japan had allied themselves with the nation's military leaders to form a partnership with the Axis nations while the French, British, and American alumni had been very much in eclipse. Many of them had worked in the Free Thai underground, in association with Allied intelligence agencies. At the end of the war, they became the dominant faction in the bureaucracy and the government. The prime minister, Pridi Phanomyong, a French alumnus, had been drawn from their ranks. The coup d'etat of 1947 had chased Pridi into exile and very sharply reduced the influence of the American, British, and French alumni. They chafed under the rule of their military chiefs, most of whom had been active collaborators with the Japanese. Therefore, the American Alumni Association was more than just a social group. It had a very significant political dimension as well.

Many of the alumni came from old aristocratic families that had a sort of hereditary hold on some ministries in the government, dating back to the days of King Mongkut. The Devakul family, for example, had long dominated the Foreign Ministry, and many of its members served either as ambassadors of Thailand abroad or in responsible positions within the Ministry at Bangkok. Most of them had been educated either in England or in the United States. They all spoke fluent, gracious English in that gentle, elegant vernacular that is peculiar to the Thai aristocracy.

We had come to know a number of Devakuls, and shortly after our arrival in Bangkok, had been invited, along with a few other foreigners, to spend some time with them at their vacation villa by the Gulf in Hua Hin. Because I was held up at the Embassy, my wife joined a group that went down ahead by train. Another straggler and I chartered a small, single-engine aircraft to be with them on the weekend. We landed on a rough strip that had been made of sand and crushed sea shells near the beach. Because of prevailing winds, we had to land on a shoreward vector and pulled up perilously close to a grove of rubber trees. When the pilot took off his sunglasses and turned around to apologize for his abrupt braking action, we saw to our astonishment that both his eyes were heavily clouded with cataracts, and he explained that they were the cause of his retirement from the Air Force. We decided to take the train back to Bangkok on our return.

The weekend was a delight. The Devakuls were obviously the patrons of the small nearby fishing village, and all sorts of fresh creatures from the sea were brought to us at all hours of the day and then cooked in a variety of ways. Fruits and greens also appeared mysteriously to complement the seafood. Cool Thai beer and other drinks were constantly being offered on the great wide shaded verandah or for those on the beach resting from a swim in the coral bottomed sea. Lots of good talk, lively argument, and the tender, teasing humor of the Thai lasted late into the mild evenings, when the fragrance of frangi-pangi blossoms made sleep especially welcome.

One of those evenings, we decided, on the spur of the moment, to join the people of the fishing village, who were celebrating one of the frequent holy days that are a constant excuse for a party in Thailand. We brought along three or four bottles of Mekong, the local Thai rice whisky, and placed them, along with a Coleman lantern, on the beach near the village. Then, to the steady rhythm of a few primitive strings, flutes, and drums, we all joined barefoot in the graceful ramwong. This is a slow, sinuous dance in which the couples move as part of a large swaying circle, making flowing, flirting gestures with arms, hands, legs, and feet, but never touching each other. The very attractive village girls, shy at first in dancing with foreigners, soon relaxed to their coquettish ways; and the young, wind and sea hardened village braves, awkward at first with their pale-skinned partners, were soon cavorting with suggestive, mildly obscene movements to the persistent tempo of the drums. Although the girls never drank, the young men would occasionally break pattern and dart toward the lantern for a hearty swig of whisky, returning flushed and confident to the ramwong line.

This party went well into the night until the whisky and the fuel in the lantern were both exhausted. By that hour, a large pale moon had filled the eastern sky and a few low clouds scudded past it. We walked arm in arm along the beach to the villa and settled in pleasant satisfaction on the chairs and couches of the unlighted veranda. Hardly had we spread out when we began to hear a strange, low, rumbling noise from the direction of the village. Then, the noise took shape as a slow stampede of cattle thundered down the beach in front of us. They moved at a pace somewhat between a lope and a dash, and seemed in no particular panic. The mottled moon hung above them, while the speckled mist gave them a ghostly outline as they pounded down the beach. There must have been three hundred of them, coming out of the haze to the north and disappearing quietly to the south. No one stood or pointed. We merely lounged there and watched in curious amusement. When they had disappeared, we quietly speculated among ourselves as to the cause of what we had seen. Some suggested that a few lads from the fishing village, with a little too much whisky under their belts, had gone to the fields and deliberately stampeded the communal cattle in our direction as a good-natured shivaree. Others felt that the noise of our party had vexed the herd into action. But the consensus was that they ran by because it was such a lovely night for a run on the beach.

It was shared experiences such as this that brought us close to our Thai friends and made it natural that we would join with them in celebrating their alumni association festivities. Its annual celebration had always been a gala event, with music, dramatic skits, and other acts to warm up the preprandial atmosphere. This year it was to be held at the Suan Amphorn gardens, adjacent to the royal palace. A tent had been erected for the stage and proscenium; a dance floor had been installed, and the whole area was bedecked with Thai and American flags around tables for perhaps four hundred guests. I had agreed to join with three other Americans from the Embassy in a barbershop quartet. We were to be the lead act in the second half of the vaudeville.

The guests were all in place in folding chairs arrayed in front of the stage by eight o'clock and, remarkably for Bangkok, the performance began exactly on time. In the front row, resplendant in their white military uniforms, were the new Prime Minister and most of his general officer colleagues who held cabinet portfolios. Other senior political, business, and government figures were sprinkled through the audience. They

The Ends of Empires

all enjoyed the clever, somewhat pointed, skits of the first part of the program enormously.

After an intermission, the barber shop quartet lined up behind the curtain, ready for the second half of the show. When the curtain parted and we launched into our routine, we could see that the entire front row, formerly occupied by the Cabinet, was empty. As we sang our way through our repertoire, we could hear much commotion and consternation behind stage. When the curtain finally closed, we went back there and found a scene of angry confusion. We also found all our Thai friends, clad outlandishly in the costumes worn in their skits, armed to the teeth with pistols, submachine guns, and carbines.

It took us a little while to learn that the dinner and ball had been carefully rigged as the occasion for a coup that would return the pro-Allies government to power. The military cabinet, innocently enjoying the Yankee pranks and songs, was to be bagged and taken prisoner. Other elements of the plotters were even at that moment advancing on the royal palace to take the young king into custody and convince him to support the action. Former Prime Minister Pridi was aboard a private yacht proceeding up the river and a column of marines and navy men was moving on the capital overland from their base at Sataheep.

We Americans at the party, feeling more than a little unhappy at having been decoyed into this affair, decided to gather up our wives and leave. We discovered, however, that the exits from the gardens were very firmly blocked from the outside by units of military police, who ordered us back to our tables and, indeed, commanded that the dinner dance should proceed as scheduled. There was a lot of hasty hiding of weapons in the bushes and elsewhere as our Thai hosts realized their coup had failed and decided to carry on the party as if nothing had intervened. We heard a few bursts of gunfire over the palace walls, the clanking of tanks and armored cars in the neighboring streets, and some louder artillery explosions to the south and east of the city. But most of the noise was drowned out by the dance music, which lasted until nearly two in the morning. At that point, we were told we could leave, and it was politely suggested that we drive straight home with no detours.

That morning, after very little sleep, I was awakened by the assistant military attaché. By this point, I had left the commercial section and had been placed in charge of the consular section. In that capacity, I had, among other concerns, responsibility for the welfare of all Americans in the country. I was informed that a group of Americans who ran the Seventh Day Adventist hospital were caught in the cross fire between the army and the marine column that had penetrated the outskirts of the city from the south. The attaché had a scheme to extricate them. He intended to drive over to the army command post and arrange a cease fire. He had already talked with the navy-marine leaders and had obtained their acquiescence. I was to go to the navy signal station on Wireless Road, which was serving as rebel headquarters, and he would telephone me there. Then, I would drive the short distance to the Seventh Day hospital, gather up the Americans, and lead them back to safety. When I reached the signal station, I would telephone him, and the two sides could resume shooting at each other.

I rigged a pillow case as a white flag on the extended radio antenna of my little blue Ford and drove off to the signal station. Mortar shells were falling a few hundred feet short of the station and the crackle of rifle fire seemed everywhere. The neighborhood reeked of cordite. Young marines and sailors crouched in the hedges along the road, scurrying forward a few feet at a time, and winging off rifle shots in the general direction of the army defenders. An artillery piece was being slowly wheeled into place and its muzzle depressed for point blank fire. The houses and gardens in this pleasant,

The Ends of Empires

westernized neighborhood were incongruously quiet in the morning sun. In due course, the telephone call came, and, sure enough, the firing ceased. I got in my car and began to drive slowly down Wireless Road in the direction of the hospital, my white flag fluttering. One hundred yards short of the hospital entrance, a machine gun opened up ahead of me, and without waiting to test its accuracy, I swung into the nearest driveway, racing up its gravel toward the house ahead. As I skidded to a stop, I realized I was in the compound of the Netherlands minister's residence. To my surprise, he and his wife were having breakfast on their front terrace, accompanied by their tall, elegant second secretary, who was a close friend of ours.

As if it were the most natural thing in the world, they invited me to join them and had their No. 1 boy set another place at the table. By this time, the cease-fire had completely collapsed, and the full scale of rifle, machine gun, and mortar exchange had been resumed. Since there seemed little other choice, I joined the Dutch at their breakfast. Suddenly, a squad of marines came tumbling through the front gate and began to set up a mortar and machine gun position in the front garden. The Dutch minister was not amused, and, turning to his second secretary, said, "Jan, tell him he can't do that. This is diplomatic property!" Jan, who was about six feet four, uncoiled himself from his breakfast and ambled out to the garden. Standing fully erect, he towered over the tiny Thai. He tapped their leader on the shoulder, explained the situation as best he could, and made shooing motions to indicate that the unit should go out the gate it had entered. After a certain chatter among his subordinates, the Thai officer drew himself up to salute Jan, bowed his apologies in our direction, and withdrew. We continued eating our breakfast.

By the time we were finished, so was the fighting. Under some sort of truce worked out over the telephone, the navy units agreed to withdraw and return to Sataheep. The army agreed not to pursue. The coup attempt was over. One reason for the navy's failure was the fact that the navy command had neglected to calculate the tides and had been required to wait over three hours to make a ferry crossing, thus delaying their arrival in Bangkok well beyond the scheduled hour for coordinated action. But, the principal cause of failure was the government's advance knowledge of the secret plot and the preventive action it had taken to frustrate it with a minimum loss of life.

Because of the key role in the plot played by the American Alumni, because of the presence of so many Americans at Suan Amphorn that night, and because some American swashbucklers were on Pridi's yacht as well as among those who penetrated the royal palace, the Thai government moved very cautiously in the aftermath of the aborted coup. They were apparently not quite sure how much the U.S. government might have been involved. For that matter, the British were suspect as well since there were also U.K. citizens on the yacht and in the palace. Hence, a Thai navy admiral was cashiered and a few of the plotters were discreetly advised to leave town, but very little other retribution was meted out. To this day, I am not sure in my own mind whether there was some half-cocked CIA involvement in the action.

The denouement of it all came a few days later when I was visited by a captain of Thai counterintelligence, who acted as liaison with our consular section. He told me very politely that there was an American registered in the Oriental Hotel, who had been a conspirator in the misbegotten action and who had, indeed, been seen in the palace on the night of the fiasco. I recognized the name he gave me as that of a former OSS officer, who was the son of a U.S. senator. He said that Thai authorities intended to arrest the American the following afternoon, but left the clear impression they would be relieved to avert that unpleasantness if he were to disappear on his own volition. I thanked him very much for this information, and he retreated smiling.

As soon as he had left, I called the manager of Pan Am, the only U.S. airline flying to Bangkok in those days. His flight had just left and the next was not due for two days. He said BOAC had a flying boat going out to Singapore that evening. While I was looking up the BOAC telephone number, my phone rang and John Bull, the appropriately named BOAC manager, called to ask if, by any chance, I needed a seat on his plane for an urgent traveller. He said he had a U.K. subject with the same imperative requirement and could save a place if I got my client to his office in an hour's time. I thanked him roundly and called my driver for the trip to the Oriental Hotel. The desk clerk there was a lieutenant in counterintelligence, and he smiled broadly as I came in. Without being asked, he gave me the room number and the name of the former OSS officer.

The doors on the rooms of the Oriental in those days were latticed, with an outer set swinging outward and an inner set swinging inward. Both opened from the inside. I knocked twice on the door before a voice answered. When I identified myself, there was a pause and then a brief command to wait. I could hear the latches being lifted on both sets of doors and then heard the inner set swing shut again. When I was told to come in, I moved slowly, opening the outer doors and pausing a moment before I gently swung the inner two ahead of me. As I entered the room, there against the wall stood my quarry crouched in shooting stance, with a Colt service .45 aimed at my chest. He was red eyed, trembling, and looked as though he had been drinking heavily.

It took about five minutes of gentle persuasion to convince him that I had come to arrange his departure. When I finally succeeded, I asked him to give me his revolver. Reluctantly, he snapped on the safety and handed it over. I slipped out the cartridge clip and unchambered the round he had been aiming at my chest. He picked up his few belongings and we started out. At the desk, I handed the empty Colt to the clerk for safe keeping. We arrived at the BOAC office with time to spare. John Bull and my British consular counterpart, with another white-lipped client in tow, suggested we join them in the BOAC van for the quick trip to the launch landing that was just to the south of the Oriental Hotel. John took his two charges aboard the launch and made the short trip to the Solent flying boat moored to a buoy in the Menam Chao Phya. He embarked his two passengers and returned to the landing to await the rest of the travellers.

The British consul and I decided to have a gimlet on the Oriental terrace and see the flying boat actually airborne. In fifteen minutes, she had been loaded, her engines started, and she slipped her mooring. The launches cleared a way for her in the busy water traffic of the river and she lifted lazily off the surface just as the sun began to sink behind the tower of Wat Arun. When we called for the check, the desk clerk came instead to inform us that there would be no charge. I reached into my pocket for the cartridge clip. Inserting the extra round on top of the spring loaded rack, I handed it to him and wished him good target practice. He exploded with glee.

— 3 —

The commercial section of the American embassy in Bangkok sold rice and bought tin. The rice we sold was owned by the United States Department of Agriculture, which, in 1948, was still subsidizing American crop production through preemptive buying. The tin we bought was for the account of the Reconstruction Finance Corporation, which was still operating a smelter in Texas City. That smelter had been built during the war years, when the prime sources of tin in Southeast Asia had been cut off from the United States. It had been designed to utilize the low-content Bolivian ore that was not profitable to smelt in peacetime. After the war, the RFC attempted to keep the smelter competitive by blending the Bolivian ore with the richer concentrate from the Dutch Indies, British Malaya, and Thailand. Purchases of Dutch and British-controlled ore were arranged in Washington. We purchased the Thai tin in Bangkok.

It soon became apparent that the amount of tin ore being offered to us in Bangkok significantly exceeded the normal amount of production from the surface mines in the south of Thailand. The assumption, therefore, was that some of the product we purchased must have been smuggled from Malaya. This made much economic sense because we paid in dollars, while producers selling in Malaya were required to sell to the British Treasury for overvalued, inconvertible pounds sterling, and let the Treasury skim off the dollar profits as well as pocket the foreign exchange. The British protested to the Thai about this incursion into their official monopoly. The Thai asserted that no Malayan tin was crossing into their territory. Washington wanted to know the facts. Consequently, I persuaded the air attaché to fly me south and leave me in the town of Songkhla, just north of the Malayan border. He agreed to come back in a week to pick me up.

Songkhla was a sleepy little town that was one of the two principal tin ports of Thailand, and the documented port of loading for most of our tin purchases. It had a beautiful, palm fringed bay, with coral sand and crystal clear water. Freighters and ore carriers called there about once a week. Commerce in the town was run by the Chinese, but the one tolerable hotel was operated by the Royal Thai Railways. Although it had about six rooms, I seemed to be its only guest. The first night I was there, a half dozen large rats fought over a cake of soap I had foolishly left uncovered in my room. After that, I slept with the light on.

In checking with Chinese tin merchants, who exported the product of small, independent producers, I was assured that there was no smuggling across the Malayan border. I was also provided export figures that were only about a third of the totals that appeared on the consular invoices presented to us in Bangkok by shipping agents handling cargo originating from Songkhla. In order to shed some light on this anomaly, I decided to watch a loading operation in the bay. I bought a can of Argentine beef, a bottle of beer, and a loaf of rice bread from a Chinese shop and hired a samlor driver to pedal me out to the beach. With the promise of a good tip, he agreed to come back for me at sunset.

I watched a vessel take on tin from a couple of small barges; and then, when the loading was completed, move out past the mouth of the bay and anchor again. There, at a point I calculated to be just beyond three miles, she was soon surrounded by larger barges which slipped up from the south. She continued loading operations through nightfall. In the morning, from the window of my hotel room, I could see that she was gone. The mystery of tin smuggling was solved. The Thai were technically right. No tin crossed their frontiers. But, it was documented as of Thai origin and, hence, evaded British export and exchange controls. Back in Bangkok, examining the consular invoices, I discovered that most of the tin exports originating from Songhkla were for the account of a large British owned syndicate that operated a few scattered mining properties on Thai territory. The bulk of its operations were in Malaya. It seemed to be entirely an internal British scam, with no overt external complicity.

The British syndicate was run by a colorful Australian, who had started life as a prospector, prospered greatly just before the war, spent the war as a prisoner of the Japanese, and returned to the tin fields ahead of everyone else. He was a ruthless old buccaneer, who looked like a relic from the Spanish Main. The next time he came to call on me with an offer on a lot of tin ore, I told him what I had seen in Songhkla. He studied me a moment and asked what I intended to do about it. I said my job was not to enforce British regulations, but to buy high quality tin ore at the lowest possible price. He grunted and reduced his price a notch below the prevailing Bangkok rate. From there on, Sir Arthur (the old rogue had been knighted) and I became fast friends, and I bought his tin ore at the lowest prices on the market. This arrangement continued up to the time I left the commercial section and took over consular matters at the embassy. After that, I lost touch with Sir Arthur and hadn't seen him for some time when I was transferred to Calcutta.

My wife and I, accompanied by our six-months-old daughter, decided it would be more convenient for us to travel by ship to Calcutta, rather than fly on a plane that left Bangkok in the small hours of the morning. We booked passage on a Jardine coastal freighter operating out of Hong Kong and undertook to board her at Penang, off the Malay coast. Penang served as an entrepot for the northern Malay states, as Singapore did for the south. Moreover, the island had a large tin smelter and two luxury hotels where the British miners and rubber planters from the interior came occasionally to rest and relax. We chose to stay in one of them, the Eastern and Oriental, until our ship came to port. We learned from the Jardine agent that she was operating three days behind schedule. The hotel was a godsend after the primitive circumstances of Bangkok. The running water worked, the rooms were screened, and a crisp, starched Chinese ayah was provided to take care of our child. We settled in for a comfortable rest.

At our first breakfast, we discovered that the dining room staff was all Indian. Each table was assigned to a specific room, and each had a tall bearer, in gleaming white, with a cockaded turban and a towel over his arm. As we sat down at the table to which we were directed, we were pleased to see another American, who was the consul at Ipoh, approaching from the entrance. We invited him to join us, and discovered he was on a three day visit, since Penang fell within his district of responsibility. We noticed that there was some grumbling among the bearers at this development, but paid no particular attention to it.

The three of us went sight-seeing that morning and, shortly after noon, returned to the hotel for lunch. As we were having drinks on the terrace before entering the dining room, we were greeted by still a fourth American, the CIA station chief from Singapore. When the four of us eventually headed for our table in the dining room, we discovered that it was set for only two people and that the two extra chairs had been removed. Our companions quickly swung up chairs from adjoining tables and our bearer grudgingly set places for them. The service was surly, and we were made acutely aware that we had boorishly infringed upon the hotel's inviolable system of seating each guest at his own table.

That evening, a Saturday, was "gala" at the hotel. That meant black tie for dinner and a dance orchestra to enliven the proceedings. Once again, we four Americans gathered for drinks on the terrace and then proceeded to our table. This time, we discovered that all spare chairs within reaching distance had been removed and that each nearby bearer stood in steadfast guard over his domain. We were left standing, looking for someone to resolve our problem. Suddenly, from an alcove dais adjoining the dance floor, came a large rumble, and I looked to see old Sir Arthur headed our way. In white dinner jacket and black tie, his faced seemed more florid than ever, and he picked his way among the tables like a farmer in a field of corn. As he approached, I could see the smirks growing on the faces of the Indian bearers. The Yanks were about to have their comeuppance.

This all turned to consternation as the old sourdough threw his arms around me, and breathing gin into my face, upbraided me for not letting him know we were staying in his hotel. "Don't ya know I own the bloody place?" he exclaimed. He was

The Ends of Empires

entertaining a large group of friends that evening, he said, but arranged that we should dine with him the following evening at the Penang Club, which was a short distance from the hotel. We waved him our thanks, and, by the time we turned to our table, found that it had mysteriously sprouted four chairs and was being rapidly set for four people by some assiduous, obsequious bearers.

Dinner at the Penang Club proved to be our first introduction into the ways of the raj. For starters, my wife was not allowed to enter the front door; and when I took her around to the ladies' entrance at the rear, I was not allowed to enter there. We nearly left at that point, but decided, instead, that the whole exercise was enormously amusing and fell in with the pattern by which the British had ruled their vast empire through a mere handful of superior administrators.

Sir Arthur's dinner was then succeeded by Sir Arthur's Daimler sedan and a nice young Scottish lad as sight-seeing guide, and, finally, by Sir Arthur's private tender to take us alongside our Jardine ship, when she was finally ready for boarding. This manner of arrival naturally served to catch the attention of the salty old captain, who met us at the gangway and apologized for the rusty, sooty condition of his ship. She was an old tub, especially built for the China-India coastal trade. Although she carried general cargo, she also had a considerable load of passengers. Only eight of these travelled first class, in relatively spacious cabins above decks. About 120 more travelled " 'tween decks," in steerage. These were almost entirely Indians, or "Lascars," as the captain called them. They were separated from the upper decks by heavy grills and barred passageways. The entrances to this area were guarded by White Russian strong men, armed with submachine guns. Except for the chief engineer and the ship's doctor, only one other officer at a time was allowed to be in the "Lascar area," and the protection against piracy was never relaxed.

As we were heaving the anchor to short stay, the captain

suddenly called a halt to the process of getting underway and ordered an immediate search of the ship. He had smelled the musky odor of durian, and had a strict order against permitting any of the "passion fruit" aboard his ship. Because of its alleged aphrodisiac nature, Lascars had fought over durians in the past, and some had even been killed as a result. He was determined to throw the durian overboard. Eventually, it was found in a first class cabin, the property of a prosperous Indian merchant who surrendered it only after a loud argument and who, thereafter, never emerged from his cabin, having all his meals handed through his half-opened door by the Chinese mess stewards.

It was a smooth passage to Calcutta, with a two-day stop in Rangoon. There, unfortunately, my wife contracted an infection in her ear from swimming at the Kokine Club and suffered considerably the rest of the way to Calcutta. The ship's doctor, a gentle Jewish refugee from Vienna, did not have the means aboard to treat her, but kept her fairly comfortable until we arrived in Calcutta and then hustled her to another Jewish refugee friend who practiced there, and was able to arrest the infection.

We were soon comfortably settled in a large furnished flat in a government owned building. A staff of household help was rapidly recruited, and we were assured that our car and our possessions were en route. A few days after our arrival, we decided to dine out in what was described as Calcutta's best restaurant. It had been established well before the war in the Grand Hotel by an Italian named Firpo, and I had eaten there once in a transit through Calcutta shortly after partition.

It still made an effort to retain some touches of grandeur, but it needed repainting, the upholstery was worn, and the decor was faded. However, the bearers still wore their impressive uniforms, the orchestra was in black tie, and the napery gleamed white. Nevertheless, it was nearly deserted.

We were seated with a great flourish. The orchestra tried an American tune, and the headwaiter suggested cocktails. My wife made the mistake of asking for a daiquiri. The headwaiter and the bearer disappeared for a long time. I finally called over one of the other bearers and told him that, if there was any problem about the daiquiri, my wife would join me in a whisky and water. I was assured that there was no problem, and, after several more minutes, the drinks finally arrived.

The color of the daiquiri didn't look right, but we could see three or four eager faces peering through the oval windows of the kitchen door to see how it was received. And so, after a slow, careful taste, my wife pronounced it very good, even though she could hardly finish it. After that, the service was splendid, but the food was abominable. It was the last time we ever went to a restaurant in India to eat anything other than Indian food. It symbolized, in its way, the passing of the old British raj. Many of the features of the colonial era eked out a slow transformation, and there were still, during our stay in Calcutta, such things as clubs that did not permit Indians to membership, events that were limited to "Europeans," and a small garrison at Fort William to protect us "against the sepoys." But India, as the British knew it, faded into history while we lived there, and was replaced by today's India, with a world view and a character of its own.

— 4 —

Living in Calcutta in the aftermath of the British raj proved an interesting experience. We few Americans were assimilated into the British community and treated as "Europeans." As such, we had access to the Saturday Club and other symbols of power and status. But, we had very little access to the Indian intellectual and literary figures who accounted for the irascible brilliance of Bengal. My own duties with the consulate general were largely commercial and threw me into the business groups who thrived in this old imperial port city.

In those days, we were far less concerned with export sales than we were with purchasing scarce raw materials to feed the maw of our expanding economy. The two critical items wanted from Calcutta were jute and manganese. Jute was the victim of partition and manganese a casualty of the railroad. Partition had awarded all the jute growing areas in the swamplands around Dacca to the Muslim state of East Bengal, a wing of newly created Pakistan. All the mills, warehouses, and processing areas were along the banks of the Hooghly River, in Hindu West Bengal, a province of India. Although both elements of the industry were operated by British companies, and managed by indomitable Scotsmen, the tension and turmoil that afflicted the border area made it almost impossible for those companies to fulfill their orders.

The Hindu and Muslim communities were still literally at each other's throats a year after partition, and battles were constantly breaking out in the border areas, which left hundreds killed and mutilated in the most atrocious ways. Since the border was only a few miles east of Calcutta, it was not unusual for us, while driving outside the city, to come upon a massacred village, where bodies with gaping, gory wounds were displayed alongside the highway, presumably to whip up the fury of revenge. I remember one Sunday when we were returning from a Chamber of Commerce picnic held just north of the city. The British executive secretary of the Chamber, who was a retired major from the Indian Army, had a Muslim driver, who rather foolishly wore a cap that identified himself as such. As our caravan of autos was passing through the old French enclave of Chandenagore, most of us raced ahead to get past a railroad grade crossing ahead of a slow freight train. The major and his driver, bringing up the rear, were forced to stop and let the train pass. While they were stopped, a Hindu crowd formed and dragged the driver from the car. The major jumped out to save him. Both were so thoroughly butchered by the mob that their bodies could never be reassembled.

The Ends of Empires 105

The violence was not confined entirely to religious feuds. It also colored the politics of the city, and for that matter, the everyday conflicts that were bound to erupt in such crowded circumstances. The sidewalks of the city had been built wide by the old colonial engineers who created the entrepot on the mud flats of the Hooghly. But, the human tide that was constantly in motion on them during the daylight hours overwhelmed their broad expanse. If something occurred to block the movement of pedestrians, for example, along the borders of Chowringhee, one of the principal thoroughfares, tens of thousands of people were backed up, friction would develop, and fights would break out.

On the huge maidan, or park area, which provided open space in the center of the city (and, incidentally provided a field of fire for the guns of Fort William) gatherings of one sort or another were always in progress. Some of these were political, but many were religious, or ceremonial. The Communist Party, under instructions in those days to provoke violent revolution in India, found the gatherings ideal for their tactics. Almost every evening, they precipitated a riot in which at least a half dozen and sometimes as many as a hundred people were killed. These usually took place fairly near our office building, and were clearly visible from our windows. They almost always delayed us in getting home from work at the end of the day.

We watched the Communist technique and wondered at the fact that they could succeed in it time and again. From their point of view, it was very inexpensive and almost assured of success. A small group of their young thugs, never more than twenty, would gather in an alley near the point where the day's procession debouched into the broad expanse of the maidan. At that point, the original marchers, no matter how well organized, bunched up because they were inevitably joined by curious young stragglers and the hordes of unemployed who had nothing better to do. The Communists waited until the marchers were stalled, compacted, irritated, and uncomfortable. Then, at a given signal, they would mount a flying wedge into the procession, swinging chains, clubs, and other weapons at the hapless and confused marchers who, naturally, fought back. The uproar would attract the riot police, who were always stationed along the route of march. The police, with shields and lathis, would swing into the crowd and head for the disturbance. Just as they arrived and were bearing down on the center of the melee, another signal would sound and the Communists would withdraw into an alley that led to their preplanned escape route. As the last of them left, their leader would toss a grenade or fire a pistol at the leading ranks of the police. The bedlam that followed would last a good ten minutes and leave an assured number of dead on the pavement.

If the crowd reaction was severe enough, the riot swirled off into the working quarters of the city and lasted well into the night. Trolley cars and lorries were overturned and set on fire. Whole sections of the city were cordoned off, and the fires glowed against the black smoke that covered the evening sky. This sort of occurrence was so regular for most of our first six months in Calcutta that we came to take it for granted.

Even when the nights were not wracked by riots, their misery was appalling. Hundreds of thousands of refugees from the Muslim areas had streamed into the city and had no place to live, no means of livelihood, and no food to eat. They slept at night on the sidewalks, and whole families had their reserved areas of pavement, which they guarded with their lives. Every morning, a portion of these people were found dead where they lay, and municipal lorries, with death crews, moved slowly along the streets, picking up the corpses and carrying them to the burning ghats along the banks of the Hooghly. It was exactly as it must have been in the European cities at the times of the Great Plagues.

We "Europeans" lived isolated from all this misery, in a

special quarter of our own, with high walls, gardens, and durwans. The durwans, or guards, were invariably Ghurkas, those tough little Nepalese veterans of the British Army, who chose to supplement their pensions by working for foreigners in Calcutta before returning to their native mountains in Nepal. The men guarded our homes and their women cared for our children. They were the baby-ayahs who arrived early in the morning, bathed, dressed, and fed the children, presented them to their parents at the breakfast hour as happy, angelic offspring, and then took them off for a morning frolic on the maidan.

Every morning, about the hour when we European men left for our offices, a whole stream of flashy prams, each pushed by a Ghurka ayah in a gleaming white sari, with a gold and jeweled bangle in her nose, moved out to the northern end of the maidan. There, in a special grassy area, surrounded by trees and protected by the motherly statue of Queen Victoria, the ayahs gathered, and their wards gamboled on the lawn. A loose cordon of Ghurka durwans strolled casually around them, chatting and flirting with the ayahs, their sharp kukris swinging easily in the scabbards that hung from their web belts. All hell might be breaking loose at the other end of the maidan, but nothing ever disturbed the idyllic peace of Queen Victoria's precious domain. No Bengali dared approach within hailing distance of this sanctuary.

We were part of this scene. Our daughter was appropriately blonde and curly, our pram was gleaming, our ayah was slim and stern and efficient. As for our durwan, he was properly fierce. He had a ferocious looking black moustache, his uniform was always creased and clean, his boots were polished, and his brass buckle gleamed in the sun. He was not really "our" durwan, because we lived in a building belonging to the consulate general that had four flats. However, since we were the only family there with a child and since I was beginning to get grey hair, the durwan decided that he should report to me. Perhaps he appreciated the fact that I always returned his heel-clicking, whip-lashing hand salutes with a proper navy snap.

In any event, he arrived one morning at my office, accompanied by our senior Anglo-Indian clerk to act as his translator. The caste system was such in those days that an Anglo-Indian, a person of mixed Indian and English ancestry, was always the senior clerk even if the office contained Bengalis, Madrasis, or others who had college educations and other attributes objectively superior to the genetic advantages enjoyed by the burra-babu. As a matter of fact, Anglo-Indians were already in short supply. They had had a special niche in British India and were beginning to lose it with the disappearance of the raj. They had run the railroads, the post and telegraph service, and a few other functions that the British, after the Sepoy Rebellion, would not trust to Indian hands. Since most of them descended from the illegitimate offspring of British troops, they had no political constituency to support them in the new dispensation and saw no future in India. As fast as they could afford it, they were flocking for "home" in a Great Britain they'd never seen, or in Australia, where their British passports permitted them to pass for Englishmen.

It was their departure in such large numbers that had brought about the collapse in the former efficiency of the Indian railway system. This, in turn, was the cause of the breakdown in the supply of manganese through the ports of Calcutta and Vizagaputan to the blast furnaces of a western world that needed steel to rebuild from the ravages of the recent war. Our Anglo-Indian clerks were pressed into service largely to try to influence rail shipments long overdue for American consignees. Their success was limited.

But, this particular morning, our Anglo-Indian clerk stood in the door of my office, with the durwan just behind him. In a parade ground voice he'd probably heard as a boy, the clerk announced the durwan's arrival. The durwan, in turn, performed a salute that would have done justice to Kipling. The heels of his boots rang, his right hand quivered at attention, his moustache bristled, and his kukri was slapped to his side by his left forearm. While holding this salute and looking at a point six inches above my head, his voice rang out with bellicose ferocity. The clerk, also standing at attention, barked the translation: "Sir, Durwan requests your permission to kill Mr. Lynn's cook, Sir!" Startled as I was by this demand, I leaped to my feet, stood in a brace, and in my best quarterdeck manner, shouted, "Permission not granted!" This was, in turn, shouted back in translation to the durwan, who, without batting an eye, shouted a phrase that was translated as "Thank you, Sir," executed a snappy about face, and marched out, followed by the clerk.

After he had gone, people from other offices came to my office door to ask what the commotion had been all about. Among them was Mr. Lynn, our neighbor in the second-level flat. By this time, the clerk had returned from seeing the durwan out. He explained some of the background, including the fact that the Lynns' cook, who was a Christian, had apparently strayed too close to the women's shower in the servants' quarters while the durwan's wife was there, and that honor demanded some revenge. I asked whether honor had been satisifed by my firm denial of permission and was assured that it had been. I then asked what would have happened if I had found it amusing to grant permission. The clerk, who was also a Christian, drew a hand sharply across his throat, gave a little shrug and a crooked smile, and shuffled back to his desk.

— 5 —

There were only a couple of Indians with whom I had any intellectual association during our stay in Calcutta. My introduction to both of them came about because of my duties in following the trade union movement in that port city. Most organized labor at that time worked on the docks, in the shipyards, and among the heavy industries strung along the Hooghly river. It was the focus of a vigorous political party recruitment campaign that was contested by the communists on the one hand and by the Indian Congress party on the other. There were also a number of maverick groups, such as Trotskyites, who were minor contestants in the field. A great deal of political power was riding on the outcome of that campaign.

As a result, our labor attaché from New Delhi visited with me often, and we spent a lot of time in the hiring halls, coffee houses, and trade union offices during the campaign. In one of those coffee houses one morning, he introduced me to a patrician old man with flowing hair and careless dress that seemed charismatic. He spoke English with the familiar lilt of a Bengali, but he was accompanied by a worn looking European woman, wearing a sari. He was the legendary M.N. Roy, and she was his Austrian wife of nearly thirty years. Roy had been one of the original associates of Lenin, Trotsky, and the early Bolsheviks in the Third International. His first assignments were in the Mexican Revolution, the Chinese Revolution, and other aborted communist efforts in the third world. In due course, he fell out with Stalin; but, because he was a foreigner, he escaped the executions and assassinations that eliminated most of his Russian associates. He had rusticated in his Indian homeland, but far away from his native Bengal. He had established an ashram in Dehra Dun, north of New Delhi, where he espoused something that he called Humanism, and he became an outspoken anticommunist. He and his wife had been drawn to the Calcutta campaign like old fire horses to a bonfire.

My meeting with him that day was the first of many. I discovered that he had made that particular coffee house his headquarters and held court there every morning. Many of those who frequented the place had no idea who the old man was and listened to him out of curiosity. He was therefore grateful for an audience of one who would ask him questions about his past and let him ramble on about his days with Borodin, his efforts to recruit Zapata, and his bitter excoriation of Stalin, who was, at that moment, at the peak of his power in Moscow.

We used to sit there, day after day, at the rough wooden table, balancing on small crude stools, and drinking cup after cup of the aromatic Ootocomoond coffee, served in small, fragile, mud-colored pottery. As each cup was finished, it was smashed on the cement floor. This was done both as a sanitary precaution and as a signal to attract the bearer. After a couple of hours of this routine, the floor around our stools would be covered by a heap of pottery shards, but the conversation was never exhausted. If only the cassette recorder had been invented in those days!

The other man I met during that trade union campaign who was of intellectual interest was the leader of the Indian National Trade Union Congress (INTUC) organizing drive in Calcutta. He was a college graduate, a Fabian socialist, very much influenced by his studies of the British trade union movement, and a man who was distressed by the corruption, violence, and demagoguery that characterized the campaign. Although he was not himself from Calcutta, he had learned the Bengali language, the patois of the dock workers, and the politics of the city. He was a tremendously hard worker and had captured the imagination of the uneducated but shrewd laborers from the bustees. He was supremely confident that he would hand the communists a shattering defeat in Calcutta.

Every day that I visited the campaign territory, I usually ended my visit with a call at the INTUC headquarters, in an old storefront in the warehouse district. It was a pleasure to talk with this idealistic, intelligent young man and to catch his enthusiasm and honesty as he assayed his chances of success. Just two days before the final vote, I found him brimming with confidence, and concluded that I could report to New Delhi that the communists seemed headed for defeat in Calcutta. I headed back to the office to write my report.

The heavy traffic delayed my progress, and it took me longer than I had calculated in getting to the office. Much of the delay was caused by a large number of fire engines and police vehicles moving through the streets, going, I assumed, to one of the many fires that always afflicted the overcrowded city. When I finally arrived, I was startled to have our rather prim Anglo-Indian receptionist throw her arms around me and usher me into the consul general's office. It seems that a hand grenade had been thrown into the INTUC office shortly after I had left there, killing all those inside and setting the place on fire.

Shortly after this event, we were invited to dinner by a Marwari merchant who had begun doing considerable business with the United States. Marwaris came from the Bombay side of the subcontinent and were known as sharp practitioners. They were also usually wealthy, with very little sympathy for the Bengalis. This particular merchant was selling textiles to New York and had begun to develop quite a lucrative trade. But what attracted me most to his acquaintance was his traffic in musk pods. These are the fatty glandular products taken from the musk ox, which exists largely in Tibet. I was fascinated to learn how the trade in that item actually reached Calcutta and, from there, went on to the perfume industry of the United States and France. So, I went to call on the merchant in his shoddy, crowded offices in the bazaar area of the city. Although he was as oleaginous as I had expected, there was something ingratiating about him, and I accepted his dinner invitation without reservation. He said it would be in his family home and invited me to bring another American couple "so as not to be lonely."

The directions he gave us to his house took us into the most squalid bustee area south of the city where the day laborers from the docks lived. Their hovels had no electricity or sewage. Water came from standpipes spaced about every two hundred yards. Cows wandered everywhere and cow dung was the cooking fuel. As we passed through it in the last light of evening, an acrid smell permeated the fetid air. Eventually, as we neared the river, we came to a huge crenellated white wall. Directly ahead of us was a gate flanked by two watch towers. In each tower stood a guard, with a submachine gun at the ready. We thought we had arrived at a prison. But a uniformed bearer was there outside the steel gate, and it swung open as we approached. The bearer motioned us through and on to a driveway bordered with flowering trees. The drive curved toward a huge white building of modern construction, and beyond it we could see small colored lights in large plane trees that stood between the house and the river.

The whole compound, which must have covered a dozen acres, was like a fairy land in contrast with the surrounding bustees. The house was built with a large central area where the head of the family and his wife lived, with two wings containing four spacious apartments for the four sons and their families. The high surrounding wall continued down into the river and was extended out in the stream on stone quays. There were watchtowers and armed guards every fifty yards.

We four Americans were ushered into the midst of the family, with the father, mother, four sons, and four daughters-in-law all resplendent in colorful clothes and dripping with jewelry. A squad of bearers poured whisky and brought tasty small chow. The opulence increased as the evening went on. The culinary climax came with dessert, when we were served small sweets wrapped in thin sheets of solid gold, which we were urged to swallow intact "as an aid to digestion." After dinner, the ladies were given small flasks containing attar of roses that they were asked to use and keep.

Then, we were all invited to inspect the air raid shelter. It was a spacious, air-conditioned apartment built underground, fully furnished and stocked with food enough to last fifty people for a month. My merchant friend, who turned out to be the eldest son, took me quietly aside to show me "another room." It was a vault the size one finds in a large commercial bank, with the same sort of locking devices. As he took me in, I could see that the walls were lined with shelves, and the shelves were loaded with gold and silver ingots. There were also steel boxes of loose pearls and other precious stones. When I asked what all this hoard was worth, I was told "about five million sterling." At the time the pound exchanged for about five American dollars.

When the evening was over, we were waved off into the night, passing through the heavy gate into the all-encompassing misery of the bustees. We had difficulty sorting out our feelings as we drove home, wondering how the pampered Marwaris could live in such obscene opulence alongside their wretched Bengali neighbors. Less than two weeks later, we had part of the answer. The papers were filled with the story of a riot in the bustees and murder at a luxury mansion on the banks of the Hooghly. The stories said that poor Bengalis had stormed the gates of a Marwari compound seeking food. Armed guards had fired at the mob, and four people had been killed. Two guards and the head of the Marwari family had been arrested for murder. I never did learn the ultimate price of Bengali justice in this case.

Because of the violent atmosphere in Calcutta, we wanted a holiday in more attractive parts of India. When we were able to do it, we took advantage of an invitation to spend some time in the hill station of Nainital with a former Indian classmate my wife and I had known in graduate school. He had married an American girl and had brought her back to India. The change from Calcutta was dramatic. The town was high in the foothills of the Himalayas, set above a crystal lake at about 7,000 feet, with crisp air, clear skies, and a view off to the snow-capped giant mountains in the north. The house

The Ends of Empires 115

was gracious, the mountain people friendly, and the whole visit a delight.

We probably should have ended our vacation there and headed straight back to Calcutta, where we could savor the memories. But we wanted to see the Taj Mahal and the Red Fort, as well as other sights of northern India. So, our host drove us down the mountain to the train station where we could catch a train and travel overnight to Agra. He insisted on buying the tickets and managed to get us two bunks in a coupe, which was one-half of a small sleeping car containing only four bunks and a private bath in a separate compartment. In addition to the two bunks that we had paid for, he had without our knowing it purchased the other two as a present for us and pocketed the tickets, so that we would have the compartment to ourselves. He gave us strict instructions that we should, in no case, open the compartment door because the compartment had been completely booked. With these instructions and many more on how to lock the door, he saw us safely shut inside and bid us goodbye. Two minutes later, there was a sharp knock on our door and a demand, in the sing-song gichi accent of the Anglo-Indians, to see our tickets. I unlocked and opened the door to find our friend Hari there, glowering in mock anger about our failure to heed his instructions and keep the door locked against all pretenders. We accepted his scolding, and two minutes later the train pulled out of the station into the dusk of the Indian plains.

As we descended lower into the valley of the Bramaphutra, the temperatures climbed. The compartment was not airconditioned, but the two windows, on either side of the coupe, were fitted with wooden louvers. I pulled down both the glass panes on the outside of the window frames and raised the wooden louvers on the inside. They were held up in place by pegs that fitted loosely at their side. We were tired after our stay in the mountains, and the slow sway of the train made us drowsy, so we undressed and went to bed. My wife took the lower bunk and I took the upper one.

No sooner had we got in bed than the louvers on both sides of the train began to rattle fiercely. It was clear that something outside was shaking them, and my wife turned on the light so that we could see what it was. At this point, one of the louvers came loose and in came the hairy red arm of a big rhesus monkey. Fortunately I had reached for the louver as it started to fall and was able to slam it back up on the monkey's arm and force its withdrawal. However, as I put the holding peg in place, it was apparent that it wouldn't be able to resist indefinitely the constant rattling the monkey was inflicting on it. The same was true of the other window, which had not yet given way but was being severely tried on the other side.

We were passing through the monkey forests on the edge of the plain, and these big, pesky beasts, which plagued the villagers there, had obviously learned the scavenging opportunities that abounded on the trains. A whole horde of them had dropped on the roofs of the cars and were roaming up and down the length of the carriages, trying to force their way into the compartments where food and other loot awaited them. As defense against them, we tumbled out of bed and prepared for their assaults. I took one shoe in each hand and sat on the edge of the upper bunk, where I could swing in the direction of each window. My wife stood on the floor of the compartment prepared to lunge against whichever louver began to fall and slam it back in place. Whenever a holding peg tumbled and a hairy arm or head appeared, I clobbered it unmercifully with the heels of the shoes, and my wife slammed the louver shut. There was no way we could figure to reach out and raise the glass panes without letting a monkey in. And there seemed no way we could lock the louvers in place except for the totally inefficient system of pegs. This assault continued for nearly two hours as we chugged across the Indian landscape. Eventually, the marauders seemed to drop off, and we relaxed our vigil sufficiently to lie back on our bunks and turn out the light. But, I kept my trusty shoes at hand and tried not to fall off to sleep.

As the first light of dawn began to break and as we pulled out of a small station where we had stopped, I began to hear the rattling of louvers again, apparently in the compartment next to ours. I came awake and grabbed my shoes. My wife snapped on the light. Sure enough, one of the louvers was being banged and was starting to give. I sprang at it just as it dropped, with both shoes swinging. Both heels found their target and there was an instant howl of pain. It came not from a red rhesus, but from a pink mouth in a dark human face, which fell back and tumbled from the carriage onto the gravel roadbed. My wife slammed the louver back in place and we both stood there, on the swaying floor of the compartment, clutching each other, shocked at the inhumanity of it all! It was not the sort of background against which to appreciate fully the cool, classic white marble beauty of the Taj Mahal that afternoon and evening.

Chapter Four

Occupying Japan 1950–1952

I<small>N</small> 1950, I WAS ASSIGNED to Tokyo, in a position euphemistically designated as a "political adviser" to General MacArthur. At the time my assignment was made, we were preparing to wind up the five-year occupation of Japan that had followed the surrender in Tokyo Bay. It was our intention to negotiate a peace treaty and reestablish the sovereignty and independence of our former enemy. It was my assumption, therefore, that my functions in MacArthur's headquarters would be primarily directed towards the peace process.

However, after we left Calcutta and before we could arrive in Japan, the North Koreans attacked across the thirty-eighth parallel, and the entire situation in Tokyo took on a different complexion. MacArthur's headquarters, which had assumed all the trappings of a shogunate, had suddenly to be transformed back into a military operation. Generals, colonels, and sergeants who had grown soft and sedentary in the service of the occupation had suddenly to squeeze back into combat gear

Occupying Japan 119

and head for the summer mud of Korea. MacArthur himself, who had been devoting most of his effort to the metamorphosis of Japan, turned all civilian aspects of his job over to his deputy chief of staff and devoted himself full time to directing his troops.

During the occupation years, he had proven himself a remarkable administrator. Although most of the senior military members of his staff were second rate, he had attracted to his headquarters a talented group of civilian specialists, who had succeeded in transforming the former feudal society of Japan. Among these were people such as Wolf Ladejinsky, who became a close friend of ours. Wolf was a specialist in land reform who designed and supervised the break-up and redistribution of the old feudal land holdings to the individual ownership of the small farmers, who had previously been sharecroppers or serfs on those large estates. He understood, better than any other expert at that time, the sophisticated requirements of credit arrangements for the farm family, of seeds and fertilizer, and of marketing systems. He was therefore able to break up the estates and turn them into more efficient, more productive, and more prosperous agricultural units than they had been under the feudal system.

It was MacArthur's genius that he could understand such things, endorse them, and make them work. He would hold long private sessions with Ladejinsky, give his blessing to a project, let Wolf write up the instructions, and then order his staff—and through them, the Japanese nation—to execute the project. He gave Wolf a brevetted rank of major general, so that he could live comfortably in the old Imperial Hotel and not have to worry about such trivialities as running a household. This distinction was taken as a supreme insult by the peacock generals—and their wives—who were the other permanent occupants of the hotel. They spent most of their time worrying about their perquisites, keeping their splendidly tailored uniforms cleaned and pressed and their boots polished.

Wolf, in contrast, wore baggy tweed suits, pockets bulging with scraps of notes, smoked a pipe and let the ashes scatter on his vest. His hair was seldom cut and never combed. The generals called him "the ragpicker" and muttered among themselves that he was "communizing" Japan.

Of course, what Wolf and MacArthur were doing was just the opposite. By instituting a land reform program and making the small farmers prosperous beyond their dreams, they were building the base of a contented countryside of conservative small landowners who owed their fealty to the American Supreme Commander, and, together with him, to the Liberal Democratic Party, which was in power in Tokyo and was the beneficiary of their contentment. It is significantly through Wolf's successful work that Japan has been a peaceful, prosperous, and friendly ally of the United States ever since.

There were other such evidences of MacArthur's visionary brilliance, largely at variance with the reactionary resistance of his stodgy staff, that should earn him credit among historians for the success of the postwar occupation of Japan. Unfortunately, much of this evidence became obscured in the aftermath of his arrogant confrontation with President Truman and his potentially disastrous proposals for military policy in Asia. But, of course, they are preserved in Japan, where his name is venerated and where the imprint of his presence is represented by the vast transformation of an entire people.

In the summer of 1950, much of this success hung in the balance. The North Korean attack, launched without warning and pressed forward brutally, overwhelmed the South Korean units and the small American garrison force. Mild panic began to spread to Tokyo. Some American families began to evacuate, and no new dependents were allowed to accompany those military and civilian personnel being assigned to MacArthur's headquarters. The State Department was shrewdly able to convince the Pentagon to let my wife and daughter accompany me on the grounds that, having come from Calcutta, I was merely making a move "in theater" and was not being newly assigned. No one in the Pentagon cared to assert that Calcutta was outside MacArthur's theater of operations, and so our travel plans stood.

By the time we arrived, the headquarters was a pretty somber place, and many of its senior officers were off in Korea attempting to stem the Communist advance. We were moved into temporary living quarters at the old Imperial Army Headquarters facilities at Inguchi, which had been converted to apartments and christened "Pershing Heights." Most of the families there were without their husbands and fathers, who were in Korea. It was not a joyous atmosphere, since death notices were quietly delivered daily by senior chaplains who tapped solemnly on apartment doors. As the North Korean onslaught pressed down on the last remaining American redoubt in the Masan Perimeter, we were finally assigned permanent housing and moved to the University precincts in the Hongo District.

The headquarters—called SCAP, in abbreviation of Supreme Commander, Allied Powers—was still concerned, under its deputy chief of staff, General Hickey, with the problems of running Japan. The system for doing this had been perfected over the five years of occupation. There was a Japanese government, fully intact, with a democratic system of voting, a parliament, political parties, a cabinet, and, of course, an Emperor. But, intervening at the top of this system was SCAP. Japanese bureaucrats could function, Japanese political decisions could be made, Japanese policies could be proposed, but nothing could be authorized until confirmed by SCAP. The instrument of ukase in which all authority rested was the SCAPIN, acronym for SCAP Instruction. The business of the civilian side of SCAP headquarters was to draft and issue SCAPINS. Once these were signed by General Hickey, they became the supreme law of the land. Some of the more controversial drafts were sent back to Washington for approval before being issued, but routine matters were put on paper, cleared with relevant sections of the headquarters, and sent to the general for signature. Once signed, they were issued to the Japanese for compliance.

Of course, by 1950, each headquarters section worked closely with a counterpart ministry of the Japanese government, and these policy issues were thrashed out in advance with relevant ministerial specialists. Where all were in agreement, no problems arose. It was only when two or more ministries were at odds and the prime minister chose not to force the issue that SCAP truly had to make internal Japanese policy by Solomon's judgment.

I was assigned, on my arrival, to the Diplomatic Section. We had three functions. One was to operate as the foreign office for SCAP; the second was to deal with the allied powers associated either with the occupation or the war in Korea; and the third was to create a Japanese Foreign Ministry and Foreign Service, in anticipation of a peace treaty terminating World War II. At the beginning, I worked largely on the first two functions, because a peace treaty seemed a long way in the future. Then, with the great tactical success of the landings at Inchon and the complete reversal of the fortunes of war, emphasis began to switch once again towards the treaty. My attention turned to the creation of a new Japanese foreign affairs establishment.

Our offices at that time were in the old Mitsui Bank building in downtown Tokyo, a few blocks away from MacArthur's location in the Dai Ichi insurance building. They were sumptuously appointed, with thick carpets, panelled walls, and fireplaces. In these quarters, another Foreign Service officer and I vetted those Japanese diplomats who were proposed by their government to represent Japan abroad.

Most of them had spent the occupation years, since their ministry had been disbanded, doing menial liaison work with the United States armed forces. A few of their colleagues, whose records indicated overzealous fascism or treachery against our interests, had been jailed or purged as war criminals. The rest had worked as translators, expediters, or assistants in U.S. engineering units, air bases, and other such locations. Their arrival on the thresholds of our offices was their first reintroduction into the polished world of diplomacy. They arrived in morning coats and striped trousers smelling of mothballs, with their rough thick-soled workshoes in sharp contrast to their other regalia. Although their appearance before us was largely a formality occurring after we had checked their records, they entered with great deference and were obviously nervous about their future. We made every effort to treat them as colleagues rather than subordinates, and when we finally congratulated them on their new assignments and walked out with them to the elevators to wish them well, they fairly burst with relief and satisfaction. For many years after, as I was assigned around the world to various posts, these Japanese diplomats were often the first ones to welcome us to a new country, to treat us as old friends, and to remember that traumatic moment when their lives had returned to normal.

What we were doing with them was assigning them to "Overseas Agency Offices," to establish embryonic embassies so that they could begin to function efficiently once a peace treaty had been signed and full sovereignty restored. They could handle commercial and consular matters, but real diplomatic substance continued to rest with SCAP pending the treaty. This meant that we in the Diplomatic Section had to negotiate arrangements for the establishment of the Overseas Agency Offices with potential host countries. Sometimes that was not easy, especially in those Asian countries where Japanese military brutalities were not forgotten.

In 1951, for example, we were having difficulty getting agreement from a number of Southeast Asian countries, and it was decided that I should undertake a mission to a number of those capitals to press the negotiations. The trip proved surprisingly successful, and the Japanese were enormously impressed by my prowess. In actual fact, the agreements came rather easily. In Rangoon, as it developed, our proposal had not been answered merely because the Foreign Ministry had misplaced the file. I will always remember squatting on the floor of an old army building with the vice minister of foreign affairs, who was barefoot and wearing a long-yi, picking over dusty files that were tied with fading red ribbons until we found the formal SCAP proposal. I returned to his office the next day, and he smilingly presented me with an affirmative reply signed by the minister.

In Colombo, the Foreign Office official had the file all right, but seemed quite vague about an answer. The afternoon after seeing him, I was approached by his brother at the Galle Face Hotel where I was staying, and asked to tea. After tea, he took me to his jewelry shop in the arcade of the hotel and told me how much he longed to have a similar one in the Imperial Hotel in Tokyo. When I assured him that could be arranged through a Japanese Overseas Agency once it was established in Colombo, he advised me to be prepared for a call from his brother the next day. Hence, I left Colombo also with an agreement in my pocket. That was the way the trip went.

By the end of that year, we had established the Japanese in nearly every country except those of the Communist bloc. Their Foreign Ministry had been restored, and they were once again in touch with most of the outside world. With these preparations in hand, they would be able to make a smooth transition to sovereignty. It only remained for a peace treaty to be negotiated and signed.

— 2 —

In the spring of 1952, we began in earnest to develop a peace treaty with Japan. Although the main outlines of such a document had been laid down as early as 1947, the Stalinist drive that began the Cold War and culminated in the attack against South Korea had delayed action for five years. The Truman Administration, keenly aware that 1952 was an election year, sought to remove the treaty process from partisan politics by appointing John Foster Dulles, a prominent Republican, as chief negotiator. He carried out his mission with relentless zeal and, within a few months, had a draft document that he considered viable. As a gesture of courtesy to the State Department contingent in Tokyo, he showed us the draft before he took it back to Washington and asked for our comments.

Being a brash young man, I wrote a memorandum criticizing the draft because it omitted any provisions for the disposition of Korea, which had been a Japanese colony before the war, and because its clauses dealing with Okinawa were inconclusively vague. Dulles, who had battered his considerable talents against these apparently intractable issues without avail, must have been justifiably exasperated by this upstart criticism, but managed to concede, in very good grace, that both comments were valid. Instead of giving me the back of his hand, however, he arranged that I should be assigned the task of remedying these defects as a follow-up to his continuing effort to press the treaty to signature and ratification in its admittedly incomplete form. Consequently, I soon found myself in the position of mediator between Japan and Korea in an effort to resolve the issues that were holding up confirmation of the independence of the Korean state from its former colonial master. A rather formal negotiating process was established.

The Japanese delegation was headed by a senior Foreign Ministry official, Koh Chiba, who later became a distinguished Japanese ambassador to several countries in Latin America. Koh had been born in San Francisco, where his father edited a Japanese language newspaper. He had been educated in the public schools of his native city and came back to

Japan in the 1930s to get his university training. Although he was clearly recognized under Japanese law as a Japanese citizen, he was, by accident of his birth, also recognized under United States law as an American citizen. Therefore, when he was given this negotiating task, Koh thought it prudent first to clear the books by formally renouncing his American citizenship. He came to me in considerable embarrassment about this matter, because the act of "renouncing" in the Japanese culture carried with it a pejorative connotation that he felt might be insulting to Americans. In fact, it was a simple and painless procedure, which I had one of our vice-consuls accomplish with him in the privacy of my office.

The Korean delegation was also headed by an American-born negotiator. He was the Korean ambassador to the United States, a physician who was a native of Hawaii, where he had developed a successful medical practice and married a Caucasian American wife. I don't believe Dr. Chang ever bothered to renounce his American citizenship. In fact, I think he rather enjoyed it.

The two delegations began their meetings in the neutral arena of our conference room and readily agreed upon certain ground rules. The first was that the language of negotiations was to be in English. The second was that I would keep the official record of the proceedings, and only that record would be a valid document of their various understandings. And the third was that I would be the sole spokesman for the negotiations and the only contact with the press. I would, however, clear any statements and communiques in advance with the two sides. On this basis, we began to move rather briskly ahead with the discussions and, in the course of a few meetings, had resolved a number of issues between the two sides. Our progress was impressive enough to warrant a rather flattering message of encouragement from Dulles, who was then in Washington, shepherding his treaty through the political process that would lead to its international ratification at the San Francisco conference shortly before the presidential elections in the United States.

However, it soon began to emerge that there were two very thorny issues on which the two sides were far apart. One concerned the current and future status of those Koreans who were resident in Japan. Many had been brought to the country as forced laborers in the mines and other heavy industries. However, they had settled into their new society and had no desire to return home to their war-torn native peninsula. The Japanese, on the other hand, wanted to deport all of them in the shortest possible time. The problem was further complicated by the fact that these Koreans, like their homeland, were sharply divided between communists and bitter anticommunists.

The second major issue concerned the property settlement that would go with this imperial divorce. The Koreans, naturally, claimed not only all the tangible property in Korea or in Japan that was clearly identified as Korean, but also a vast sum that they attributed to Korean origin as well as a considerable amount for reparations. The Japanese were prepared to offer very little in the way of restitution and nothing for reparations.

As these issues came to the fore, the negotiations bogged down. As the mediator, I began to shuttle between the two principals, probing for any compromise that might emerge. On the issue of the residents, it appeared that differences could be narrowed. By talking to the two sides, I finally got them to agree that the residents could remain for some period, but that there would be a time limit on their stay. Then I began to try to close the gap in the number of years' residence, which was still at issue. Eventually, they were only seven years apart.

One day, Chiba came to see me and said, in confidence, that he would be authorized to split the difference in the residence time, by agreeing on a limit that was three and a half years greater than Japan had proposed. It looked to me like a breakthrough, and I felt that, if agreed upon, we could put together a treaty, leaving the reparations issue for subsequent negotiation between the two governments. I was so ecstatic that I decided to prod the process along by a talk with the Koreans. That same afternoon, I arranged an appointment at the Korean embassy. In my talk with the Koreans, I took the line that the differences on the length of residence ought to be resolved. I said that the seven-year gap was largely a "mathematical" problem rather than a question of principle and that I hoped it could be resolved by "mathematical" means. Without saying so explicitly, I was urging them to split the difference with the Japanese, as I knew the Japanese were prepared to do.

Unfortunately, my insistence that the time limit was not a matter of principle touched a tender Korean nerve. My pleasant interview began to turn into a torrent of rhetoric. The Koreans present outdid each other in describing and defending the "principles" that were at stake. (Not the least of these was the prospect that the communist Korean group would roundly castigate them for selling out all Korean residents, and would demonstrate against any agreement with Japan.) By the time the interview was over, I was sorely aware that I had not advanced the compromise in any way. Indeed, my well-intentioned intervention had seemed to exacerbate the issue.

My chagrin was more than doubled when, as I was being seen out of the embassy, I encountered Koh Chiba, sitting in the waiting room and obviously startled to see me there. By attempting to pave the way for his overture, I had acted only to rehearse the Korean arguments against his move and to whet the emotions with which they were advanced. His compromise proposal, on which I had placed such high hopes, was rejected out of hand. I think Koh never really forgave me for my gauche initiative, and the negotiations shortly collapsed. It was nearly fifteen years before they could be resurrected and successfully completed. It was my most graphic lesson in Talleyrand's diplomatic dictum, "Surtout, pas trop de zèle!"

On the Okinawa issue, which Dulles had also bequeathed me, I hardly fared better. The failure with respect to Korea had considerably squelched my confidence, and I decided to move on Okinawa with much greater reserve. I discussed the prospects with my colleagues at some length while the date for the San Francisco Conference drew near. Suddenly, an opening fortuitously presented itself. One of the secretaries in our office was a sweet young South Carolina belle who was married to an army major, and who had escaped the evacuation of military families by becoming an employee rather than a dependent. Although her secretarial skills were limited, she was a decorative addition to our staff.

One day she came to me to say that her husband, who had just returned to the headquarters staff in Tokyo after infantry duty in Korea, had been assigned to the Plans section and had been asked to prepare the military proposal for the post-treaty status of Okinawa. She confessed that "Duke," her husband, knew absolutely nothing about Okinawa, and she was aware, from typing some of my correspondence, that I had been working on the subject. She wondered if I would be willing to help Duke with his task. Naturally, I leaped at the opportunity and, in effect, wrote Duke's staff study. The proposal suggested that, rather than leaving the vague "residual sovereignty" formula that Dulles had incorporated into his peace treaty, we move shortly after ratification of the treaty to terminate our occupation of Okinawa and return the territory to the administration of Japan. Simultaneously, the Japanese would enter into a security agreement with us under which we would station troops and forces in Okinawa in accordance with a "status of forces" agreement that was sketched out in the staff study.

SCAP headquarters, at the time I did this study, had

undergone sharp changes from the heyday of MacArthur's occupation regime. MacArthur himself had been fired in his encounter with Truman. Ridgway, who replaced him, was primarily concerned with terminating the Korean war. He cleaned out the residual MacArthur staff and brought in new people, who regarded the Occupation as an ephemeral matter coming to an end with the Peace Treaty. They were not overly concerned with matters they regarded as political. Consequently, once Duke's staff study had accumulated all the proper tabs, clearances with staff sections, and signatures, it sailed through the Chief of Staff, who signed it and sent it off to the Joint Chiefs of Staff in Washington. Through our separate channel of communications, I alerted the State Department that the proposal was en route and received a very favorable response. It looked as though the tricky question of Okinawa might be resolved.

Then, suddenly, that bubble also burst. When the Joint Chiefs received the SCAP proposal, they went through the roof of the Pentagon. Back from Washington to Tokyo came a rocket, not only rejecting the proposal but instructing the headquarters to burn all copies of the staff study. I never have dared follow up the consequences to poor Duke's military career.

— 3 —

At one point in my Tokyo tour, I was invited by one of my fellow officers who spoke fluent Japanese to visit the Sugamo prison, which housed the Japanese war criminals sentenced by the international tribunal. By the time I went there, most of the minor offenders had been released, and only the hard core remained. A few of these were former political leaders of some stature; but most of them were small unit commanders from the Imperial Armed Forces whose troops had committed atrocities during the war or former prison guards who had been particularly beastly to Allied prisoners of war.

They were a tough looking lot.

On the visitors' day when we were there, several members of their families were also visiting and they stood in small clumps throughout the prison yard. Very few of the prisoners unbent to play with their children or to show any affection for their wives. Instead, the families seemed to be making short, rather formal reports, while the war criminals, in their baggy grey prison uniforms, with close cropped hair, stood stoically by, occasionally nodding their heads to acknowledge some information. It was not a scene brimming with tender emotions.

After a short while, it was announced over the speaker system that a Buddhist ceremony honoring war dead would be held at an open air auditorium where a small stage was erected. Prisoners and their visitors were invited to attend. People began to drift in that direction and we followed, standing on the edge of the crowd. Soon a group of about a dozen monks, clad in flowing robes of various colors, and with shaven heads, mounted the platform and began to chant. After about ten minutes of this, one of them, who seemed taller than the rest and who wore black robes decorated with a white lotus, stood up to the microphone. In a clear, quarterdeck voice, he began to address the assemblage. I got a running translation from my colleague.

The speaker identified himself as former naval captain Wada and said he had been in command of the garrison forces at Iwo Jima when it had been overrun by the Americans. He said he felt a great responsibility for those under his command who had been killed and buried unceremoniously in the volcanic ash of the lonely island. He felt it his duty to recover their bones, return them to their families, and bring their souls to peace with their ancestors. He said that for that purpose and for the purpose of returning other bones from other battlefields, he and a group of companions had formed the White Lotus Society and had pledged themselves to dedicate the rest of their lives to the noble search. He hoped he could have the support of the prisoners and their visitors in this commitment.

After finishing his speech, Wada returned to his colleagues, chanted a bit more and then pronounced the ceremony at an end. He came down from the low platform and wandered among the spectators. There was much reverential bowing and greeting, but, as far as I could see, very few words exchanged. As he drew near us, I asked my associate to attract him so that I could engage him in conversation. When he was brought to me, he surprised me by speaking fluent English and by shaking my hand with a firm grasp. He explained the English by telling me that he had been Japanese naval attaché in London for three years and had learned such Anglo-Saxon ways as the handshake. He was a smooth-talking, self-confident, gregarious man who obviously enjoyed attention. When he learned who I was, he was delighted to settle into conversation. I told him I was interested in his White Lotus Society. He asked for my card and said he would invite me to a dinner with its leaders. We left, while he continued his rounds among the small knots in the prison yard.

Within a week, I had received the promised invitation, and within two weeks another officer and I presented ourselves at a western-style restaurant in a somewhat less than fashionable part of town. We were met by our affable host, dressed this time in a sturdy blue serge double-breasted suit. It was not necessary to note the areas near the cuffs of the sleeves where the four gold stripes had been removed to realize that it had once been a naval officer's uniform. We were led into a formal Victorian dining room where a dozen or so sturdy men stood rather awkwardly deployed, all wearing exactly the same clothing as our host. I was, in effect, a class reunion among former naval persons.

Throughout a sometimes edible British-style meal of meat,

potatoes, and brussels sprouts, our voluble host explained at great length the lofty purposes of the White Lotus Society. As Scotch whisky flowed with abundance, he also explained a lot about his past experiences, especially those in naval intelligence. He told us how he had purloined the "Brown Code" from the U.S. consul general's safe in Kobe five years before the war. He regaled us with tales of his exploits in tapping into U.S. military communications from across the border in Baja California just before Pearl Harbor. And he expressed high admiration for U.S. technical intelligence, but left the impression that, on a personal level, Japanese performance was superior.

Before the evening ended, Wada brought in a cameraman who had apparently been waiting in the wings. He set up an old fashioned tripod camera, with a black silk hood, bellows adjustment, glass plates, and a squeeze bulb to activate it. He arranged the dinner guests in formation and took half a dozen photos. When we received copies of them a few days later, they looked like the sort of scenes one used to see in biographies of Sun Yat Sen. The Japanese, with their shaved heads and dark jackets, stood sternly at attention while the two American novitiates bore slightly silly looks of mild amusement.

Wada used delivery of the photos as an excuse to come visit me in my office at the Mitsui Building. This time he was attired in his priestly robes, with the White Lotus rampant. Further conversation with him convinced me that the Buddhist affectation was a fraud and that he had no more claim to wear the robes than I did. He gave me glowing reports on the organizational success of his enterprise and presented me with a formal petition to take a group of his followers to Iwo Jima to search for bones. With this last action, he trapped me into a further and continuing association with his program. Because the U.S. continued to administer Iwo Jima, I had to make a recommendation about whether to permit the trip to take place. This meant that I really needed to know more about Wada and the White Lotus.

Consequently, when I received another invitation to dinner from him, I again accepted. This dinner was to be traditionally Japanese in a geisha restaurant district in the northern part of the city. Inquiries indicated that it was a restaurant patronized (and perhaps owned) by the big Japanese fishing companies. This association immediately caused me some concern, and I began to see how shrewdly Wada operated. It seemed that he had obtained some financing for his undertaking from these companies through former navy cronies who had naturally begun to operate the big fishing fleets. Through them, he learned that, among my collateral duties, was that of fixing "the MacArthur Line" governing the ocean areas where these fleets were allowed to fish. Every month, I arbitrarily drew a line on the map of the Pacific Ocean permitting the Japanese to fish a little further from the home islands and circulated it to allied governments to determine if they had any objections. Only the Koreans were adamantly opposed, and I had long since ceased moving the line further in their direction. But gradually, I was expanding the prosperity of the fishing companies eastward and southward by my monthly cartography.

Hence, it should not have been entirely a surprise to me to find that I was the guest of honor at a luxurious restaurant that had been taken over for the evening; that the heads of all the major fishing companies were there with their personal geishas; and that Wada was presiding as host. He had a racy looking geisha at his side and presented me, on my arrival, with a stunning young girl who spoke impeccable English. Geisha dinners are sybaritic by almost any standards, but this one excelled. Guests were taken, on arrival, to private dressing rooms where they were permitted to undress and enter a common bathroom, with washing tubs, soap, cloths, and bath attendants to scrub down. Then, once clean, they were led to selected rooms for the traditional soak in a hot tub before donning a freshly ironed yukata and moving into the dining room. When I was led to the room with my hot tub, I was rather startled, when the shoji was slid back, to find a tub in the shape of a fishing dory, already occupied by a pink-skinned mermaid who turned out to be my English-speaking geisha.

As I slid in beside her, she was appropriately demure, but began a carefully structured conversation with ease. She had been well briefed on who I was and what I did. She answered my questions with candor and told me that she was not a regular at the restaurant, but had been especially imported because of her fluency in English. That facility had resulted from her childhood in Hawaii and a careful studies program after the war. It was her intention to leave her geisha indenture within three years, when her contract was finished, and go to college. In the meantime, she was earning good money in her chosen profession.

After a few minutes, we finished our soak, she dried me off, clothed me in my yukata, and bowed me through another shoji towards the dining room. There I joined the Japanese camaraderie in a fairly boisterous dinner. My geisha companion joined me as soon as I was seated and much food and sake ensued. Through it all, Wada acted as the leader of bilingual discussion, the spinner of yarns, and the master of merriment. The geishas played their usual little games, they danced, played instruments, and kept the chatter light. Not once in the evening was the subject of fishing rights or Iwo Jima ever mentioned. I kept a close eye on Wada, even though his dominance of the evening made that unnecessary. He was hardly priestly in his behavior, and the mutual play between him and his geisha partner was anything but monastic.

As the evening was drawing to a close, Wada was quite flushed and apparently a little drunk. He and his partner mounted the little stage where the geishas performed and did a burlesque on the stately kabuki theater, to the uproarious merriment of the guests. After this obvious success, they turned to a somewhat more lewd routine and soon descended to the obscene. They finished with Wada ecstatically submitting to a public performance of mock fellatio by his partner, as most of the room burst with applause.

One old fishing magnate, however, and his rather refined companion were obviously uncomfortable, and I soon found him looking down the table at me. When our eyes met, I gave a brief nod. We both stood up, and bowing to each other, left the room together with our distaff companions skittering along in tow. We dressed in silence and were seen off to our cars by the two geishas and the proprietess of the restaurant. Wada was not there to say goodbye, and I never saw him again. I did, however, years later, see pictures of him and his companions, all in their robes, blessing some bones on Iwo Jima.

On one final task in Tokyo, however, I did have more constructive success. After the Peace Treaty was ratified, we very rapidly concluded a Security Treaty, which was, indeed, a separate but integral part of the peace package as far as the United States was concerned. Under the Security Treaty, provisions were made for the continued presence of United States forces in Japan, but in the status of allies rather than occupation troops. In order not only to symbolize the change but also to work out the practical consequences of the change, a Joint U.S.-Japan Committee was established.

In organizational terms, the SCAP headquarters was abolished. In its place, the military created a significantly smaller Far East Command, with responsibilities exclusively in the military field. Those of us who had been State Department personnel assigned to SCAP became the nucleus of a new embassy, with Bob Murphy as our new ambassador. It was quite a different world.

I found myself designated as one the the U.S. members of the new Joint Committee, along with an Army general, an Air

Force general, and a Navy captain. We prepared for our first meeting with our newly organized Japanese counterparts by deciding upon those conspicuous aspects of the Occupation that we could dismantle and turn over to the Japanese for maximum propaganda effect. After much haggling, we agreed on two moves. The first was to vacate the Dai Ichi building, MacArthur's former headquarters immediately across the moat from the Imperial Palace. The second was to return all the golf courses except two, which were inside U.S. military installations on the outskirts of Tokyo. The Japanese accepted both proposals with alacrity and with appreciation for the good will they entailed.

But, in the American military community, there was a reaction we had not counted on. No one resented or regretted return of the Dai Ichi building, even if the new quarters were less imposing. But the return of the golf courses was quite another matter. There were several U.S. general officers who were still not speaking to me months later, when my duty in Japan came to an end and I left for Italy!

Chapter Five

Nurturing NATO
1953–1958

Toward the end of 1952, I was transferred to Italy, to help with the establishment of the new NATO alliance in that country. Because of some jumbled assignments, I did not immediately reach my new post in the embassy in Rome, but was detoured to a temporary position as political adviser to the American admiral heading the Southern NATO Command in Naples. This was an interesting experience in allied military politics. Aside from the Italian and American components of our staff, we had British, Greek, Turkish, and occasionally French colleagues. There was very little joint planning and only a limited amount of strategic cooperation.

We spent most of our time trying to fend off extraneous efforts by the French to get us involved in Algeria, by the British to entangle us in Egypt or the Middle East, and by the Greeks and Turks to engage us against each other. However, we did have some interesting exercises in working out tacit understandings with the Yugoslavs and in constructing some hypothetical scenarios for problems in Southwest Asia. We also gave a certain amount of attention to the issues which would arise if there were ever to be a State Treaty for Austria that would permit the termination of four power occupation of that country.

Aside from the concerns of the NATO command, our stay in Naples proved enjoyable. My wife was conspicuously pregnant when we arrived there, and her condition proved to be a special attraction to the warmhearted, family loving people of that city. Because of it, we were able to get a large, comfortable apartment in a new building the landlord had not intended to rent. It also gave us early entree into a circle of friends who helped us settle into the complicated life of the city. It was the cause for other unexpected insights into the Italian character. I remember, for example, one evening when we were leaving the old San Carlos Opera after a rousing performance and attempting to board a trolleybus back to the apartment. Just as my wife was mounting the steps of the bus, two large Neapolitan women came bearing down on her, in their customary scramble for transportation. Since they seemed about to cause serious harm, I threw myself against them in an old fashioned hockey block and slammed them both against the bus. Their immediate reaction was to reach for their handbags and begin to beat me about the head and shoulders; but as soon as they realized my wife's advanced pregnancy, they began to coo and coddle, helping her to a seat, standing over her, and assuring me how clever I was to prevent them from causing an inadvertent injury.

Eventually, however, we went to Rome. There, I picked up the threads of a partly negotiated status of forces agreement that would govern the stationing of American forces on Italian soil. It involved the same set of problems I had coped with in Japan, but the political sensitivities were different. The Italians had a large Communist party that was capable of causing major disruption in the country, especially through labor strikes. The government was tenuous in its control of the parliament, and it did not detect any immediate military threat that would seem to warrant all the problems that went with foreign military forces.

Therefore, the negotiation of the agreement was a lengthy and tedious exercise. However, in order to make clear that there were no fundamental differences inherent in the delays, our Italian counterparts made their stalling tactics as pleasant as possible. For example, once we had finished the actual text of the agreement, which we negotiated in Italian, we then turned to the task of conforming a parallel official text in English. The chief Italian negotiator, in preparation for this undertaking and in cadence with the slow rate of progress demanded by the domestic political situation, brought along books by Wordsworth, Byron, and other English romantics in order to parse the various meanings of English words worthy to capture the full grace and majesty of the Italian text. It was also apparent that our pace was materially influenced by the progress being achieved in Vienna between U.S. and Soviet negotiators working on the Austrian treaty. When that document was finally signed, our agreement soon emerged from limbo and was pressed to completion.

Shortly after that happened, the Italian chief of staff invited several of us who had been working on bilateral military matters to a luncheon at the Golf Club. It was a rather unusual location, because it was outside of town and because General Mancini was neither a golfer nor a member of the club. But it was a rather discreet place to meet if there was something important to say. And the general did have something important on his mind. What bothered him was the Ljubljana Gap, a natural landscape formation to the northeast of Italy which made that corner of his country especially vulnerable to the threat of tank attacks. With the departure of allied forces from Austria, there was nothing protecting Italian territory from the movement of Warsaw Pact forces through that valley except a few scattered Yugoslav troops, whose capabilities and political attitudes the general did not trust.

In a very casual and unofficial conversation after lunch, the general suggested that it might be possible to bring some of the American forces out of Austria down into Italy to plug that gap. He indicated that a relatively new military installation built for the Alpini Brigade in Trentino might be made available to the Americans under our new status of forces agreement and that airfields at Aviano and Montechiari could be used by U.S. forces, with an advanced radar warning center at Udine. He claimed there was no political posture favoring this proposal in the cabinet but thought one might be possible.

I went back to the embassy that afternoon and wrote a cable reporting the general's suggestion. Ambassador Clare Booth Luce signed it out that evening. Within a few days, the plan to fulfill the suggestion was put in motion and its substance was agreed in principle. Teams of U.S. military officers began to descend on Rome to work out the details. One of these teams was headed by a tall young brigadier of Scandinavian extraction who was in charge of personnel matters for the army headquarters in the Pentagon. He and his staff flew to Trentino and inspected the barracks being offered by the Italians. They were new, well built, and in a spectacular setting. But the general found that the sleeping space allotted to each individual soldier amounted to one or two cubic feet less than the standards ordained by the army's manuals. He therefore reported in to my office before he was scheduled to return to Washington and told me he was going to have to recommend against the barracks, and by extension, the whole deployment.

He told me this at about 5:30 one evening and said he was leaving the next morning for Washington. I called the ambassador's office immediately and discovered that Mrs. Luce had already left for her residence in the Villa Taverna. She had an official dinner with the Prime Minister that evening and had gone home to try on a new formal gown she would wear. (She had a couturier do them in Paris and fly them in with frequency.) With some annoyance she did agree to see us at the Villa if we could get there by seven. We arrived in good time and were ushered into the sumptuous living room by the rather regal liveried butler, who assured us the Ambassador would be there shortly. Within a few minutes, she swept in, strikingly glamorous even to a Scandinavian brigadier, who gulped at attention. I quickly filled in the background and then had the brigadier give his little speech, complete with cubic statistics. La Luce gave him a coy smile and then tinkled a bell for the butler. On command, he brought an ivory and gold telephone on a long extension cord, into which the ambassador purred the request that the operator connect her with Secretary of Defense Wilson in Washington. The brigadier began to get scarlet behind the ears.

Because we had access to the new military communications network, the connection took less than a minute, and that clear belllike voice filled the silence in the large room. "Charlie? I have one of your bright young generals with me here in Rome and he has a problem." On it went for a few minutes more while the ambassador sketched out the relative importance of the general's geometrics and the international significance of the deployment under consideration. As she spoke, the general seemed to grow smaller and smaller. When she finally handed him the phone to get his orders from the secretary, he seemed to me to be shrinking into the pillows. Needless to say, an exception to army cubits was made for the Alpini barracks, and the deployment was set in motion.

However, when the line of communications for supplying the deployed units was designated by our Italian hosts, we had trouble from another quarter. General Al Greunther, the Allied Supreme Commander in Paris, did not think much of a supply line that ran through the Communist-controlled port of Livorno and minced no words in telling us so. Because we had used it before as an alternate supply route for Austria and because there were no other feasible options, I held out for using it and was supported by Ambassador Luce. The army's agreement did not come easily. I had to meet with and satisfy another platoon of generals before it could be done. And, in satisfying them, I had to obtain a whole battery of Italian assurances. Moreover, I had to agree that I would spend a few days each month in Livorno monitoring the arrangements and assuring that it would work. Thus began one of those comedies that could only occur in Italy.

The mayor of Livorno was a Communist. The head of the stevedoring organization which would handle all the American military cargo passing through the port was also a Communist, and his stevedores were all members of the Communist trade union. The quaestore, or head of the national police in the city was a tough little Sicilian, who was adamantly anti-Communist. The prefetto, charged with civil administration in the area, was a rather wise and cultured man. These men constituted the committee established on the Italian side to assure fulfillment of our agreement. Every month, I traveled to Livorno and, together with the U.S. Army colonel operating our port facility, met with this Italian team. We held our meetings in the palace of the cardinal, under whose watchful eye we worked out our agreements. He was a jolly and accomplished politician of the Church who took pains never to get involved in our business, but also made sure that it never failed. In all the time I was in Italy, not only did we never have a work stoppage or an unresolved labor dispute, but we also had no pilferage in the Port of Livorno. General Greunther later colorfully told us that he'd like to get a few more Communist port operations in other areas of the alliance.

All went well in our Italian military operations until Washington asked us to tighten up some of the language reflecting understandings on the issue of concurrent jurisdiction of the United States and Italian legal systems affecting our servicemen. In the course of our original negotiations, we had left the language deliberately vague because the differences between our two positions did not seem to be reconcilable except in practical application to individual instances. This flexibility did not satisfy our legalists in the Pentagon.

The negotiations on this subject were not conclusive. It finally became necessary to hand them over to Ambassador Luce to be worked out directly with the prime minister. As is usually the case in Italy, the appointment was set for the evening, after our normal business day. The ambassador had taken her papers home, to study there before going to the prime minister's office in the Palazzo Viminale. To her surprise, the Foreign Ministry negotiator asked to meet with her there before her appointment with the prime minister. She telephoned me to ask me also to be present. When I arrived, my Italian counterpart was already there, making a great plea that she not take up our disputed issue with the prime minister, but return it for resolution at the working level. I assured her we were at an impasse at the working level and pointed out that she was due for her appointment with the prime minister very shortly.

Mrs. Luce politely cut off her Italian interlocutor and got into her waiting limousine, heading, I assumed, for the Palazzo Viminale. In view of the rather curious delaying tactics by my Foreign Ministry counterpart, I decided to await her return at the Villa. After half an hour, the butler brought me the phone and said that the prime minister's office was asking when to expect the ambassador. I took the call and spoke to the cabinet secretary, explaining that Mrs. Luce should have been there fifteen minutes ago. I also told him about the intercession of the man from the Foreign Ministry in the event that had somehow caused a delay.

An hour and a half later, the ambassador returned, radiant with laughter. It seemed that her driver, Gino, having understood her to say "Palazzo Quirinale," had taken her to the president's office instead of the prime minister's. Since she had been studying her papers en route, she didn't notice where she was until she got there. Although she apologized for her mistake and tried to leave, the president asked her what was on her mind and, since her mind was filled with her brief, she blurted it out as she had intended to do with the prime minister. The President, who was thoroughly unbriefed on the subject, said it all sounded quite acceptable to him, but asked to be excused because his train was waiting at the station for a trip to northern Italy.

By the time Mrs. Luce made her appointment at Palazzo Viminale and explained the reason for her delay, the prime minister had already had words with the Foreign Ministry man who had tried to preempt his meeting and was not feeling kindly toward officious bureaucrats. When he also learned that the president found the Ambassador's proposal acceptable, he was thoroughly willing to make a generous gesture and agree to it. The ambassador's evening was a success. As I left my Villa to get my car, Gino, the driver, ran after me to explain the misunderstanding and to hope he hadn't caused any serious problems. To his astonishment, I told him he was a diplomatic genius.

— 2 —

The Dutch were different from other people I had dealt with in Asia and the Mediterranean. They had an obsession with truth. While others, almost as a matter of course, spun elaborate webs of circumlocution rather than unveil unvarnished facts, the Dutch were direct to the point of being blunt. In other societies, interlocutors would be especially imaginative in developing the nuances of disinformation, particularly if bad news were involved. In Holland, citizens male and female of all ages seemed to find constructive catharsis in conveying the worst tidings in their most unadulterated form.

Consequently, when I was first assigned to our embassy in The Hague in the winter of 1955, I found the change in professional climate something of a cultural shock. It did not take long to realize, however, that the direct Dutch approach constituted honest alliance in the truest sense of the word. Except for a tiny Communist party, all elements of Dutch society in those days considered themselves strongly committed to the ideals of NATO and looked to the United States for leadership. If they told us blunt facts and occasionally unpleasant ones, they were truly performing their Calvinistic duty of comradeship and cooperation.

Their attitude, of course, induced a certain reciprocity. And, since I had spent some time in Southeast Asia and was in considerable sympathy with the Indonesian effort to get rid of Dutch colonialism, I often had rather sharp words for my host country's policies with respect to their former colony, and particularly with respect to their dilatory tactics regarding West New Guinea. While most of the Dutch whom I met respectfully differed with me on this subject, I became aware that there were some, especially in the Labor Party, who agreed with my criticism. But they were too loyal to their nation to say so publicly. Eventually, some years after I had left The Hague, one of those senior officials informally gave me the formula which the Department of State was able to use to mediate the dispute between Holland and Indonesia successfully.

I soon came to have great respect for the way in which this plucky little country conducted its national affairs. It had survived the ravages of war and German occupation, the loss of its empire, and the reorientation of Europe in surprisingly good shape. Although it took care of its own interests meticulously, it was not selfish or insensitive to the needs of others. It was, in many ways, a model democracy. However, in that period, its society was still marked by the residues of the religious wars that had wracked its history. The principal social division in the country was between Catholics and Protestants, with additional subdivisions within the ranks of the Protestants themselves. Each family knew exactly where it stood on these religious frontiers and behaved accordingly. As a result, most services were duplicated everywhere, even in the smallest villages. There were usually two bakeries, two butcher shops, two greengrocers, and so on. One was Catholic and was patronized only by Catholics. One was Protestant with a Protestant clientele.

When we first moved to The Hague, my wife was not aware of these niceties and developed the pattern of her patronage on the basis of the best service or goods provided in each shop. As a result, she had a mixed shopping profile, with some purchases made in Catholic shops and some in Protestant. This naturally confused the good burghers and caused all manner of curiosity in trying to establish some rationale for such odd behavior. There was even some speculation that we might be Jewish, but the butchers were able to dispel that from the knowledge of our nonkosher dietary habits. It titilated my wife to leave them wondering.

Given the excellent education system in Holland—I should say systems, since there were Catholic, Protestant, and a few public schools—most Dutch spoke French and English in addition to their native tongue. As a small nation of traders, they realized the need for a polyglot culture, and spread it widely in their secondary education. They often joked about their own language, which, in strict national character, is rather blunt, practical, and far from mellifluous. Because of its limited utility, very few foreigners bothered to learn it.

However, I decided I would learn Dutch and began studying it in the first six or eight months I was in The Hague. One reason for this determination was the fact that my embassy assignment was to work with the Partij von der Arbeid, the Dutch Labor Party, most of whose members were working class citizens with limited formal education and a pronounced lack of fluency in English or French. Another determinant was my desire to read the excellent Dutch press, which had extensive coverage of political and economic events of interest.

As the result of my effort to learn their language, my Labor Party associates were far more forthcoming and congenial than they might otherwise have been. They always welcomed me to their headquarters in Amsterdam and even let me sit in on their internal meetings, partly to show the depth of their commitment to our alliance and partly to demonstrate that they had nothing to hide. When I would go to the Tweede Kamer, the lower house of parliament, to improve my Dutch by listening to the debate, Labor members would leave the floor and visit with me in the gallery to provide an insight into the politics of the debate.

This close association that I had with the Labor Party was carefully observed by the Soviet embassy, especially in the parliament, where one of their officers, who also spoke Dutch, usually monitored the performance of the communist party, which was in the process of disintegrating into two bitterly contesting factions. The result was a Soviet assumption that I was the principal CIA representative in the country and that our chosen instrument was the Labor Party. In due course, I was approached by the chief KGB representative, who acted as first secretary of the Soviet embassy, and invited to lunch. He suggested that I bring a colleague and indicated that he would do the same. I brought our second ranking CIA man, while he brought a Second Secretary, who was a legitimate officer in the Soviet foreign service. At the end of the meal, our host ostentatiously passed the bill to the Second Secretary, who paid. This was presumably to avoid any impression that I was being bribed by the KGB. A few weeks later, I hosted a return lunch for the same participants. I conspicuously passed the bill to my CIA colleague, who paid. The reciprocal lunches became a regular monthly event until I finally left The Hague. Neither we or the Soviets learned very much of significance from them, but, courtesy of the KGB and the CIA, I enjoyed some excellent meals during that period.

My Dutch language ability also had another pleasant consequence. Through it, I became an honorary first secretary of the Luxembourg embassy. It came about in the curiously homey way in which formal diplomacy was practiced in The Hague. The Luxembourg ambassador was a distinguished gentleman who later became his Duchy's foreign minister. He had a large house and, because of the close geographical and political relations between Holland and Luxembourg, a conspicuous presence. But, since his business was rather limited and he was only a few miles from the seat of his government, his thrifty parliamentary masters saw no need to provide him with a large professional staff. He had one secretary-receptionist and one code clerk, and that was all.

The ambassador was the first to admit that he didn't need a staff of diplomatic secretaries for his chancery, but he did feel their absence when he tried to carry out his representational functions. As ambassador from one of Holland's partners in the Western European Union and other such entities, he felt the need to entertain Dutch cabinet officers and to reciprocate the invitations they tendered to him. In the ambiance of Europe in those days, this usually meant formal dinners of the white tie or black tie variety. The ambassador found it hard to greet his guests at the door of his large house, accompany them into the drawing rooms, engage them in conversation, introduce them to others, and tend to their interests. In short, he needed a first secretary, preferably equipped with an attractive wife.

After we had met the Luxembourg couple several times, the ambassador approached me with an amusing proposition. He asked if I would be willing to be an "honorary first secretary" of his embassy and if my wife and I would be willing to help him and his wife at social functions. Since they were very pleasant people and lived rather close to us, we accepted. Hence, for the rest of my tour, I got to know most of the

Dutch cabinet at least as well as my ambassador did, and I also gained some new perspectives when discussion around the dinner table, usually in French, centered on European matters and occasionally on European views of the United States. It was a useful dividend to "serve" in two embassies simultaneously.

But the Dutch were not always seriously engaged in business, and when they unbent a little and enjoyed themselves, they were a very pleasant lot. They usually took care to do this in circles where they knew everyone else and had known them for some years. That often meant that relaxation generally took place either in the confines of a private home or in one of the small private clubs that inconspicuously abound in Amsterdam and The Hague.

One of those clubs, called, I believe, "De Kring," is oriented largely towards artists, writers, and amateurs of the arts. Its pride is a huge mural, which covers an entire wall of the principal social room of the club. The mural is the combined product of the artistic members of the club, each of whom has painted a portion in conformance with a mutually agreed design. On the day after Christmas each year, the mural is painted over with a fresh coat of paint and the club is closed to its general membership. Only the artists who have agreed to participate in the project are allowed to remain in the club, which stays fully staffed, especially in the kitchen and the bar. The artists then face the task of agreeing on an artistic plan for the new mural, dividing up the work on it, and completing the work so that it can be unveiled and inaugurated at the stroke of midnight on New Year's Eve. The product, which in some years is an invaluable masterpiece, graces the wall of the clubroom for the remainder of the year, but is doomed to extinction on the day after Christmas. This process has been going on for generations, and will probably continue into the future.

In settings such as this, Dutch friends are inclined to drink

Nurturing NATO

enough alcohol to lay aside their inhibitions and engage in rather heavy-handed humor. Sometimes this takes the form of elaborate practical jokes, or, on birthdays and other such occasions, appears in carefully crafted poems of doggerel, usually with a certain amount of biting reference not always appreciated by the target of the poesy.

When informality and proper decorum came into conflict, the Dutch of those years were often confused. Things have changed sharply since that time, but I recall putting a number of crusty innkeepers to a rather severe test. It happened in the late summer of 1956, when I decided to explore the country on bicycle. Holland has a wonderful network of *fietspads*, or bicycle paths, that permit a biker to go almost anywhere without having to fight heavy automobile traffic. Using a map of these paths, I laid out an itinerary that would take me in a circular path around the great Zuider Zee, which dominates the center of the country, and take me through almost every major town in the course of about eight days. I figured to ride approximately a hundred miles a day and spend the rest of the time poking into nooks and crannies inaccessible by automobile. Once I had fixed my itinerary, I looked up the best hotels along the route and wrote to them on embassy stationery asking for reservations. Most of them were categorized by European standards as "luxe" and prided themselves on their dignity and their cuisine, usually in that order. I didn't specify in my letters the means of conveyance by which I would arrive, but the embassy seal on my letterhead assured me rapid confirmation of reservations and, usually, the best accommodations available.

There was always some consternation at these establishments when I rode up to the elaborately uniformed commissionaire at the polished entrance, asked him to park my bicycle, and strode into the elegant lobby in my biking clothes, with my saddlebags over my arm. After recovering from his assumption that there must have been some mistake, the desk clerk usually accompanied me nervously to my room or suite, obviously wondering what I would wear to the dining room, where some guests would be attired in black tie. It was always amusing to see the obvious expressions of relief when, after a good hot bath, I showed up once again in the lobby wearing a jacket and tie that I produced from the saddlebags and a good clean shirt that was the product of the overnight laundry service those luxe hotels used to provide. Sometimes, the staff had recovered enough so that my morning departure became a matter of some ceremony, with the commissionaire producing my cleaned and polished bicycle in a gesture of great flair.

When we left The Hague, our Dutch friends gave us a great farewell. They chartered one of the tourist boats that plies the graceful canals of Amsterdam, stocked it with plenty to drink and with Dutch delicacies such as herring, sausage, and cheese. They sprang a derelict accordian player from a local lockup and stationed him in the prow with a bottle and a freedom to improvise. We sailed and sang and drank for an hour or so and finally moored near an old restaurant, in which they had reserved the second floor for a private party. The meal, the toasts, and the poetry were bountiful. We left that country with a great sense of sympathy for a very civilized people.

Chapter Six

Foggy Bottom
1959–1963

WHEN WE RETURNED TO Washington in 1958, I had been out of the country for thirteen of the previous fifteen years. The managers of the Foreign Service thought it was time for me not only to become reacquainted with the country I represented, but also to get a little experience in the way the Washington end of our foreign affairs bureaucracy functioned. Therefore, they assigned me to the Department of State, in Southeast Asian affairs, back in the region where I began eleven years before.

It was toward the end of the Eisenhower administration, and those in charge were clearly running out of steam. John Foster Dulles, who had been secretary of state for six years, was stricken with cancer and had to retire. The system of alliances he had established was beginning to run into trouble. Eisenhower himself, who had suffered a serious heart attack, was further discouraged as he began to see his hopes for some sort of understanding with the Soviets founder on the arrogance of Khrushchev's conviction that his system would "bury" ours. The cold war had reached new and more dangerous dimensions as new technologies made the possibility of total mutual destruction more tangible.

In Southeast Asia, the hopes we had raised by our postwar support of decolonization had begun to sour. The newly independent nations had long since forgotten their earlier gratitude to the United States as the champion of their independence and had, instead, begun to look on us as an "exploiter" from which they needed to be "liberated." Nowhere was this attitude more pronounced than in the former French colonies of Indochina, and no antagonist was more bitter and fanatic than the Lao Dong party that controlled North Vietnam. Much of our effort in the Southeast Asian area at the Department of State was directed toward development of a policy to contain the thrust of Chinese communist hegemony into Indochina, and, beyond that, to the wealthy prize of Indonesia, finally liberated from Dutch colonial control.

Those last two years of the Eisenhower era took on the aspect of a rear guard action. In foreign affairs, we were almost everywhere on the defensive. No great new initiatives were set in motion during that time, but a number of tactical moves were proposed to try to recoup some of the ground we appeared to be losing in the Third World. In general, I worked with congenial people in the State Department, the Pentagon, the CIA, the White House, and the Congress. Many of them had backgrounds similar to my own—college just before the war, military service during the war, and government service after the war. The war had been the major factor in our lives, giving us a broader scope of interest in the world, convincing us that something needed to be done to improve the state of mankind, and persuading us that we were capable of influencing that improvement. We were used to success and frustrated by failure.

I learned to operate in the bureaucracy, although I never really enjoyed it. I began to find my way around Congress and made a number of friends on the Hill. I knew many members in both houses from having worked with them as host and escort during my years in Rome. The care and feeding of visiting congressional delegations in that great city were developed to imaginative art forms. I remember once, for example, when a well-known senior member of Congress disappeared from his hotel during the middle of a visit. His colleagues in the delegation insisted that I not make any attempt to find him and felt convinced that no foul play was involved. However, when he had failed to reappear on the eve of the delegation's departure for points east, I finally persuaded them to let me go to the Italian police.

With great discretion, I approached the police captain whose section had responsibility for dealing with foreign embassies. I laid out our problem as delicately as I could and stressed the national importance of the missing congressman. He soothingly clucked his tongue and told me not to worry. He said my missing solon was ensconced in another nearby hotel, was with a "nice girl" who would not rob him, and that he would be sobered up in the course of the evening. Then he would be returned to the delegation's hotel during the night and be prepared to leave the next morning. Sure enough, the next morning our errant legislator was there at the breakfast table with all his travelling companions, bright and chipper as the rest. Neither he nor they mentioned his absence as I gathered them up and took them to the airport. He rejoined the junket and went on to become chairman of his committee. Although we never in any way alluded to the lapse in Rome, he was always a staunch supporter of mine on the floor of Congress or in committee battles thereafter.

Partly because of acquaintances such as this, I was asked to escort a group of congressmen around the world in 1959. The group had its own airplane, borrowed from the air force, and a number of staff people from various committees as well as from departments of the executive branch. It was a trip that consumed the better part of a month and went to a large number of countries. On the whole, my congressional charges were a pleasant, convivial, and relatively conscientious lot. Occasionally, however, one or more threw over the traces and required acts of salvage.

For example, there was the night in a cabaret in Istanbul, when things got a little out of hand. Two of the members had imbibed rather heavily before dinner, and the effect of food seemed to spur them on to more heroic acts of indulgence. When they insisted on going to a cabaret we passed en route back to the hotel from our dinner engagement, I decided that I had better stay with them to head off any international incidents. One of them was a gentleman farmer very fond of horses, and the other was a gentleman very fond of girls.

It so happened that the cabaret that evening appeared to feature both a horse and a bevy of girls. The horse did tricks for a scantily clad equestrienne who rewarded his performance by a great deal of nuzzling and ultimately a considerable amount of erotic rubbing of bodies. The bevy turned out to be not girls at all, but a group of French transvestites whose silicon injections were very deceptive. By the time the cabaret performance was over, my two congressmen were intoxicated not only by their beverages but also by the spectacle they had seen. Each egged the other on until both bolted for the area behind the small stage. I settled the bill with the waiter and rushed to join them. By the time I arrived, one had the horse and rider firmly in tow, and the other had a transvestite on each arm. They were heading out the back door of the cabaret and moving toward the hotel, which was a newly constructed Hilton of rather grand design.

The equestrienne had been persuaded that she and her mount could give a repeat performance of her act in the grand foyer of the Hilton to a large and appreciative international audience who would reward her generously. The transvestites had been tempted by other more private rewards for more private performances. It was clear their gallant escort had no idea of their true sex and thought he had a couple of cuddly chorines in custody. It took me some time and some fairly graphic maneuvers to prevent a scandal. My first breakthrough came when tactile tests revealed to the girl-fancier the folly of his illusions. He sobered up with a bolt and then assisted me in decoupling his colleague from the equestrian act. By the time we actually darted into the Hilton lobby, both honorable members were ready to flee to their rooms. The next morning they were sheepishly grateful and became my friends for life.

Other events in my Washington tour had a less puckish cast. For example, there was another time in 1959 when I thought I had really got my feet in the flypaper. It happened as a result of the prevailing mania for civil defense. It was the conviction of the time that a nuclear war could be fought and won, albeit with enormous casualties on both sides. In order to prepare convincingly for such a holocaust, a great shelter program was prepared. The paragon of these shelters was a huge installation burrowed in the rock of the Blue Ridge mountains, where the operations of the United States Government would be transferred in case of attack. Each department had a number of "key" personnel designated to go to this gigantic bunker and operate from its belly once nuclear attack seemed imminent. In order to make these preparations realistic, the "emergency management" people decided to simulate the action in a dry run that would last for three days. A number of us on the "key" list were given a limited warning and instructed to gather at the shelter. We were about one third of those who would actually be accommodated there in "the real thing." Therefore, the actual business of government was not severely curtailed while those of us in the bunker played out a "war game" that was scripted to an exchange of nuclear weapons with the Soviet Union.

Further in the interests of realism, the managers of this

program decided that they should simulate living conditions as closely as they could. Hence, although there were beds for all of us, they sealed off two-thirds of the dormitories and instituted a system of "rotational rest." This presumed that one-third of those present were on duty, one third engaged in such matters as eating, shaving, etc., while one-third slept. It was patterned on navy life at sea. Lots were drawn to determine who was in which third. I drew the third third, which meant that, after the end of a full working day in Washington, I would have to wait another sixteen hours before my allotted bunk would be available. I was not amused.

Because the war game plan was pretty sketchy, I had very little to do during my eight hour duty period. When I was relieved at midnight, I then had eight more hours to while away before I slept. This prospect vexed me. As something to do to stay awake, I decided to explore the underground maze. After ten or fifteen minutes of meandering, I came upon one complex of rooms that was decidedly superior to the rest. Upon examination, I discovered that it was "the White House area." I also discovered that not a soul was in it. The very comfortable beds, the private showers and the luxurious appointments overwhelmed my sense of duty. I chose the best accommodations, closed the door, turned off the light, and slept for eight hours. When I awoke, I went back to the working area and had breakfast. By this time, my third of the group still had about six hours of sleep before duty was scheduled. Given this prospect, I picked up my suitcase and clothes, moved nonchalantly back through the corridors to my newfound quarters, showered, shaved, and changed to fresh clothes. After reading awhile, I returned to join my duty section for another boring eight hour game session. Then, after the evening meal, I went back to my "quarters" for another good night's sleep.

The next day, at duty, I was startled to hear my name called over the speaker system. I was asked to report to the office of the man who was directing the project. When I did, I was distressed to find four burly young men with very grim faces and the unmistakable look of the Secret Service. It seemed that the Soviets had shot down one of our intelligence aircraft, that the nation had gone to a state of limited alert, and that the president was actually transferring his operations from the White House to the bunker, where his presence would coincide with the last day of our exercise. The Secret Service had come ahead to the bunker to double-check the president's quarters and had found evidence of an alien presence in the room as well as an unmade bed that had obviously been slept in. The evidence, in the form of my suitcase, pajamas, and dirty laundry, was spread on the director's desk. I was, I assumed, under arrest.

The director, a former Republican governor who had been defeated in the last election and given this job as a political plum, looked stern and forbidding. He looked at the evidence, looked at me, and looked at the Secret Service. "Gentlemen," he said to the latter, "I'll take care of this." With this assurance, the four muscle men trooped out and the governor closed the door behind them. As he turned around to face me, he began to laugh in nearly uncontrollable laughter and pronounced my trespass the "damndest thing he ever heard." And, he concluded, "to think I've been sleeping on one of those wretched bunks!" With that, he hustled me and my baggage out the door. That night, I also slept on one of those wretched bunks.

My next near encounter with Eisenhower occurred when another of our planes was shot down. This time it was the U-2 flown by Gary Powers. That event occurred as Eisenhower was at the outset of a major world tour that was to take him to Europe, to the Soviet Union, and to Japan. By the time he got to Paris, however, Khrushchev had reacted to the U-2 incident by withdrawing his invitation for the visit to Moscow.

The stunned delegation, still committed to the Tokyo visit, cabled back to Washington for recommendations on what should be done.

I happened to be the duty officer in the Far East bureau that weekend and the cable came to me early in the morning for action. By the time it was decent to wake up anyone of higher authority, I had drafted a reply, which I sent to my superiors for clearance. It recommended preserving the planned trip to Tokyo, but filling in the time gutted from the schedule by the Soviet disinvitation through some hastily arranged stops in Asia. I proposed Manila, Taipei, and Seoul. By midmorning, in the absence of any better ideas, my draft was approved and sent off to Paris as the official Washington recommendation. Word came back from Paris that evening that the president had approved the recommendation and had directed that the changed itinerary be organized.

Since the proposal had been my idea, I was instructed to organize the trip. By the time the crestfallen president and his delegation returned to Washington from Paris, I had most of the details in place. Manila, Taipei, and Seoul would be delighted to receive the president. Transportation, communication, and security arrangements were in train. Communiques were prepared. Speeches and toasts were written. Background books were assembled.

Tom Stevens, the president's appointments secretary, called me over to the White House and went over the plans. He thought they were fine and passed me along to Andy Goodpaster, the president's assistant. He also approved but took the added precaution of naming me "coordinator" for the trip so that I would be on tap along the way in case anything slipped. I therefore found myself on Air Force One as Eisenhower came aboard and we took off for Asia. As we were leaving, we began to get reports from Tokyo that Press Secretary Jim Haggerty, who was "advancing" the trip, had been roughed up on his way to Haneda airport to leave Japan. When we arrived in Anchorage, Alaska, to spend the night, Haggerty was there to greet us and gave us some harrowing accounts of his problems in Japan. By the time we reached Hawaii, our embassy in Tokyo had reported that the communists were using the U-2 incident as cause for major riots. The Japanese Government, however, insisted that all was under control and the visit should continue.

In Manila, discussion in our delegation of the visit to Japan became heated. The Secret Service and some of the staff were dead opposed to risking the president's life for the sake of a visit. The president himself, even if he might have shared those views, insisted that he had given his word and would go unless the Japanese asked him not to. At the Malacanang Palace, before going to a large rally in Rizal Park, he told me to open a direct telephone line to Doug MacArthur (the General's nephew, who was at this time our ambassador in Tokyo) and to keep regularly in touch with him. He told me to call Andy Goodpaster, who would have a telephone in Rizal Park, if any important news came.

About a half hour after Eisenhower left, Doug MacArthur told me that the Japanese prime minister had just concluded that the visit would have to be cancelled. I telephoned Andy at Rizal Stadium, and he informed Eisenhower just before he spoke. The old soldier never missed a beat. He carried on his performance exactly as scheduled. That trip, however, and the dual disappointments of Moscow and Tokyo, seemed to me to be the end of the Eisenhower administration. When we got back to Hawaii, Eisenhower decided to hole up in the Marine base at Kaneohe and canceled his appointments in Washington. He sent most of us back to the capital on the backup plane and concentrated on playing golf. He was fed up with the way the world had gone and was ready to let someone else try. He never had his old bounce again.

The bounce, instead, came from a new quarter. The campaign of John F. Kennedy in 1960 captured the imagination of most of America, and not least, of those whom he called "the junior officers of World War II." I fell into that category and was caught up in the enthusiasm for this new young president. I had known him and not been terribly impressed when he was a young congressman. But, as he swept into town and brought a retinue of many others I knew well, I was swept along and into the enthusiasm of the new administration. Those first few months were heady ones and invited new ideas and new challenges. I put forth some thoughts on China and on Laos, which had become a crisis era. Kennedy accepted both suggestions and plunged me into the middle of his foreign policy activities. Before too long, I found myself in Geneva as Averell Harriman's deputy, negotiating with thirteen other delegations about Laos.

— 2 —

The negotiations on the neutrality and independence of Laos dragged on through 1961 and half of 1962. The event was something of a circus, with fourteen nations being represented at the Palais des Nations in Geneva. The Chinese, for example, used it as a training program for their foreign ministry, which was just beginning to emerge from the isolation of the communist revolution. They took over an entire hotel in the city, and bussed nearly two hundred of their bureaucrats to the meetings, where they sat in serried ranks in the visitors' gallery, with notebooks spread on their laps, busily filling them with mandarin characters. When it became apparent that nothing was going to be quickly or easily resolved, the senior diplomatic representatives from each country, who had other more pressing things to do, quietly slipped away from the conference, reduced the size of their delegations, and left more junior subordinates in charge. Thus it came about that I became acting head of the United States delegation in the fall of 1961.

Geneva was a pleasant city in those days, with a great number of excellent little restaurants and many nearby diversions. But hotel living, even in the most pleasant and efficient Swiss ambience, can eventually begin to pall. I decided in due course to find an apartment in the city and to try to live a somewhat more normal life. Two other members of our delegation—John Czyak, our legal adviser, and Bill McCrae, our military representative—had the same idea and readily agreed to share an apartment. John, a refugee from Polish concentration camps, was also an excellent cook and loved to tinker in the kitchen. The three of us found a spacious furnished flat and set up housekeeping there.

John was also an excellent pianist, with a profoundly sentimental addiction to Chopin. Although we did not have a piano in our apartment, we discovered an excellent concert grand in the very gracious bar of a hotel not too far away. This bar, presided over by an attractive young lady named Lilly, became a favorite place for Americans from the various official delegations in the conference city of Geneva to gather in the late evening for after-dinner drinks. When most of the Swiss, who retired early, had left the bar, we could usually prevail upon John to give us informal concerts of Chopin, Liszt, and Tchaikovsky. These always ended promptly at midnight because Lilly, acutely conscious of propriety and of the police station across the street, insisted on rigorous application of the city ordinances.

Our living pattern settled into a routine which involved endless speechifying at the conference table, sporadic negotiations on the text of a draft agreement with the British and Soviet cochairmen, long consultations with friendly delegations, reports back to the State Department, and a considerable amount of entertainment among the different delegations, the Swiss gentry, and the large press corps. In pursuit of peace and understanding, we dined and drank quite often with the delegations who were our adversaries. Since it was contrary to United States policy in those days to break bread with the

Chinese, this meant that our eligible adversaries were largely limited to the Soviets, the Poles, the North Vietnamese, and the Pathet Lao. Since we misjudged the independence of the North Vietnamese, we felt the only ones among these who really mattered were the Soviets. Hence, we and they spent quite a bit of time socializing with each other.

Once settled in our apartment, we decided to invite the three senior members of the Soviet delegation to a home-cooked meal, prepared by John Czyzak and containing a few Polish and Russian delicacies. I functioned not only as host but also as bartender. My ministrations, John's meal, and our boisterous dinner conversation in mutually fractured French made the evening a grand success. When it was over, we proposed a visit to Lilly's bar and Chopin on the concert grand. Our proposal was readily accepted by our Soviet guests, and we set off in great good spirits on a balmy night.

Although it was nearly midnight when we arrived, Lilly sized up the situation very quickly and slipped out to explain to the adjacent police station the need to bend the city regulations slightly. The police understood and required only that Lilly close the windows to confine both the music and the Soviet-American harmony within her four walls. Chopin, cognac, Tchaikovsky, and schnapps flowed on for at least another hour. Our Soviet guests, a bit maudlin by this time, were blissfully oblivious to the time. Finally, close on to 2 a.m., one of them glanced at his watch and, abruptly, all three of them rose to bid us a warm but hasty farewell.

When we returned to the apartment and tackled the dirty dishes before retiring, we were vaguely aware of a number of automobiles parked on our quiet street where none usually stood after dark. We also had some sense that room and closet doors seemed unusually ajar. But we attributed this to the fact that we had left the place on the spur of the moment and had not put things back to their normal order. About half an hour after our return, most of the cars on our street started their engines and quietly drove away. By the time the apartment was tidied up, everything seemed to have returned to normal.

When we went to the office that morning, I found a request from our CIA representative for an appointment. He came in accompanied by a man from our consulate who was responsible for liaison with the Swiss police. They had a fascinating story to tell. It seems that the Soviet delegation, housed in a suburban villa owned by their government, went into a state of high alert about 1 a.m. that morning. A number of vehicles moved out and headed for various destinations. One went to the airport, another to the railroad station, and three or four to the residential district where our apartment was located. From the ever-efficient Swiss police, it was learned that our apartment had been surreptitiously entered by two men who stayed there for nearly fifteen minutes before stationing themselves in some shrubbery down the street. At about 2:30 a.m., the whole exercise seemed to have been called off, and the automobiles returned to the Soviet villa, which resumed its normal solemn quietude.

That afternoon at the Palais des Nations, the Soviet delegation was on the scene early and clearly waiting for our arrival. Our three guests of the night before, looking a little drained, came to greet us effusively. The head of the delegation, a senior ambassador, thanked us heavily for our hospitality and apologized for staying so late. In a gently lowered voice, he expressed the hope that "everything was all right" with us. I replied with great nonchalance and did not in any way indicate that we were aware of the misunderstanding the late night had caused at the Soviet mission. There may have been some subconscious reflection in my demeanor of my astonishment that men of this seniority could have been suspected by their watchdogs of defection, but I tried not to show it.

Shortly after that event, the Soviets chose to reciprocate our hospitality. They invited the three of us who had been their hosts, as well as our CIA associate, to dinner at their villa. There, accompanied by their senior KGB representative, they greeted us with great warmth. The villa was decorated in a sort of Victorian plush, with much dark panelling and heavy bourgeois touches. The dinner was excellent and was clearly laid on as an extraordinary gesture. Mounds of caviar, numerous varieties of Russian vodka, Russian wines, and Russian fruit were on the table. The pièce do résistance was a huge pheasant under glass, which our host, with Freudian confusion, kept referring to as "peasant." When it was over, I asked if we could toast the cook. Although this proposal caused a little confusion, our host accepted, and the KGB man went to fetch him from the kitchen. The chef, who was a stocky Russian peasant wearing a towering white hat, a slightly stained apron, and about three days growth of stubble, was a little bloodshot when he appeared with some embarrassment in the midst of the "gentlemen" diners. However, when apprised of our purpose, he readily fell in with the idea of a toast.

He darted back into the kitchen and soon reappeared with a large tumbler, filled nearly to the rim with vodka. Although our Soviet colleagues visibly blanched at this libation, the ambassador gamely translated the words of my toast and they all lifted their champagne glasses and gently sipped the wine. We all then stared in fascination as the cook tilted his tumbler on end and in one continuous gulp, drained the entire contents as his contribution to our civility. Then, with a face-splitting grin, he bounced back to his kitchen. The Soviets, with practiced diplomatic aplomb, shifted attention away from their proletarian countryman by engaging us in congenial conversation as the demitasse service and after-dinner liqueurs replaced the dessert and champagne. They radiated good will and optimism about the outcome of our conference. They were especially flattering in their appraisal of our new young president.

While we were enjoying all this, I noticed the swinging

doors of the kitchen opening ever so quietly. Then, I saw a large white hat protrude into the dining room, followed by the flushed, slyly grinning face of our chef. Everyone else except for the Soviet sitting next to me was too engrossed in the conversation to notice what was happening. My immediate companion, who did see it all, began to make funny little noises in his throat and stared at the kitchen door. Suddenly, the chef leaped into the room in a commanding presence that attracted everyone's attention. It was clear that he was, by now, quite drunk, and in his hand he held the large kitchen tumbler, once again filled to the rim with vodka. In a loud, slurred voice, he proposed a toast to the "Amerikanski" and raised his glass on high. The Soviets froze in terror at the sight. Suddenly, the KGB man leaped to his feet, locked both arms around the hapless cook, spun him around, and propelled him back into the kitchen. Try as we might, we couldn't really pick up the spirit of the dinner after that happening, and the evening ended rather early. On our way home, we concluded that the KGB was really quite an overworked organization.

— 3 —

The fall of 1962 was an enormously busy time. We had completed the Laos agreements that summer, and I had arranged to take a brief vacation with my family in a house that we had rented on one of the Delaware beaches. While we were there, a summons came from Washington. I was asked to go to the capital and report to the White House. No further details were provided. We had fortunately taken two automobiles to the beach, so that I was able to depart in one and leave the other for my family. When I reported in, I was told to be prepared to leave the next evening with General Maxwell Taylor for a trip to Asia. President Kennedy had decided to appoint Taylor, who had resigned from the Army in a dispute with the previous administration about military strategy, as chairman of the Joint Chiefs of Staff. Taylor felt he needed to update his information on Asia, and particularly on Vietnam, Thailand, and Indonesia before assuming his new duties. He and Navy Captain Worth Bagley and I spent about two weeks looking into all the potential trouble spots before returning home.

Two days after we got back, I was at the White House again. This time it concerend Laos. It was apparent that the new neutralized government we had ordained in Geneva needed foreign exchange if it was to survive. While the sums were not great, we felt that the appearance of neutrality would be violated if the United States supplied them all. I was asked to go to London and Paris in order to seek the equivalent of a million dollars apiece from the British and the French. President Kennedy wryly assured me that he'd give me a Medal of Honor for every franc I managed to pry loose from the notoriously tight French Treasury.

In the event, I did manage to get the money I was after from both governments and was feeling pretty smug in Paris when I received a message telling me to catch the next plane home. Abe Chayes, the State Department's legal adviser, who had just arrived in Paris a few hours earlier, received the same message, and we both caught the "red eye special" that night, wondering what the problem was. The problem, of course, arose from the Soviet missiles in Cuba. Abe was plunged immediately into those negotiations. I, on the other hand, was sent to New York to handle the issue of Chinese representation in the United Nations and to free other members of Adlai Stevenson's staff for work on the missile crisis.

The atmosphere at the United Nations in those few days when the world teetered on the brink of nuclear war was tense to the point of trauma. The world's diplomats, used to arguing about petty points of difference, realized that the whole globe could go up in smoke if Khrushchev's audacious gamble in Cuba should result in an actual exchange of missiles between the superpowers. I was left in the General Assembly

Foggy Bottom 169

to deal with the relatively secondary issue of Chinese representation, while the real focus of attention lay in the Security Council, where Stevenson was dealing with the problem of the missiles in Cuba.

There were, nevertheless, interesting developments in the General Assembly. There, the drive to seat the communist regime from Peking in place of the nationalist regime from Taipei had regularly been led by the Indian delegation, which seemed to relish the chance to antagonize the United States for its traditional stand in opposition to this proposal. I had organized the American voting position that year, and anticipated a very close call. In fact, because the vote was going to be obscured by a lot of secondary skirmishing in the Third World, involving such questionable entities as Mauritania and Outer Mongolia, I had expected serious trouble. In a tactical move to gain certain dubious support, I had persuaded the Chinese Nationalist representative, George Yeh, to agree to a deal that would give Outer Mongolia a seat at the same time as Mauritania, in order to gain Arab abstentions on the China vote. This deal ran contrary to Taipei's traditional view that Outer Mongolia was a puppet creation of Moscow and did not merit recognition as a nation. As a result, poor George lost his job to the jealousy of a lightweight, ambitious young foreign minister, who was a Kuomintang political hack. We won the decision on representation by only two votes, and the Mauritania-Outer Mongolia deal was obviously a necessity. However, the thing that had really made the victory possible was an Indian abstention.

Relations between New Delhi and Peking had been in a state of decline for some time prior to the vote. The depth of the deterioration had first become apparent to me in Geneva. I had been at a reception given by the Swiss Government after the successful completion of our negotiations on Laos. It was held at a lovely old building in the medieval part of the City of Geneva. During a lull in the festivities, I had stepped outside to admire some of the carved masonry and had stumbled on an alcove where Krishna Menon, the Foreign Minister of India, was in animated conversation with Marshall Chen Yi, the Foreign Minister of the People's Republic of China. They were both taken aback by my sudden intrusion.

I had gotten to know both of them fairly well during our long negotiations. They were, each in his own way, rather colorful characters. Krishna was a consummate fraud. He made long, histrionic, rambling speeches designed to show his own education, but which were usually offensive in one way or another to the bulk of his auditors. He was an unpopular figure to most diplomats. Chen Yi, on the other hand, was a throwback to an eighteenth century Chinese war lord. He had been a successful military commander during the communist revolution and the political commissar of Shanghai. He used his combined political and military leverage to take control of the Foreign Ministry in the Peking government and to run it like a private fief. It is questionable that he had much ideological commitment to Marxism.

When Chen Yi had given a large party to mark the end of the negotiations, he had flooded the American delegation with invitations, even though our two countries had no diplomatic relations. Secretary of State Dean Rusk, as head of our delegation, decided that it would be too sensational for him or Averell Harriman to attend the affair, but decided that I, as the third ranking member of our group, could go to demonstrate our appreciation of the cooperation Peking had shown in signing the Laos agreement. I took our lawyer and our CIA representative with me. Our appearance at the Chinese villa caused consternation, since none of them expected we would deviate from our usual practice of rejecting all Chinese overtures by frostily ignoring them. However, Chen Yi had risen to the occasion by treating me with great bonhommie, toasting U.S.-Chinese friendship over and over again, and requiring me to join him in countless gulps of biting Mao Tai liquor.

I had also had an extraordinary experience with Krishna Menon during the conference. The Indian delegation had played a rather important role in the proceedings as the principal neutralist representative at an enterprise seeking to develop a neutralist resolution of the Laos crisis. I had worked very well with the Indian deputy, Arthur Lall, and, on several occasions, had hammered out constructive solutions through him. On one such instance, he and I needed to reach agreement early one morning in order to resolve one issue in an afternoon session. We met at his hotel in the morning, worked out an understanding, subject to the concurrence of Krishna Menon. We therefore took our text to the latter's bedroom, where Arthur knocked on the door. Recognizing the voice, Krishna asked him to come in. When we did, we were surprized to find the Indian Foreign Minister seated at a table, tucking into a large plate of fried eggs and bacon. He was clearly embarrassed by my presence. It was his cherished reputation to be a vegetarian, to eat practically nothing at all, and to survive largely on water and a few ascetic bread crumbs. He quickly accepted our compromise language and seemed very glad to see us leave his suite.

These were the two men I discovered in earnest conversation at the Swiss reception. Menon immediately took the initiative, hooking me with his ever-present cane and attempting some rather feeble joke about the difficulties India and China were having in the Ladahk area northeast of Kashmir. He tried to suggest that the problems were all the result of minor misunderstandings and would soon be resolved. Chen Yi, on the other hand, did not consider their discussion amusing. He fixed a stern eye on me and said, "I just told him we would give them a bloody nose unless they get out of our territory!" And he jutted his jaw at Menon, as I tactfully withdrew.

The development of this conflict, even though it was reflected in the UN General Assembly, was, of course, obscured by the more deadly confrontation unfolding in the Security Council. As soon as the vote on the China representation question was finished in the Assembly, we all broke for the Council chamber. There, Stevenson was just beginning his statement, accompanied by the blown up photographs of the missiles the Soviets had brazenly denied they were installing. After that session, Arthur Schlesinger and I dashed for the airport and caught the shuttle back to Washington. I remember sitting on that plane with thoughts of the coming holocaust gripping my mind and marvelling at Arthur's insouciant ability to consume the trip by writing an anonymous review of a movie he had seen the previous evening.

Within a few days, however, the crisis was resolved and the world stepped back from disaster. It was then that the India-China problem came to the fore. Chinese forces attacked sharply in both the Ladakh and Northeast Frontier regions, and the Indians fell back in disarray. They screamed in distress for assistance from all those nations Krishna Menon had spent several previous years excoriating. The official reaction in Washington was sympathetic but rather cautious. Even though the public press reaction was emotionally critical of China, our official conclusion was that they had been recklessly provoked by the Indians.

President Kennedy decided that it would be wise to coordinate with the British before reacting to the frantic Indian appeals. A team of us from State, Defense, and CIA flew to London to meet with our British counterparts. Symbolically, our meetings were held in the old, elaborately panelled East India Room at Whitehall, and I turned out to be the lead-off speaker. When I gave our official assessment of the situation and of Chinese intentions, the British seemed enormously relieved that we did not reflect the emotional bias of the American press. We quickly agreed to put together a joint U.S.-British mission to visit India and provide appropriate assistance. The mission was to be headed by Averell Harriman for the U.S. and Duncan Sandys for the British. Within another two days, we were on our way to New Delhi.

The Indians were in a panic. Their troops, which were always of indifferent quality, had totally collapsed in the face of the Chinese human wave tactics that we had experienced in Korea. In the Northeast Frontier Region, whole battalions, including a number of senior generals, had surrendered and given up strategic territory with no real resistance. Their leaders in New Delhi were prepared to believe that hordes of Chinese were about to swell over the Himalayas and invest the valleys of the Bramaphutra. At the same time, they suspected that their Pakistani neighbors were collaborating with Peking in a massive plot which would chew up the subcontinent and dissolve the Hindu nation. We and the British were not convinced that anything so cataclysmic was afoot. We believed, as Chen Yi told me, that the essential Chinese purpose was to give the Indians "a bloody nose" and to resolve the frontier question once and for all. We could hardly see any desire on the Chinese part to take over the squalid human morass represented by the Bramaphutra and Hooghly river systems.

Consequently, our prime focus was on attempting to use the trauma of India's consternation to get her leaders to face their station in the world a little more realistically. We rather hoped that their panic would lead them to respect the fact that Pakistan had behaved quite honorably by not attacking them in their distress. We tried to use this circumstance to guide them to some broader understandings with their neighbors, especially in Kashmir. We attempted to bait this inspiration with the moderate amount of military assistance they might need to reestablish their position on their northern frontiers. For awhile, it seemed we might succeed. Krishna Menon was fired, and Nehru acted reasonably. The old civil servants in the foreign and defense ministries proved to be solid bastions of common sense. In working with them and their counterparts in Pakistan, we thought, for a brief moment, that we might have had a breakthrough of reason in the subcontinent and be able to put an end to that senseless religious violence that I had earlier experienced in Calcutta.

Unfortunately, when prospects looked brightest, they were destroyed by that old diplomatic nemesis, an excess of zeal. Flying back from Karachi after our apparent success there, Duncan Sandys could not contain his prospects for a brilliant success. Without consulting with our American contingent, he went straight to Nehru's house at about 2:30 a.m., waking the prime minister from a sound sleep and insisting that he agree then and there to the deal we had arranged with the Pakistanis. Whether or not Nehru ever would have agreed is questionable; but there was no better way to have assured his obstruction than by having a clumsy colonial stamp into his bedroom at an ungodly hour, breathing whisky onto his countenance.

Our success on the subcontinent was, therefore, somewhat less than complete. We did, nevertheless, establish a reasonably equitable arrangement with the Indians, set up a modest British-American supply line for their armed forces and stabilize the overreaction to the Chinese attack. Our ambassador, Kenneth Galbraith, who had been a strong partisan of the Indians in this somewhat ambivalent situation, pronounced himself satisfied. In celebration of that circumstance, he arranged a press conference at the embassy to pass on the results of our consultations to the media. At the time he arranged it, Harriman and I were busy preparing the report to the president. Galbraith, nevertheless, urged me to get Harriman to attend and, with some reluctance, Harriman assured me he would.

When the time came for the conference, which was being held in the embassy's meeting room, I reminded Harriman of his promise. He asked me to go and save a place for him at the opposite end of the room from Galbraith. As I came up the stairs to the room, Galbraith met me and asked where

Harriman was. I assured him that he was coming and suggested he start the proceedings. He therefore took his place at the head of the large table and began to speak. All the reporters and all the television cameras turned to focus on him. I slipped into the seat at the foot of the table and watched the conference begin.

Within a minute, Harriman came into the room and tapped me on the shoulder. I rose and ceded my seat to him. In a flash, all the reporters and all the cameras turned in his direction, leaving Galbraith in the shadows. From my vantage along the wall, I could see him fume, but then mellow as Harriman manipulated the press with great style and candor. By the time it was over, the press tumbled rapidly out to file their stories. Harriman returned down the stairs toward his office. I felt a large hand on my shoulder and looked up into Galbraith's craggy face. "Bill," he said, "Now I know what it's like to be had by an expert like Ave."

— 4 —

Once we had concluded an agreement for cessation of hostilities in Laos, we were keenly aware that it could only succeed if we were to get a similar agreement with respect to Vietnam. However, in Vietnam, the structure of forces was sharply different than it was in Laos. Among the Laotians, there was no real stomach for battle, and the so-called Pathet Lao faction was nothing more than a handful of leftists who acted as a front for the Lao Dong party of North Vietnam. Most of the political establishment was neutralist and, although the armed forces were vocally anticommunist, they had no great desire to express their sentiments through military action. In Vietnam, by contrast, the two contending forces were bitter, violent, and itching for battle. There were no neutralists of any stature.

Consequently, there was no great impetus toward negotiations in Vietnam and no strong neutral figure such as Souvanna Phouma who could act as a catalyst for compromise. Nevertheless, in 1962, President Kennedy favored negotiations rather than increased conflict if some avenue to discussions could be found. He authorized Averell Harriman, who returned to Geneva for the final rounds of the Lao negotiations, to try to find such an avenue. Harriman discussed the subject with the South Vietnamese negotiators at Geneva and found them willing, in principle, to consider negotiations, but adamantly opposed to doing anything to initiate them. He then decided we should try the North Vietnamese. We approached the head of the Burmese delegation to see if he could arrange a discreet private meeting for us with the North Vietnamese. Our Burmese friend was an Anglo-Burman named James Barrington, who was permanent secretary in their Foreign Ministry and a very accomplished diplomat. Jim soon got the North Vietnamese foreign minister and Colonel Ha Van Lau (who later became Hanoi's ambassador to the U.N.) to join us for tea one afternoon in his hotel suite.

Barrington lived in a rather modest hotel directly across the street from the larger Railroad Hotel that housed the South Vietnamese delegation. Harriman and I decided that the presence of the North Vietnamese Zis and the American Cadillac outside this small building would be conspicuous to the curious and particularly upsetting to the South Vietnamese. So we decided to walk to our rendezvous at the hotel and approach it from the rear. We found ourselves picking our way through some of Geneva's back alleys and entering the hotel through the service exit.

Once in Barrington's rather small suite, we discovered that our Vietnamese counterparts were already there. The foreign minister, Ung Van Khiem, was a small, stocky man who dressed in bulky Soviet suits with the sleeves so long that they covered his chubby hands when he stood. He seemed to speak only Vietnamese and Russian, and when he had delivered his bombastic speeches at the conference, they had always been translated into French. He did not receive us graciously, and there was probably very little grace in his makeup.

Ha Van Lau, on the other hand, was urbane, French-educated, and an accomplished diplomat. His origins were allegedly bourgeois, but he had been a fervent member of the communist Lao Dong party since his youth. He greeted us cordially.

Once Jim Barrington had accomplished the introductions and provided the tea, he withdrew to a small, windowed alcove and ostentatiously pretended to read a book. Harriman and Ung sat on a stiff backed sofa, while Ha and I deployed ourselves on chairs facing them across the tea table. It was an awkward effort. Harriman spoke in English, which I translated into French for Ha, who then translated it into Vietnamese for Ung, who responded in Vietnamese, which Ha translated into French, and I translated into English for Harriman.

No matter in what language we might have spoken, the results would have been the same. Ung was brutally, arrogantly negative. The language he used was didactic, and even Ha seemed to wince a little as he translated it. The North Vietnamese refused to concede that they had any role in the South Vietnam fighting. They insisted the whole turmoil was the result of Ngo Dinh Diem's repression of the population. Since Diem was able to be repressive only because the United States provided him with the means, peace would come to Vietnam only when the United States withdrew support from Diem. Then, "the people of South Vietnam would know what to do."

Harriman was marvelously patient with this insulting little thug and never showed a flash of anger. He probed every possibility of negotiation, offered every opportunity to let Ung make some acknowledgment of the scores of thousands of North Vietnamese troops that we knew to be engaged in the fighting, made every attempt to examine some process short of war, but was incessantly rebuffed. He permitted his inner anger to show through only at the end of the long, futile hour when, standing up and towering over his stubby interlocuter, he told him that he seemed to be in for a long, tough war. We trudged back those same alleys we had ascended in somber disappointment. Harriman, who took great pride in the unvarnished accuracy of his diplomatic reporting, instructed me to draft his assessment of our session to the president in bleak, unpromising terms, but to draw no independent conclusions, leaving those to the sober judgment of the president himself.

Our return to Washington in the summer of 1962, following the success of the Laos negotiations, was overshadowed by our concern over the deteriorating conditions in South Vietnam and the apparent intractability of that problem to diplomatic solutions. However, before we had much chance to brood about those things, the Cuba missile crisis and the India-China border war intervened. It was thus well into the winter of 1962 and the spring of 1963 before the administration could turn full attention to Vietnam.

My first serious involvement with Vietnam was in the form of a war game, organized by the Joint Chiefs of Staff. In order to provide maximum objectivity, the Chiefs had engaged the Rand Corporation to draw up the rules of the game and to act as control team. The opposing red and blue teams were to represent all elements of the Administration that would presumably be involved if we were to intensify our involvement in Vietnam. The game would be played out as a command post exercise, in an effort to project how the Vietnam situation might unfold over a span of about ten years, given certain assumptions that would be introduced into the proceedings from a script prepared by the control team. In principle, those assumptions were neutral, and their results on the outcome of the game would be determined by the way in which the red and blue teams reacted to them.

The two opposing teams were organized on separate echelons. The senior group functioned on the policy level and met only sporadically during the play of the game. The other group operated at action level and was in constant session eight hours a day during the week that the game consumed. The blue team policy chief was John McCone, the head of the CIA, and its action chief was an air force general. The red team policy chief was General Maxwell Taylor, former chief of staff of the army, who was then in the White House as senior military adviser to President Kennedy, and I was head of the red action team. On my action team, I had a marine general, colonels from the army and air force, a navy captain, some senior intelligence officers, and civilians from relevant government departments and agencies.

Taylor, who dominated the red team policy group, instructed me to play the game according to the rules of guerrilla warfare, accept heavy casualties, exploit propaganda opportunities, and be brazen about disregard for the truth. He particularly wanted our action group to play upon any and all weakness we could find in the traditional military doctrines of our opponents and the civil processes of a democracy. He took some relish in casting himself as the figure of Ho Chi Minh and encouraged me to think of myself as General Giap, the case-hardened military commander of North Vietnam's troops. We launched into the game with zeal.

By the end of the week, at a time frame representing the winter of 1972, the game had played itself out. Our red team (North Vietnamese) forces were everywhere on the map of Indochina. We had overrun most of Laos, and we controlled the countryside of South Vietnam and the cordillera extending into Cambodia. We had taken severe casualties, but our structure was still intact, and we had solid support from the Soviet Union and China. We had extended and demoralized the forces of South Vietnam. But, most of all, we had bogged down 500,000 American troops in the quagmire of Indochina and had involved a large portion of the U.S. Navy and Air Force. We had caused great expenditure of the United States budget on this feckless enterprise and had provoked great agitation and unrest in the American population, especially on university campuses. Moreover, we had all but isolated the United States in the United Nations and in world public opinion. We had driven the U.S. Congress to the brink of revolt over the seemingly endless war.

John McCone, as leader of the blue team policy group, concluded that his organization ought to call it quits and cut its losses. The experience of that game made him a dove on Vietnam then and forever more. He felt that its projections were accurate and that the shadows they cast before them should be heeded as real. He did not like what he foresaw if the U.S. engagement in Vietnam continued down that predictable path.

Other participants drew different conclusions. Some of the air force officers, in particular, felt that the control team was unrealistic in its scoring of certain actions. They felt, for example, that control was wrong to let the red team persist in its military operation in the face of an unremitting U.S. air assault against targets in North Vietnam and along the Ho Chi Minh trail. They felt that control was also wrong in letting our red hit and run tactics succeed against some of their installations in South Vietnam. I specifically remember their cry of foul when my guerrillas were able to infiltrate and blow up a large number of U.S. aircraft at Bien Hoa airfield in a game-time calendar of late 1964. I remember this so graphically because I recall looking out the window of my airplane in November 1964 as I was leaving Vietnam to return to Washington to be sworn in as ambassador to Laos and watching black smoke billow from the airport at Bien Hoa, where a guerrilla attack had succeeded in blowing up fuel, ammunition, and a number of U.S. aircraft.

The devastating results of the game prompted a high level

review of its proceedings and conclusions. This was held in the spring of 1963 in the National Military Command Center, deep in the bunker that was popularly portrayed in the film "Dr. Strangelove." Assembled there for that occasion were Secretary of State Dean Rusk, Secretary of Defense Robert McNamara, National Security Advisor McGeorge Bundy, General Maxwell Taylor, all the Joint Chiefs of Staff, John McCone, and a score of others. The presentation of the game's results was made by a JCS staff officer and the Rand director. The discussion that followed was acerbic and blunt.

The brunt of the criticism came from General Curtis Le May, chief of the air staff, who felt the conclusions were unrealistic. He contended that control had given inadequate weight to the ability of the air force to interdict North Vietnamese logistics, to shatter their operations, and to destroy their morale. He became caustic in his insistence that we should ignore the dire indications of the game and pursue our national interests fearlessly. He waved his cigar and said "This is the way we lost Czechoslovakia." At this point, Mac Bundy, who had been sitting through Le May's diatribe and growing redder and redder in the face, leaned forward and said, "Curt, I didn't know you ever *had* Czechoslovakia." The atmosphere grew tense and silent. Everyone in the room sensed the possibility of an open confrontation between the president's man and the quintessential military mentality. Dean Rusk and Robert McNamara stepped smoothly in and defused the situation at this point preferring to let the argument be pursued in a more intimate arena with fewer spectators.

A number of assignments were handed out as a result of this war game. Among them was another war game, with broader participation and broader scope. I played in that one also, as a member of the policy team acting as the representative of China. It came to roughly the same conclusion as the first game and produced many of the same criticisms. It also produced a very large crop of senior military officers who, unlike Le May, found the results convincing and sobering. This game produced two other assignments for me. One was to head up an interdepartmental team to study whether there were any bombing targets in North Vietnam that might make a strategic difference to Hanoi's pursuit of the war if they were destroyed. (We concluded there were not, with a dissenting opinion from the Air Force.)

The second assignment was to work out with Mike Forrestal of Mac Bundy's staff the text of a joint resolution that the president might present to the Congress in order to precipitate a "great debate" on whether or not legislative and public opinion would support an extensive pursuit of the military effort in Vietnam. The paper itself was never used in the Kennedy administration. However, in 1964, after the Tonkin Gulf incident, a significantly foreshortened version of that paper was provided by President Lyndon Johnson to Senator William Fulbright, Chairman of the Senate Foreign Relations Committee, and pressed rapidly through both houses of Congress as the Tonkin Gulf Resolution. Lyndon Johnson always referred to it as the "Fulbright Resolution" and carried a copy of it around in his pocket whenever he wanted to point to the legal justification for his extended and frustrated pursuit of the war effort.

— 5 —

In the spring of 1963, the Soviets were misbehaving again. They were being obstreperous in Berlin, mischievous in the Congo, had violated the neutrality agreements in Laos, and, after the 1962 missile crisis in Cuba, had left behind there the combat brigade which Jimmy Carter belatedly discovered in 1979. President Kennedy felt he could not tolerate all these activities without making some remonstrations, but he did not wish another major confrontation so soon after the 1962 crisis. In these circumstances, he did what other presidents had done before him; he decided to send Averell Harriman to Moscow for some plain talk with the Soviet leadership. His instructions to Harriman were quite generalized. He wanted to caution the Soviets against pushing him too hard, but he pretty much left it up to Harriman to make the point in his own words.

Harriman set about his mission in his usual austere way. He had a minimum number of briefing papers prepared, limiting them to factual presentations on the various issues that were disturbing the administration. The delegation he assembled to accompany him on this mission consisted of two assistants: Mike Forrestal from the White House and myself. His travel plans involved three seats on a commercial airliner to London for brief consultations with the British and, subsequently, three seats on a Soviet jet from London to Moscow.

The Soviet plane was the first jet they had placed in commercial service. It was, in fact, a converted Tupolev bomber with certain modifications designed to accommodate passengers. The amenities were crude, the cabin service was clumsy, and the aircraft performance was not up to international passenger standards. But it was a nice touch to arrive in Moscow on a Soviet plane. We were met at the airport by our ambassador, Foy Kohler, and taken to his residence as Spasso House, where we were to spend our time in Moscow. Arrangements had been made to meet with Gromyko and the Foreign Ministry staff, and Gromyko undertook to host a luncheon at which other senior Soviet officials would be present. Khrushchev had agreed to see us but, typically, no exact time for the meeting had been fixed.

It was a damp, late spring in Moscow, and the ice was just breaking up on the river. The leaden skies and the drably clothed Muscovites all contrived to produce an atmosphere of dull depression. Although we didn't know it at the time, it was the period when Khrushchev was being pressured into retirement. The general climate did not seem auspicious for the opening of new understandings with the Soviets or the closing of old grievances.

Our meetings with the Soviets soon confirmed our worst predictions. Gromyko was at his legalistic, pettyfogging prime. He and his subordinates led us through all the most frustrating variations on their propaganda themes and presented all the half-truths and convolutions which were their diplomatic stock in trade. They never had facts available to discuss the issues we wished to raise and they inundated us with allegations and accusations on matters irrelevant to the topics we attempted to pursue. Harriman was doggedly patient through it all, occasionally using a little heavy sarcasm on Gromyko, but generally biding his time until he could see Khrushchev, on the grounds that only one man made decisions in Moscow and it was not worthwhile to squander energy and emotion on subordinates. In due course, we were informed that we would have a meeting with Khrushchev in the Kremlin in the middle of the afternoon of the last full day we had scheduled for the visit.

When we arrived at the chairman's office, the same one previously used by Lenin and Stalin, the ebullient, rotund little peasant dictator greeted us with jokes and laughter as if we were a political delegation from the hinterland. He and Harriman compared notes on the previous arrangement of furniture in the room and on other banalities before he permitted us to get down to business. At last he, Gromyko, Kornienko from the Foreign Ministry, and Viktor Sukhrodev, the interpreter, ranged themselves along one side of the green baize covered table. Harriman, Kohler, Forrestal, and I sat on the other side, and the discussions began.

Khrushchev was an interesting study of a discomfited dictator. He twisted and dodged. He constantly changed the subject. He held up some ore samples that were on his desk and held forth at great length on the mineral wealth of the Soviet

Union, the prowess of its agriculture, the success of its industry, and the glorious prospects for its future. Harriman kept boring in, bringing him back to the points at issue, forcing him to respond to the matters of our concern.

Finally, Khrushchev reached the end of his rope. His face reddened, the top of his bald head glowed. He struck the table with both fists, and then he jumped to his feet. He pointed to a spot on the carpet in front of him and said, "Berlin is a bunion on your big toe! If you touch my troops in Cuba, I will put my foot in Berlin like this!" And he graphically ground his heel into the carpet at the spot indicated. His face grimaced and Sukhrodev, in his translation, mimicked the anger in his voice to perfection. Then, the performance over, Khrushchev abruptly sat down with a leering grin on his face.

Harriman viewed this whole episode with what President Kennedy used to call his "crocodile" look. His eyes were half-lidded, his long jaw drawn into a pose of disapproval, and his general demeanor suggested that he had just seen some lower form of reptilian life on the slimy banks of the serene river of his domain. Quietly, and without any abrupt change of pace, he suggested we draw the proceedings to a close. He proposed that a brief communique be drawn up with an anodyne description of our talks, and Khrushchev, in great relief, readily agreed.

The meeting adjourned as Harriman and Khrushchev rose from the table. Gromyko, Kornienko, Kohler, and Forrestal set about drafting the communique. I joined Harriman, Khrushchev, and Sukhrodev as we stood in front of Stalin's massive old desk for informal chatter. As we talked, Harriman took a small keychain from his pocket and began to fiddle with the three or four small keys it contained. Suddenly, the chain parted and one of the keys tumbled away. It was dusk by now in the Kremlin and growing dark in the office. The large Persian carpet which had served Khrushchev so well in his dramatic gestures about Berlin was a pattern of dark geometric designs easily able to camouflage a small key.

I bent over the carpet in the vicinity of the spot where Harriman had been standing and began to run my hand through the tuft, searching for the key. In a flash, Khrushchev was also hot into the search. He had dropped on all fours and was rooting around with great animation. In deference to his zeal, I also got down on my hands and knees and began to emulate his method of search. Suddenly, he scooted into the broad alcove under the old Stalin desk. I darted in along side him. At this point, he began to make deep chortling sounds, to snort something unintelligible, and to nudge me repeatedly in the ribs with his elbow. The intrepid Sukhrodev, leaning over us with hands braced on the edge of the desk, translated his master's observations with great relish. "I will find Harriman's key and I will have the key to Harriman's millions! Then I will take his fortune and balance the Five Year Plan!"

All this commotion distracted the dutiful diplomats at the table who were toiling over the wording of the bland communique. Kohler later told me that he turned around to see two rumps protruding from under the desk while Sukhrodev shouted his translations and Harriman tried to convince everyone that the missing key was of no significance and that we should all abandon the antic search. In due course, Harriman prevailed and we assumed a vertical posture once again. The communique was finished, read, and approved. The meeting was over, but Khrushchev, gleefully stuck in a single groove, kept repeating his refrain about having the key to the Harriman millions. On this incongruent note, Kennedy's effort to modify disruptive Soviet behavior came to a close.

We piled into our limousine and headed rather despondently back to Spasso House. As we were passing out the gates of the Kremlin, I asked Harriman if he had looked for the missing key in the cuffs of his trousers. "Of course!" he sputtered, "That was the first place I looked." But, absently, just to be sure, he ran his finger again through the cuffs and sheepishly said, "Oh, my God. Here it is." And he held up a tiny key. The ever-affable Kohler suggested that he would telephone Sukhrodev upon return to Spasso House to let Khrushchev know the missing key had been found. At this mild suggestion, the Old Crocodile turned and snapped, "That," he said, "is the most stupid idea I've heard today. Of course we won't call them!" And we didn't.

— 6 —

The Alliance for Progress was one of the centerpieces of the Kennedy Administration's foreign policy. By the fall of 1963, steps were needed to give it greater momentum, especially in the effort to make it less unilateral. The intention was to model its future on the Marshall Plan, in which the American contributions acted as a catalyst for greater European initiatives toward common actions to enhance the prosperity and political vigor of the European democracies. The theory was that Latin American countries, brought into greater coherence through the efforts of the United States, would work more closely with each other and would develop cooperation in their continent.

Since Averell Harriman had been one of the most successful leaders of the Marshall Plan, it made sense for the Kennedy people to turn to him to breathe new life into the Alliance. As undersecretary of state, he had a brief for all issues and all continents, even though he admitted to very little knowledge of or experience with Latin America. Nevertheless, under the stimulus of such enthusiasts as Arthur Schlesinger, Ed Martin, Bill Rogers, and others, he soon developed a great interest in the opportunities for positive actions by the United States. He assigned me to work out some concrete ways in which he might be able to be helpful.

In due course, we came up with a proposal to develop in Latin America the equivalent of the European group known as the OECD, which had developed priorities among development projects in Europe and had grown into a clearinghouse for programs that eventually led to the Common Market and the European Economic Community. It was decided to launch this proposal at a meeting to be held in São Paulo, the burgeoning industrial metropolis in Brazil. The hope was that a uniquely Latin American executive group, under the direction of a distinguished Latin American economist, could do for that region what the bureaucrats of Europe, under the prodding of Jean Monet, had done for the Western Europeans. The plans were set in motion and the meeting was scheduled for mid-November.

In the meantime, the Argentines had turned ornery. A new government in Buenos Aires had decided to nationalize the rather puny petroleum industry that had been developed in some limited oil and gas fields discovered by a few American companies in the southern region of the country. They were of relatively insignificant value and had no very bright future. Therefore, rather than making any compromises to retain them, the world's major oil companies were prepared to retaliate against their seizure by cutting off Argentina from all access to the purchase or distribution of petroleum and petroleum products. In those days, they still controlled the means to make such a boycott truly effective and thoroughly disastrous to the fragile Argentine economy.

The White House did not like the prospects of this development and felt it was important to head it off before it reached an irreversible impasse. It was decided that the United States Government should take the initiative to talk the Argentine Government out of its nationalization program and avert the chaos that would result, not only in Argentina, but in all Latin America, where an oil boycott orchestrated by American petroleum companies would be seen as Yankee aggression. Since there was already a plan to have a Harriman mission in behalf of the Alliance, the Argentine dimension was added as a logical extension of that undertaking.

In November, we departed in two echelons for Latin America. The larger contingent, headed by Ed Martin and containing such impressive assistants as Carl Kaysen, Pat Moynihan, Bill Rogers, and others, headed for São Paulo to prepare the meeting at which we would launch our proposal for CEAP, the Latin American equivalent of OECD. A smaller group went on just to Buenos Aires, where we would attempt to work out some understandings with Argentina before joining the rest in Brazil.

Given the circumstances, our visit to Buenos Aires did not go too badly. It was clear that the government realized it had gone out on a limb with its nationalization proposal and was looking for a graceful way to retreat. Although our embassy, under the colorful Ambassador Rob McClintock, was doing its best to make such a retreat possible, the local representatives of the oil companies, who had a surprising degree of involvement in local politics, seemed intent upon inflicting maximum embarrassment on the Argentine administration. Therefore, while we were able to see a way out of the prevailing impasse, it obviously would have to involve decisions by the home offices of the major oil companies. Hence, we worked out the outlines of a settlement, but asked that it be held in abeyance until we could meet with the top management of the oil companies on our return to Washington. A meeting was set up in the State Department for the afternoon of November 23, shortly after we would return to Washington.

Before leaving Buenos Aires, Harriman was asked by McClintock to participate in one brief reception he had arranged. It was a gathering of the surviving members of the Argentine national polo team, which had dominated world polo in the 1920s, and had been swept out of its preeminence in the latter years of the decade by an aggressive young team from the United States, which had met them in Buenos Aires and defeated them roundly in a series of cup matches. The captain of the American team had been a lanky young swell from New York named Averell Harriman.

McClintock had arranged for the Argentines to come for a late tea in the family quarters of the palatial embassy. By the time Harriman and those of us who were with him swept in after a brisk negotiating session with the Argentine president, there assembled were the erstwhile gauchos of the polo circuit, hunched over in their chairs, leaning on canes, and otherwise testifying to the weight of their years. Harriman, only a few days away from his seventy-fifth birthday, was a figure of health and vigor. That summer, in an annual ritual softball game between the State Department and the Japanese embassy, he had played second base and participated in a double play. The contact with his old polo rivals touched him but, at the same time, depressed him. Poor McClintock, who had turned them out to provide a pleasant surprise for his distinguished visitor, realized it had somehow or other gone a little stale in the happening, and had not provided exactly the nostalgic touch he had planned for our departure.

But, none of this lingered long as we plunged into the heady confusion that reigned in Brazil. It was the epoch of Julao Goulart, the leftist president who had deliberately decided to shake up the established order in that giant country. We met with his ministers in Rio de Janeiro, with him and his flamboyant wife at their surrealistic palace in Brazilia, and with the industrial oligarchy in São Paulo before joining the U.S. delegation at the conference being held on the campus of the new national university. The ground for our proposal had been carefully and professionally prepared. The institution we sought was unanimously established, the secretary general we favored was overwhelmingly elected, and the work of the conference was considered a great success. We topped it off with a rather sumptuous banquet at the Automobile Club in São Paulo to celebrate Harriman's seventy-fifth birthday.

After that celebration, I returned to the deserted offices

of the U.S. delegation on the university grounds to find the telephone ringing. When I picked it up, I was amazed to find a White House operator on the other end, telling me that the president was calling. Before I could ask why, the familiar Boston twang was in my ear, informing me that the *New York Times* coverage of our meeting was supercilious and emphasized the "juggernaut" nature of our procedure in obtaining our objectives at the conference. When I asked the president what he wanted us to do about that, he replied that I should "tell Tad Szulc (the *New York Times* correspondent) to pull his hat down over his ears." With that, he rang off, and the phone went dead. It happened that the first person I met upon emerging from our improvised office space was Tad Szulc. I conveyed the president's message forthwith, to Tad's embarrassment and ultimate amusement. It was the last chore I ever performed for President Kennedy.

We returned to Washington on the evening of November 22. I arrived in my office early on the following morning and proceeded through the check list of actions always taken on return from a mission abroad. High among these in recent months had been the requirement to inform the vice president of actions resulting from the mission. The White House, largely at Bobby Kennedy's urging, had felt it important that Lyndon Johnson should not consider himself deliberately isolated from foreign policy issues. We were therefore under standing instructions to make personal reports to him on the substance of our activities. Knowing that Johnson was an early riser, I put in a call to his office to ask whether he wanted a briefing on our mission from Harriman or myself. I was surprised when the White House operator put me through to the vice president himself. Having been out of the country, I had not realized that he and the president were in Dallas and that I was calling him in his hotel room at about 6:00 a.m. He was, in any event, up and about and couldn't have been more chatty or pleasant about dismissing my apologies for calling him at that hour. He didn't see any need for a personal briefing and went on, in his gregarious way, to tell me what a great day it was going to be in Dallas. A few hours later, the president was mortally wounded by the bullets of an assassin.

Ed Martin and I were in Harriman's office preparing for our meeting with the oil company executives when someone burst in the door with the news that the president had been shot. Harriman himself was at the other end of the hall meeting with George Ball, who was acting secretary, to inform him of our work in Buenos Aires and São Paulo. Dean Rusk and part of the cabinet were airborne en route to Japan. Ed and I immediately started down the corridor to Ball's office. As we arrived in the anteroom, a tearful secretary informed us that the president was dead. We opened the door to Ball's office and found him and Harriman seated on the edges of their chairs in front of a television set, holding their heads in their hands while the voice of the announcer repeated the awful news in a tremulous, incredulous voice.

As soon as the shock could be surmounted, a numbed group of assistants and staff assembled, and Ball began giving the instructions necessary to set in motion those actions a nation needs to take when its leader is assassinated. Ed and I were conscious of the score or more of senior oil company executives assembled in the waiting room and recommended to Harriman that we be allowed to dismiss them and fix another date for our meeting. To our astonishment, the ashen-faced Harriman, who had become a close and affectionate friend of the young president, drew himself up and said, "Life must go on. Bring them in."

The meeting was disastrous. Those of us on the government side of the table were in shock and could concentrate on the Argentine oil problem only with great difficulty. The oil executives were a mixed lot. Some of them seemed to sense our devastation and sympathize with it. Others seemed to look on our distraction as an opportunity to put over some fast proposals that we might accept just to get them out of the room. Finally, one brash young vice president proposed that "the new president" write a letter which would play upon the pathos of the assassination and seek a speedy, favorable settlement of the nationalization threat. An older company representative, seeing the wrench this crass suggestion had caused on our side of the table, suggested the meeting be adjourned to a more appropriate time. Pete Collado, an Esso man who had been formerly in the Foreign Service, moved in to make appropriate expressions of condolence, and the meeting broke up inconclusively. We then set about the arrangements for the funeral and the enormous influx of international dignitaries we expected for that event.

The next few days were a period of national neuralgia. Those of us concerned with the countless details of preparing the diplomatic aspects of the funeral welcomed the preoccupation of our time and attention demanded by that exercise. My only respite from that flood of protocol, schedules, and ritual was to take a half hour away from the office in order to stand in the silent, shuffling crowd along Independence Avenue as the caisson bearing the casket of the late president made its muffled way toward the Lincoln Monument and Memorial Bridge. Then, I returned to my office to make the last-minute adjustments necessary to receive the hundreds of foreign dignitaries who would come back from Arlington Cemetery for a light buffet lunch and the discreet, carefully timed interviews they would have with our new president, who would receive them at intervals in the office of the secretary of state.

After the enormous entourage had arrived at the department and been ushered to the reception rooms on the eighth floor, a watch officer brought me a ticker item from the machine that constantly monitors the Tass news service. It was a fairly brief report, but its tenor was ominous. It said that the assassination of the president appeared to be part of a right-wing plot to overthrow the government of the United

States and suggested that a number of prominent Texans who had close associations with the newly installed President Johnson had a role to play in this plot. After reading the piece and absorbing the malice of its implications, I took it to the office of the department's executive secretary, Ben Read. He shared my concern and had one of his assistants fetch Llewellyn Thompson, the Soviet expert, from the eighth floor reception rooms where he was in attendance on the Soviet delegation to the funeral. In short order, we had Mac Bundy, Chip Bohlen, and Tommy Thompson gathered in the small seventh floor office to develop a course of action. We rapidly decided that Bundy would go to Mikoyan, Bohlen would go to Gromyko, Thompson to the Soviet ambassador, and I to Smirnovsky, the Head of the American Division of the Soviet Foreign Ministry, who was the fourth member of their funeral delegation. All of them would be given identical messages and told that it was urgent the Tass item be killed.

The four of us went up together in the elevator and entered the foyer to the reception rooms. Television cameras had been allowed to set up there to focus on the milling throng of kings, presidents, prime ministers, and other members of the international galaxy. One alert television commentator spotted us as we arrived in phalanx, paused to locate our prey, and fanned out to encounter them. He had his camera pick out each of us as we found our respective Soviet and reported to his viewers that some concerted American action with the Soviets seemed in progress. Fortunately, events were in such a whirl that his comment evaporated on the air waves. Also, fortunately, the Soviets grasped the significance of our message, and the Tass item was withdrawn.

Once I had gotten into the reception, my own withdrawal proved impossible. The Dutch ambassador, who was shepherding Princess (now Queen) Beatrix, was receiving no attention from any official American. Once he saw my familiar face, he commandeered me to a table where the princess was resting from the day's ordeal. I offered to fetch her some food from the buffet and moved quickly to get a plate. As I swung around some slow moving guests, I saw Herve Alphand, the French ambassador, bearing down on me. He had just received his summons to bring General de Gaulle down to meet with President Johnson.

Herve had de Gaulle by one arm, and le grand general, nearly blind without his glasses, was sweeping along the table like some great frigate under a towering billow of sail, scattering lesser mortals from his path. Seeing the look of concentration on Herve's face and the lofty insouciance on that of the general, I backed a couple of steps out of the way. As I did, I stepped on the toes of someone behind me and turned around to apologize. There was the diminutive, bearded, bemedalled Haile Selassie, whose tiny polished boots I had trampled. I apologized profusely, and he very graciously made a joke about the aggressive nature of the French.

A few minutes later, after having delivered the plate to Princess Beatrix and realizing that I had not eaten since breakfast, I returned to the buffet to get something that I could smuggle quietly down to my office and fortify myself against the long evening I saw in progress. At this point, a numerous Japanese delegation approached, and we exchanged some bows of recognition. In the course of one of these, I backed up again and, once again, stepped on some toes. I swung around and, to my intense embarrassment, found Haile Selassie again. This time, he pulled himself up to his full height, cocked a finger at me, and in mock outrage, said, "Monsieur, ce devient une habitude!" I took my plate and retreated slyly down a stairwell. It was the last event in my token of farewell to President Kennedy.

Chapter Seven

War in Indochina
1964–1968

In the spring of 1964, Lyndon Johnson became exasperated with the whole problem of Vietnam. He felt it was useless to try to direct the complex bewildering American involvement in that country from Washington. He decided to pick a proconsul whose judgment he trusted, send him to Saigon, and delegate to him full responsibility for settling the problem and getting the United States out with honor. His choice for this formidable job was the chairman of the Joint Chiefs of Staff, General Maxwell Taylor. In accepting this dubious honor, Taylor was required to retire from the military and become ambassador. However, he was assured that he would also have control over the military effort in Vietnam, and that General Westmoreland would be his direct subordinate. In order to tie down explicitly the scope of his authority, Taylor drafted a letter to himself from Johnson, which the president promptly signed.

Taylor was also told that he could take with him to Saigon anyone in government service, no matter what his current

War in Indochina

position. From the State Department, he chose U. Alexis Johnson, who was undersecretary, and myself. Since I had already been scheduled to go to Vientiane as ambassador to replace Leonard Unger, this choice created some confusion. It was eventually agreed that I would go to Saigon for "just a month or two" to help Taylor get established, and I would then be released for the Vientiane assignment. In the meantime, Unger would stay on post a little longer.

The American ambassador's residence in Saigon was a large concrete house with a fairly spacious garden, but located at a very busy intersection leading into the center of the city. It had been built by a wealthy French businessman and was a most comfortable place for living and for official entertaining. However, because of the heavy volume of constant traffic passing by, and because it could not be cordoned off, it was considered an insecure place for the ambassador to live. Instead, ambassadors had for some time been housed in another old French colonial home on a dead-end street that could be better protected from intruders and passersby. Taylor and Johnson, who were old friends, took over that place, and I was assigned to live in the official residence.

Consequently, as a temporary bachelor, I inherited a large establishment with an appropriately large staff of servants. There were obviously more of them than I needed to take care of me; but, because I was expected to stay such a short time, it seemed prudent not to change any existing arrangements. Moreover, the cook, butler, maids, laundress, chauffeur, and gardener all seemed a compatible bunch and lived in happy harmony in a large separate building that also housed the garage. With their spouses and children, they made for a generous retinue.

One evening, after I had been in Saigon a couple of weeks, I had enjoyed a splendid solitary dinner and was nursing a cognac while reading in the library, a room that had probably been the original French owner's office. Suddenly, the door from the pantry burst open and the cook ran in, pursued by an angry woman waving a large cleaver. Behind them came the butler and the laundress, both screaming at the top of their lungs. This procession sped through the library and out into the broad front hall before I could react and run after them. The cook made a sharp turn in the hall and headed for the dining room, where he dove under the broad table and cringed against its legs. The woman with the cleaver bent down as if to pursue him. By this time, the butler and I were able to grab her, disarm her, and propel her back against the wall.

After much further screaming and shrieking, I was able to gather that the woman was the cook's wife, in town from their family home in Can Tho. The upstairs maid, with whom the cook was living in connubial harmony, was, therefore, not his wife at all, and some of my illusions about domestic tranquility were shattered. I gave a few rather blustery master-of-the-household directives to the butler, ordering him to resolve the crisis, and went back to my cognac. By the following morning, the cook, the upstairs maid, and the wife with the cleaver were all gone. And so were my assumptions that I could manage a household without effort.

Fortunately, a temporary solution was at hand. A young foreign service couple had arrived in Saigon about ten days before this event and were staying unhappily and uncomfortably in a hotel while trying to find a place to rent. I offered to turn two connecting bedrooms of my spacious quarters into a private apartment for them if the wife would undertake to manage the house. It proved a satisfactory arrangement to all concerned for a period of a few weeks until the couple found an apartment they could rent. By that time, I had expected to be gone, on my way to Laos; but things didn't settle down enough to permit me to move until five months had passed.

Among the things that didn't settle down in those times was the leadership of the South Vietnam government. The previous stability in Saigon, enforced by the brothers Diem, had come to an end in the fall of 1963 when they were murdered in a coup d'etat. The inheritors of power from that enterprise had, in turn, been overthrown by another coup in the spring of 1964. During my tenure in Saigon, power rested rather tentatively in the hands of a pudgy general named Khanh, who was never very popular with his military colleagues.

The American military made a valiant effort to work with him and to treat him as though he had the support of the forces he commanded. At that stage, our effort was largely advisory, although our military assistance personnel actually accompanied Vietnamese units in the field. The effort had become a sprawling one, with Westmoreland's personnel increasing almost daily. His hard working chief of staff, General Richard Stilwell, had developed a two-shift working pattern to try to keep abreast of the rapid growth. He would work the normal Saigon hours, take an evening nap, then come into the office after midnight for another stretch of time that coincided more closely with the peak hours of the Washington schedule.

About four o'clock one morning, I was wakened from a sound sleep in my enormous bedroom by the sound of heavy traffic in the street outside. Going to the window and pulling back the curtains, I saw a whole column of tanks passing clumsily toward the center of town. As far back along the line as I could see, other armored vehicles and trucks carried troops in full battle regalia. It looked to be a whole division on the move. A quick telephone call to MACV headquarters got Stilwell on the line. He was aware, from field reports, that some unusual movements were afoot, but he had not as yet been able to place the location of the units involved. From my description, he gauged that they were heading for the centers of government and that an attempted coup d'etat was in progress. Taylor and Westmoreland were in the United States for a strategy meeting, so I called Alex Johnson to alert him, and we headed separately for the chancery. By the time we got there, the city center had been taken over by the rebellious troops. General Khanh was nowhere to be found. Consequently, although the coup plotters had successfully gotten their troops into the capital to topple the government, they couldn't actually lay their hands on the man they intended to topple.

We immediately reported these awkward facts to Washington and then tried to find out exactly what the situation was. As our people fanned out through the city and as military advisors reported in from units and headquarters, it appeared that the success of the coup was far from complete. The Army Headquarters Command, for example, was holding out against the coup, and the air force was decidedly opposed to it. General Khanh was reportedly scurrying around the country in a DC-3 aircraft recruiting support from regional commanders and their troops. As dawn broke, it was clear that we had a stalemate in Saigon.

Shortly after dawn, Marshall Ky, head of the air force, began to show his hand. His aircraft, conspicuously armed with bombs and rockets, began to fly menacing missions at rooftop levels above the clusters of tanks, trucks, and troops that were located at strategic intersections in the city. Although no shots were fired, all traffic had come to a halt, and the population held its breath.

During the day, arms length discussions continued between the frustrated leaders of the coup attempt and those officers who remained loyal to Khanh. In midafternoon, we learned that Khanh himself had finally come to rest in the mountain resort of Dalat, where he was holding a conference with his military leaders. It was decided that Stilwell and I would fly there to urge him to return to Saigon and take charge of his government. We drove to the airport through empty streets and were met at the terminal by the crew of our small liaison aircraft, who told us they were unable to find anyone with whom they could file a flight plan. We decided to take off anyway, since we needed to land at the unlighted Dalat airfield before darkness fell.

As we got the plane underway and began to taxi toward the runway, we were suddenly buzzed in a mock strafing attack by a Vietnamese Air Force plane. When our pilot braked to a stop, another plane came on another run at right angles to the first, clearing us by only a few feet. The pilot tried desperately to reach someone in the control tower to identify us and our mission. In due course, he got through to the tower and eventually reached Marshall Ky himself. Stilwell talked with Ky, told him our intentions, and the marshall called off his strafers. We took off and landed in Dalat just as the sun was setting.

In Dalat, we were taken to one of the old villas that had belonged to Emperor Bao Dai under the French regime. There we were amazed to find most of the senior military officers of South Vietnam, sitting about as if they were at a country house for a weekend party. Khanh detached himself from this group and invited Stilwell and me to join him in a huge, baronial dining room. He listened without comment as we urged him to return to Saigon and resume charge before the situation deteriorated further.

After we had been there a short time, there was a rap on the door, and a trim young air force pilot, wearing the dashing clothes Ky had popularized, strode across the room, saluted Khanh, and pulled an envelope from inside his flight suit. The envelope was small, lavender, and heavily scented. Khanh tore it open and read a short note. He then folded the papers into his pocket and spoke briefly to the pilot, who saluted, clicked his heels, turned, and marched out.

Khanh then asked if the United States would broadcast a statement of support for him and his government. He said that, if we did so, he would return to Saigon with us. I called Alex Johnson in Saigon, we worked out the text of a statement, and within ten minutes, we heard Johnson broadcast it on the radio. Khanh beamed his satisfaction, the assembled generals nodded their support, and we piled into jeeps to go to the airport. In a few minutes, vehicles were lined up along the runway with their headlights on to make the take off possible, and we were on the way back to Saigon with our prime ministerial quarry. When we arrived at the airport at Tan Son Nhut, Ky had arranged a gala reception. There was whiskey and champagne, all the cabinet officers, and the news that the troops which had occupied the city were withdrawing. Alex Johnson came to the airport, congratulated Khanh on his "victory" and took him aside to convey a few messages from Washington, especially some rather stern words from Max Taylor.

I used this occasion to pull Ky out of the teeming celebration. I asked if he had sent a pilot to Dalat with a lavender envelope for Khanh. He confirmed that he had. I asked if he would tell me what message his letter contained. He said, with a wry smile, that he had informed Khanh that, if Khanh was not out of Bao Dai's palace in a half hour, he would personally lead a bombing raid on the building. I then asked Ky if he knew that Stilwell and I were also in that building. He didn't blink an eye. "Of course," he said, and wiped the frost of champagne from his small moustache with a lavender handkerchief.

—2—

In the summer of 1964, the government of South Vietnam came close to collapse, not because of military pressure from the Communists, but because of internecine bickering among the political, social, and religious factions that supported the struggle against the Communists. After the assassinations of Diem and Nhu, there was particularly bitter rivalry between the Catholics and the Buddhists. The Catholics, who were the favored group under the French and who were politically represented by Diem, felt that they were the victims of a Buddhist conspiracy. The Buddhists, who were more numerous in the south than the Catholics, felt they were being subordinated to an alien religious elite who were largely northern and centralist carpetbaggers. The rivalry extended to almost all areas of daily life.

During this period, the American embassy was hard put to it to find anyone with adequate authority in Saigon to reach understandings necessary to carry out the military crusade to which our government had committed itself in defense of South Vietnam. Political figures were in constant conspiracy one against the other, and military figures were jockeying for advantage, control, or graft. It was a time for the gnashing of teeth among us Americans; and, in the course of gnashing mine, I broke a tooth so badly that it had to be extracted. This meant the construction of a dental bridge and the installation of a false molar.

The military dental clinic serving official Americans in Saigon was located in the Chinese district of Cholon, and had to be reached by a circuitous route that wandered around the large central market area. Because of the complexity of my dental work, I had to navigate this passage two or three times during a week when Catholic-Buddhist tensions were at a peak. At the same time, the "white mice," as the municipal policemen were called, had gone into some sort of work slowdown and had let the traffic snarl beyond repair, especially in the region of the market. One afternoon, as I was returning from Cholon at about the time the schools let out, the situation seemed hopeless, and I resigned myself to sitting in my car interminably. Nothing was moving except pedestrians, mostly teen-age school children, who were weaving in and out of the stalled lanes of cars.

Suddenly, as I sat in the steaming tropical heat, action exploded just about fifty feet away. Two different school groups, recognizable by the emblems on their shirts as Catholic and Buddhist, had met near the marketplace and started an altercation. Soon, schoolboys were running from all directions to converge on the scuffle, which by then had spilled onto a little park in the center of a traffic circle. The park was dominated by a small mound with some sort of statuary at the top. At the center of the fighting, sticks were being swung and briefcases used as shields.

In the space of a few moments, one of the school groups began to dominate the mound. Boys wearing shirts from the other school were being shoved and pushed back toward the traffic—except for one who had apparently been involved in the original scuffle. He was being pushed, with his arms piniond behind his back and his hair firmly in the grip of two of his captors, up to the center of the mound. His lighter color shirt stood out against the darker cloth of his rivals, and he was soon alone among a large cordon of them.

Before any of us watching this drama realized what was going on, this youngster, perhaps thirteen years old, was braced forward by those holding him, and out of the front ranks of those facing him, a half dozen small arms, belonging to children no older than fifteen, lanced out at him. There was no apparent glint of steel to indicate that the arms were tipped with knives. It was only the bright red gush of blood and the curdling scream from the boy being killed that explained the scene. Again and again those small arms struck and slashed, until the scream stopped, the face turned ashen, and the body slumped. By this time, a dozen of us were out of our cars, trying to push against the fleeing mob of schoolboys and to reach the small park. Within a minute, they had all gone, leaving only the crumpled body of the victim lying in a pool of blood. Whistles sounded at the edge of the traffic jam, and the white uniformed police made their way slowly through. Quietly and quickly, as if by some magic orchestration, the traffic jam broke and cars moved silently out of the circle into the teeming, indifferent business district of Saigon. The violence had run its course.

In one form or another, similar scenes repeated themselves throughout South Vietnam, making the war against the Communists a secondary preoccupation for much of the population. Eventually, through negotiations, tentative understandings were reached, and the turmoil subsided. The various factions began to work with each other in a semblance of unity and turned once again to pursue the war against the Communists.

Max Taylor tried to take advantage of this interval to put a firmer foundation under the collaborative effort of the Vietnamese and their American advisers. He persuaded the government to establish a group at ministerial and vice-ministerial level to involve all those aspects of government activity that needed to be coordinated in order to pursue a coherent war effort. We then established a counterpart group on the American side. The idea was that these groups could meet on a regular basis, straighten out problems that needed urgent attention, allocate responsibility for providing the various resources needed, and get on with the war. A Vietnamese senior official and I were designated the joint executives of this binational board and authorized access to all areas of the war effort in order to ferret out problems.

Shortly after we got this hopeful new enterprise underway, Khanh decided that he wished to change the form of his government in order to make it more effective. His plan was to revise the constitution along the lines of General de Gaulle's new charter of the Fifth Republic. The president of the Republic would hold most of the executive power in the state while the cabinet, headed by a prime minister, would be responsible to him as well as to the National Assembly. After some rather hasty preparations, he convened a meeting of the country's political and military leadership for a long weekend sojourn at Vung Tau, an old French colonial beach resort, to discuss his proposals. On that Friday evening, he sent word to Taylor that he hoped the senior American leadership could join his group at Vung Tau for lunch on Sunday to discuss the results of the constitutional "convention."

Taylor, Johnson, Westmoreland, and I, accompanied by one or two others from the Embassy, flew down to the coastal town on a warm, sunny day. We were met by the senior military officers in the region and escorted to a private reserve dominated by two large old French colonial villas, a small sandy beach, and a grotto with terrace carved out of a stone cliff. Khanh was there with almost all the leadership of South Vietnam, attired in bright Hawaiian style sport shirts. After much desultory social conversation, we were led to tables on the stone terrace and served a succulent bouillabaise prepared under the supervision of a Corsican cook who had been commandeered from a local restaurant. The meal lasted well into the afternoon.

Finally, Khanh and a half dozen of his top leaders took us off to a large salon in one of the villas, perched high above a crashing sea. As we sat in easy chairs, aides handed out the typewritten text of the new constitution. Written in French, it was obviously cribbed in large measure from the De Gaulle original. We were asked to read it over and offer any comment that seemed appropriate. Opportunity for consultation among the Americans was minimal because we were spread at random throughout the room. Because of its origins, it was clearly a workable document and would probably provide a more effective form of government than the less tidy arrangement then in effect. On the face of it, the form would also be democratic because it borrowed representational and electoral provisions from the French model. In practice, of course, there was a world of difference between democracy as practiced in France and the system used in Vietnam. But, in general, we could find no fundamental faults with the structure of the system proposed in this new document.

What did bother me, however, was the codicil attached to the charter. This was, in effect, a "bill of duties" for the citizen, defining his responsibilities to the state. These were generally acceptable from an historical perspective, spelling out such obligations as the duty to vote, to pay taxes, and to perform military service. However, there was no corresponding "bill of rights," spelling out the state's responsibilities to the citizen. When I made this point, Khanh responded sententiously and agreed with the need for such provisions. His manner suggested that the omission had been deliberate, in order to provide the Americans with a fault to pick and a constructive suggestion to make.

It was therefore rather rapidly decided that I should be designated to work with some unnamed "constitutional experts" who were located in another seafront villa to develop a bill of rights. The conversation then turned to the need to prepare the public for a discussion of the document, to undertake a publicity campaign on its various aspects, and to lay the groundwork for the referendum that would be entailed in its ratification. Khanh agreed that we should bring Barry Zorthian, the embassy's public affairs officer, to Vung Tau in order to provide the Vietnamese with some advice on developing such a campaign.

As dusk fell, the American group, save for myself, headed for the airport to fly to Saigon. I had called Zorthian to tell him to pack a bag, meet the plane, and come down to Vung Tau to consult on a publicity campaign. My intention was to meet with the "experts," counsel them on a bill of rights, and then fly back on the plane that brought Zorthian. After Taylor and the rest departed, I was driven to the villa to meet the experts.

They turned out to be a couple of law professors from the university plus a doctor, who was a cousin of Khanh's and who later became a deputy prime minister. They were clearly waiting for me, and the alacrity with which they produced a copy of the American Bill of Rights served to confirm my suspicions that this session had been "set up" to give us Americans the satisfaction of making a positive contribution to the process. It didn't take us long to agree on the desirability of incorporating the whole U.S. Bill of Rights, appropriately translated into French, to round out the charter. Of course, there ultimately remained the problem of translating the entire thing into Vietnamese.

By the time Zorthian's plane arrived, I was at the airport. He had been briefed by Taylor, Johnson, et al. on the issue at hand and had used his short flight on the way down to sketch out a campaign. As I recall, it was expected to stretch over about three months. He discussed it briefly with me before heading off to the villas. I climbed on the plane and went home.

About nine o'clock that evening, as I was finishing off a very light snack in the library, the telephone rang. It was Zorthian reporting on his session with the Vietnamese. Even his normally exuberant voice was depressed. "Do you know that they intend to promulgate this damn thing on Tuesday and ratify it the same day?" he asked. I didn't, but I could believe it. Especially when that was exactly what happened.

— 3 —

The hopes we had entertained in 1962 for peace in Laos were shattered by the brutal cynicism of the Lao Dong Party in Hanoi. The case-hardened old men who ran that organization had obviously treated the Geneva accords as a tactical ploy and, despite solemn promises, did nothing to remove their forces from Laotian territory. Indeed, over the next two years, they increased the numbers they deployed there even while piously maintaining to anyone naive enough to listen that they respected Laotian neutrality.

Their deployments were in two different sectors of the

country, and in support of two different objectives. Their most conspicuous presence was in the southern panhandle, or the so-called Ho-Chi-Minh Trail. About two divisions of their regular units were constantly on duty there, building, repairing, and improving the road network, protecting it against possible attack, and expediting the movement of North Vietnamese troops, supplies, and equipment into South Vietnam. Another division operated in northern Laos, on a rotational basis. It came in during the dry season, harassed and fought the Hmong people in the hills, plundered their rice and other crops, and then withdrew back to its bases in North Vietnam, when the heavy monsoon rains made its operations difficult.

Because both of these zones of activity were remote and removed from the attention of the world press, the North Vietnamese brazenly insisted that they had no forces in the country and such military activity that might occur there was the result of justifiable resistance by a largely mythical "Pathet Lao force" fighting against "imperialist repression" from the neutralist government in Vientiane. A great many of the young journalists of the western press, whose sympathies were against what they regarded as "establishment" regimes in Vientiane and Saigon, were quite prepared to accept the Lao Dong fabrications and publish them as fact. The protestations of such leaders as Souvanna Phouma were largely ignored, and the complaints issuing from Washington were discounted.

The Kennedy administration (and subsequently the Johnson administration) became rather skeptically resigned to the situation. Rather than attempting to convince world opinion of the perfidy of Hanoi, we decided to fight the Lao Dong on its own terms in South Vietnam and let the consequences of North Vietnam's defeat work its own rectification of the problems in Laos. For this reason, we proposed to concentrate our effort and our propaganda on the increasingly palpable North Vietnamese presence in South Vietnam, minimize public attention to Laos, and trust that the 1962 framework could be reestablished there after the North Vietnamese withdrew back to their own territories in consequence of their military defeat. To calibrate this campaign more effectively, in 1964 we devised a program for bombing selective targets in North Vietnam at an accelerating rate, in a plan called "Rolling Thunder."

In Laos, it was decided that, rather than revert to the large military mission and arms assistance program that had characterized our pre-1962 presence there, we would borrow from the practice of the North Vietnamese and act through a clandestine, deniable system of paramilitary assistance, with any actual fighting being done by indigenous forces. This pattern called for a lead role by the Central Intelligence Agency; but, in accordance with President Kennedy's limited confidence in that agency, their operations were to be placed under the strict control of the ambassador.

Our ambassador to Laos at the time this decision was made was Leonard Unger, an old and close friend of mine from Italy and other parts of the Foreign Service. He was a most reluctant militarist and took care in establishing the paramilitary operation to be sure it was designed to be reversible. Consequently, only a small portion of it was actually present in Laos, and all its supporting elements were housed in Thailand, under a secret agreement with the Thai. Largely because of the area where North Vietnamese attacks were taking place, but also because of the decidedly pacificistic qualities of the lowland Lao, it was decided that the primary indigenous military force would be drawn from the Hmong tribes, who bore the brunt of North Vietnamese harassment in the northern part of the country.

By late 1964, when I succeeded Unger as ambassador to Laos, the mechanism for our "secret war" was largely in place. For the next four-and-a-half years, I directed that war, and in that period, gradually increased our operations in response to more aggressive North Vietnamese intervention. By the time I left the country in 1969 , we had a Hmong infantry force of

War in Indochina

nearly 40,000 men, an airlift of transports and helicopters operating over 50 aircraft in Laos, and an air attack force with about 100 propellor driven aircraft operating in our support out of Thailand. We could also call on a rather limited number of sorties from jet aircraft of the Rolling Thunder fleet if there were particularly difficult military trouble spots created by large North Vietnamese concentrations.

Despite Soviet charges and press reports to the contrary, I never had more than 250 Americans in Laos at any time coordinating and supporting these operations. Although a few of them were military personnel on special detail for short periods, most were young paramilitary specialists from the Central Intelligence Agency or contract civilians hired through the Agency in such corporations as Air America. They were under strict orders to stay out of combat and, if and when I found those orders were willfully disobeyed, I peremptorily removed them from the country. As a result, American casualties over the four-and-a-half years were only a handful.

The kind of war I undertook to direct was strictly defensive and essentially of a guerrilla nature. Because of its unorthodox structure, Washington gave me a free hand to run it as best I could without interference. I can remember only two direct military instructions that I received in the four-and-a-half years in Laos. Since both of them, duly executed, resulted in minor disasters, there was a general resignation in the higher echelons of our government to let us do our own thing without kibitzing.

Our own thing, concentrated largely in northern Laos, was to use a prudent mixture of space and time. At the beginning of the dry season every year, the North Vietnamese 316th Division marched across Route 7 to the west and attacked our Hmong outposts. Rather than attempting to hold terrain, our troops would fall back, inflicting casualties by ambush as they went. The civilian villages they left behind contained an intelligence network that provided us accurate information on

North Vietnamese numbers and locations. As the dry season rolled on and our forces withdrew higher onto the ridges where the 316th Division found it hard to pursue, we would wait until the enemy forces were strung out on a long logistics line, with troops scattered in small units.

Then we would pick out isolated enemy troop units, cut off their food supplies by small patrols, bring them out of the villages to an advantageous location, and pounce on them with special helicopter-borne units supported by slow-moving, strafing aircraft out of Thailand. After repeating this pattern many times before the rains set in, we would then use our helicopters to move large blocking forces out to the east on Route 7, along the line of march we knew the 316th would use as it withdrew when the rains began. As the unhappy troops were slogging homeward, our Hmong would ambush them time and again, especially trying to get them positioned in a narrow valley on a day that was clear enough for air operations. Then the planes would finish them off, often hundreds at a time, while the clear weather lasted.

It was the sort of warfare that depended on good communications, rapid mobility, intrepid hill-fighters, and friendly village population through which to move. It was also the sort designed to inflict maximum damage on conventional forces at minimal risk of casualties among the guerrillas. It was, in effect, the sort of warfare the North Vietnamese were fighting against our American units in South Vietnam. On the map, it never showed any great permanent territorial gains, but it certainly prevented Hanoi from consolidating its annual effort into any lasting conquest. And, since the Lao Dong Party was so heavily committed in South Vietnam, it seemed questionable that they would augment that effort in Laos.

However, in the dry season of 1968–69, the North Vietnamese changed their tactics. Realizing, finally, that those Hmong villages they annually overran were among our most valuable intelligence assets, their advance that season was characterized by a scorched earth campaign. They levelled every village in their path and drove the women and children inhabitants westward. Although they fell back with the rains just as they had in other years, they were less vulnerable to ambush, and our strike forces were less accurate in their moves. Moreover, we were now saddled with a hundred thousand refugees who refused to go back to land that had been laid barren and could not be farmed for a number of years. Perhaps the unkindest cut, however, came from congressional critics, who managed to get aerial photos of the devastated area and accused us of having wiped it out by indiscriminate bombing campaigns.

Direction of this war effort was a tremendously absorbing and enervating task. I eventually came to live with that task on a twenty-four hour a day basis. As experience accumulated and as the months and years went by, I eventually carried in my head, just short of my subconscious, a working knowledge of our deployments, the terrain, the roads and trails, the enemy dispositions, and our aircraft availability. Many a night I was wakened from a sound sleep by a telephone call, and sitting on the edge of the bed, had to decide whether to order the evacuation of an outpost under attack, to hold on, to reinforce, to call for air support, or to mount a diversionary action to relieve the pressure on the front. It was a far cry from the normal pursuits of the striped-pants set.

All of this was made possible only through the military genius of a remarkable Hmong leader named Vang Pao. He had served as a sergeant in the French colonial forces and had gained a certain stature among the Hmong leadership. However, he was not a member of the tribal elite. Vang Pao was a wiry little man with a broad, intelligent face, and a restless air of constant activity. He had a matchless knowledge of the hills and ridges and valleys of Northeast Laos. He recruited his troops in the various villages lying in the path of the North Vietnamese menace and commanded their loyalty by the example of his personal courage. Although he had a well-equipped command post at his headquarters through the courtesy of the CIA, he preferred to be in the field where the action was.

One time, when I was visiting him at his headquarters, reports came in about an impressive victory in a surprise attack conducted by his troops against a Vietnamese outpost. It was obvious that Vang Pao was itching to go there and have a look. I suggested we take my helicopter, since it was only about twenty miles away as the crow flies. He was delighted to act as navigator.

When we landed near the site of the battle, there was mild consternation among the Hmong troops. It seemed that their report was somewhat premature and that a small number of Vietnamese were still dug into a log bunker on top of a hill, from which they were firing occasional sniper shots. Vang Pao leapt from the helicopter and took command at once. He ordered a box of fragmentation grenades brought to him at a position he took at the bottom of the hill. He had one of the company commanders line up his unit in front of him and hold the open box of grenades. Then, as each soldier moved up to that point, Vang Pao took away his rifle and handed him a primed grenade. The soldier scrambled up the hill, pitched the grenade at the bunker, and then rolled and slithered back down again. Only about one quarter of the grenades actually found their mark.

This went on until the grenade box was empty. Then Vang Pao spread the same troops out in a single cordon along the base of the hill and gave them their rifles back. At his command, they went up the hill again, holding their fire till they were a few yards from the bunker. They opened up a volley, advanced to the logs and shouted victory. Within a few minutes, they were hauling the shattered bodies of a half-dozen Vietnamese out onto the hilltop. The job done, Vang Pao immediately resumed his inspection.

Although his troops and his tribe took a tremendous, constant pounding from the North Vietnamese, he continued to be held in popular respect. If one of his senior officers was killed, he would go to the man's village, symbolically marry the man's widow, and adopt his children, thus assuring their welfare. Because of this practice, he was often depicted in the American press as a licentious potentate with an enormous family.

Like all Hmong, he was superstitious. He was an animist and believed that good and bad spirits inhabited his surroundings. Certain large rock formations, for example, were particularly sacred and were never exposed to the sounds of war. The human body was often invaded by evil spirits that had to be exorcised through baci ceremonies, which involved prayers, incantations, and tying strings around the wrists. The body had to be kept clear of foreign objects, so that nothing would obstruct the effectiveness of these spiritual purges. This last requirement caused a crisis during one dry season campaign.

Vang Pao had gone, along with some of our American relief workers, to a village which had reported a Vietnamese raid that had destroyed all its food supplies. As the party approached by helicopter, they looked carefully to be sure that cloth panels were laid out on the ground, spelling out the code of the day and indicating that the landing pad was secure. When they landed, Vang Pao opened the hatch to be, as usual, the first man on the ground. As he poised to jump, he was hit in the shoulder by a rifle bullet and knocked back onto the deck. A young American welfare volunteer, who was a conscientious objector, caught Vang Pao's M-16 as it fell, saw the North Vietnamese ambusher rising to fire again, and drilled him through the head. The helicopter took off in a hail of bullets, but with no other casualties.

The helicopter pilot headed immediately for a hospital in Thailand. I was notified in Vientiane and took another helicopter for the same destination. I arrived there fifteen minutes after the U.S. Air Force doctors had finished their examination of the patient and while the X-rays were being read. They informed me that the high-powered rifle bullet had gone clean through the shoulder and had sheared off a piece of the upper arm bone just short of the shoulder socket. They felt complete recovery was probable, but only with the introduction of a metal extender to replace the missing bone. From their professional viewpoint, it looked good. I told them about Hmong customs and doubted whether Vang Pao would accept the metal replacement, but they were vehement in their assertion that the arm would atrophy without the steel pin. They felt certain that, if they put the case clearly to the patient in terms of the alternatives, he would make the rational decision to choose his arm over his animism. I doubted it and suggested they just go ahead with their surgical procedure without telling their patient of their intentions. This they steadfastly refused to do on ethical grounds.

We finally agreed that I would explain the situation to Vang Pao in French, which the doctors did not understand, obtain his concurrence in the procedure involving the steel pin, and then let them wheel him into surgery. I did just that, but elaborated at some length on the way in which the steel would eventually melt as it was warmed by the body, and would ultimately depart from the system just like bad spirits. The doctors watched the general's face move from a frown, to resignation, to a concurring smile. When he gave his "O.K.!" they wheeled him away.

While all this was going on with regard to the battlefields in the east of the country, we also had our hands full dealing with the fractious Lao political forces that continued to jockey for power in Vientiane. Since most politicians managed, through family or other connections, to have Lao military units under their influence, political squabbles often deteriorated into military action. Since Vientiane was the locus of power, the action usually took place there. We became somewhat inured to artillery and rocket duels across the sprawling little town on the mudflats of the Mekong.

One of these squabbles took on a somewhat different dimension, however, when the head of the Lao Air Force rebelled against the machinations of several senior general staff officers. The air force chief was a young, half-Vietnamese pilot with headquarters in the southern city of Savannakhet. The general staff officer intriguing against him was from a powerful political family located in Vientiane. His apparent purpose was to bring the air force under control of his family and within his personal military direction.

When the issue came to a head, the young air force chief lost his temper and decided to take direct action. He loaded up about twenty T-28 fighter-bombers with fragmentation bombs and, flying the lead plane, took off in tight formation for Vientiane. One of our young assistant air attachés, stationed in Savannakhet, realized what was happening and radioed the senior attaché in Vientiane, who immediately notified me. I told the attaché to go at once to forewarn the putative victim of this attack. I also had our embassy security people act to stop all automobile traffic in the immediate vicinity of the general staff headquarters. A few minutes before the planes arrived in the sky over the city and began to circle their targets, both actions had taken effect. The attaché removed the targeted general and his family from their large, conspicuous house at the military camp outside the city and crouched with them in a drainage ditch while the bombs destroyed their house. The traffic near general headquarters was held at a roadblock while the bombs also destroyed the central building there. In ten minutes, it was all over. The planes had left, the dust had settled, and only the burning rubble remained. In that rubble, over forty young men lay dead, but none of the generals was even injured. These young men had foolishly taken shelter under the building after we had phoned them to warn of the attack.

As soon as I could, I passed that sobering word back to our young assistant air attaché in Savannakhet and told him to do everything in his power to prevent the returning aircraft from loading up and mounting another sortie. Then, I went in search of the acting prime minister, who came from the Savannakhet region and was a patron of the young Air Force commander. He and I rapidly agreed that the major influence in bringing this young man under control would be the Prince of Champassak, Boun Oum, who was the primary political power in southern Laos. We went to his home and tried to persuade him to fly to Savannakhet and get the airman to turn himself in.

Old Boun Oum, who recognized the seriousness of the situation, was not averse to flying south; but, for his personal and political protection, he wanted the British and Soviet ambassadors, who represented the co-chairmen of the Laos Conference, to accompany him. I knew it would be useless to ask the Soviet ambassador and finally persuaded the melancholy prince that the British ambassador would be enough. Once he agreed to that, I then had to convince my British colleague, Fred Warner, to make the trip. To his everlasting credit, Fred immediately agreed, even though the Foreign Office subsequently reprimanded him for his temerity.

We flew south in my DC-3, hoping the air force would not take off for a second attack before we got there. We were relieved, when we arrived over Savannakhet, to find the planes safely in their revetments. The air force general seemed appropriately shaken and contrite, especially when he saw his large patron, Boun Oum, lumber off the plane. The two of them closeted themselves in an airport lounge, while Fred and I waited outside. In due course, they emerged with an agreement under which the general and all those pilots who had flown in the attack would take their unarmed planes to an airfield in Thailand, where the aircraft would be turned over to American maintenance personnel and where the aviators would all be granted political exile. Frantic messages back and forth confirmed the acceptability of this to all the parties, and the crisis was over.

On the way back to Vientiane in the DC-3, Boun Oum ruminated on the events in his barracks-room French. He said that the instigation for the actual attack came from a colonel's wife. She was not just any wife. She was the sister of Princess Boun Oum. The old prince, who had once been prime minister, muttered that, if he ever became prime minister again, the first thing he would do would be to arrest his wife and her sister. It was his contention that Lao women made most of the trouble in his country.

The trouble from that attack was far from over. It took weeks to help get political and military alignments back in shape and to get an operational air force functioning again. But, helping to put all those pieces together was the sort of activity I most enjoyed. Although I don't remember, at this remove, all the intricate maneuvers, I do recall that they filled in most of the time I could spare from my principal business of running a small war.

One other function that occupied my energies was managing the large official American presence in Laos. We had all the trappings of a big embassy as well as a large aid mission. In all, there were about 2,000 Americans in my charge. Quite apart from making them all productive, I had a real problem keeping them out of harm's way as we operated in and around the edges of military action. In fact, President Johnson, looking at the colored briefing maps in the Situation Room located in the White House basement would, about every six months, be worried by those large areas of red enemy terrain pressing down on the American community in Vientiane. He would then call me back to Washington, ask for assurances that we would not all be massacred or taken hostages, and end up offering whatever help I needed. When I usually demurred on the need for more help, he would press additional money on me. Once, this was in the form of a snap decision on his part to give me $75 million that neither I nor the Department of State had asked for. I remember riding back to State from that meeting along with Dean Rusk and watching the good secretary shake his head at the president's largesse.

It must also be remembered that, all this time, I was still, in all external aspects, the United States ambassador to Laos. This meant that my wife and I had to attend all the receptions, parties, and balls that are part of a diplomat's life. It meant that I had to give speeches, cut ribbons, and entertain visiting dignitaries. In short, it meant that I had to do all those things that most observers assume are the sum and substance of an ambassador's life.

This sort of activity brought us into constant association with the other members of the diplomatic corps. Among them was a rather suspicious little French colleague with an exceedingly convoluted sense of intrigue. He was convinced, perhaps in part by Soviet persuasion, that somewhere in a dark corner of Laos, we had a large military headquarters that was conducting our "secret war." He was also prepared to assume, along with the Soviets, that we had battalions of U.S. "special forces" operating in the jungled cordillera. There was a French military mission attached to his embassy, and he commissioned the general in charge to ferret out these elements so that Paris could have a true perspective on the Yankee presence.

The general was a very upright, thoroughly professional parachutist who had spent a valorous career largely in the French Foreign Legion. In response to his ambassador's charge, he began a very detailed investigation into what we were doing. When he finally came to the conclusion that we were running our operations with a handful of young Americans and no formal headquarters structure, his ambassador refused to accept his findings. Therefore, in some frustration and after a couple of drinks, the good general approached me directly on the subject one evening at a large charity ball. When I confirmed his conviction that our "headquarters" was my office in the chancery and that the only battalions were Hmong tribesmen, he accepted those statements with relief, a relief, however, I felt was tinged with personal regret that the soldier's profession, of which he was so proud, had fallen on such parlous times.

— 4 —

Not long after I became ambassador to Laos, an attempted coup d'etat occurred. It was led by a young army colonel, who had recently returned to Vientiane from a tour of duty as military attaché in the Royal Lao embassy in Washington. While there, he had taken a number of military courses offered by the U.S. Department of Defense, including a course in what was euphemistically called psychological warfare. He was the same colonel whose wife subsequently inspired the Air Force rebellion I have recounted above. He felt himself a close friend of the United States and was strongly anticommunist, insofar as he truly understood what that term meant. Therefore, when he undertook to lead an attempted coup against the neutralist, coalition government, there were those in Vientiane who were prepared to believe that he was acting on behalf of, or with the support of, the United States Government.

For this reason, as well as because a coup could lead to a reopening of the bloody internecine warfare that had been suppressed with such effort in Laos, I decided that the American embassy had to act decisively to terminate the coup effort before it got out of hand. By most standards, the coup attempt was a rather feeble undertaking, involving only a single battalion of troops. However, since that battalion was the principal garrison force in Vientiane, it was well placed to cause trouble. Moreover, the residual effects of that psychological warfare course enabled our wily young colonel to use artifice to magnify the apparent effect of what he was doing.

The coup began in the siesta hour shortly after midday when most of Vientiane was fast asleep. The troops involved took over their assigned targets quietly and without fanfare. Among their targets was the national radio studio which, at that hour of the day, usually played a soporific series of ramwong dance records acquired in Thailand. The first sign the silent city had of anything amiss, therefore, was when the radio broadcasts were interrupted and a series of communiqués were read over the radio by a very martial-sounding young man, who announced that the coalition government had fallen and been replaced by a military junta.

After these announcements, the radio station resumed the ramwong music. Every few minutes, the music was interrupted again and another communiqué was read. Each of these communiqués announced the adherence or support of some prominent political leader or of some significant military unit to the program of the junta. By midafternoon, it was apparent to anyone accepting the substance of these radio broadcasts that the junta enjoyed the support of every important military force and nearly every well-known political personality in the country. As the young announcer proclaimed, this carefully planned and meticulously organized action was an overwhelming success.

Because the coup leaders had taken the telephone exchange as one of their first objectives and had cut all telephone service, most residents of Vientiane had no way to check with each other on the veracity of the claims being broadcast on the radio. Moreover, since the radio commanded all citizens to stay off the streets (advice that most of them were quite willing to observe), there was little possibility for people to move about to check on the information by other means.

War in Indochina

Troops had been posted at most intersections and enforced the ban against the movement of people and traffic by firing bursts of automatic rifle fire into the air whenever violators were spotted. This had the effect of reducing the city to a standstill and forcing most residents to head for cover.

The embassy had long since learned to cope with the unreliability of the Vientiane telephone system in times of bad weather as well as political trouble. We had established a network of walkie-talkie radios (a rare novelty in those days), which enabled us to communicate among our various elements throughout the city and also with the residential clusters we had on the outskirts of the city proper. Because our emergency evacuation plans included a responsibility for the British, Australian, Canadian, and other allied missions, we had radio outposts at their chanceries also.

Consequently, by activating the network and accumulating eyeball impressions from our various outposts, we were able to form an objective evaluation of the coup effort by mid-afternoon. We concluded that the troops involved were, indeed, no more than those assigned to the garrison battalion and that they were spread very thinly around town with no effective strongpoints guarded by anything larger than a squad. In fact, the largest concentration, of about twenty men, was located at the radio studio, which, we deduced, was serving as the headquarters of the rebels. One curious fact also emerged from our radio survey. There were no troops stationed at the antenna farm which contained the transmitters for the national radio station. It was unattended except for the customary civilian guard who manned the gate leading into the fenced enclosure.

With this information in hand, I held a meeting with my senior staff who were in the embassy compound. We decided we would test the effectiveness of the ban against movement in the streets by insisting on our diplomatic immunity from such arbitrary actions. An assistant military attaché and a young political officer, both of whom spoke rudimentary Lao, volunteered to conduct the test. They festooned the attaché's jeep with two large American flags and somewhere obtained a handcranked siren which they clamped on the front seat. Thus equipped, they eased out the compound gate and toward the main street. As we expected, the young Lao soldiers were somewhat bewildered by this sortie and chose, as the better part of valor, to accept the claim of diplomatic immunity rather than create an international incident. The jeep noisily made its way to the radio station.

Within half an hour, the two courageous young officers returned with confirmation of our assumptions. The coup group consisted of the young colonel and a half dozen officers on his staff. The "support" announced from all the political and military personalities was fabricated, and the communiqués were being read at predetermined intervals from a prepared script. The whole exercise was a demonstration project in psychological warfare. The report also pretty much confirmed what we suspected. The young military officers had no technical knowledge of radio. They apparently did not even realize that the radio studio required transmitters to propagate their broadcasts and that the transmitters were located elsewhere. They had therefore seized the studio, but neglected the antenna farm.

Armed with these two essential facts, we decided on a course of action. Our plan had two facets. The first was to sabotage the link between the radio studio and the transmitters. The second was to persuade the general commanding the military region to work out a surrender of the coup group, but to avoid a military confrontation that might produce bloodshed. We felt we needed to have the government's approval and sanction for what we were about to do, but had serious doubts that the government could take the actions itself. We were, in effect, the only ones trusted by both sides.

As dusk began to gather over the still quiet city, we sent

new sorties in three directions. The first went to find the prime minister and his government to inform them of our appraisal and intention. The second went to find the commanding general to seek his cooperation. And the third went to the Australian chancery to fetch the Australian chargé d'affaires.

The radio system in Laos had been constructed by Australia under the Colombo Plan of assistance and donated as a gift to the Lao nation. Wisely, the Australians had arranged for its maintenance by providing the services of an Australian technician who not only kept the equipment serviced, but also was charged with training Laotian technicians to learn the maintenance work and eventually take over full responsibility for the system. The frustrations of the latter assignment had literally driven him to drink. Hence, when, with the cooperation of the Australian chargé, we finally found the technician in the early hours of the evening and brought him to our compound, he was quite thoroughly drunk. Nevertheless, after several cups of coffee, he got the picture and agreed that the link between the studio and the transmitter could be very easily and effectively sabotaged. All he needed was a minimum amount of equipment and a dexterous assistant. We provided both through the cooperation of a half-Japanese-half-Thai mechanic, who was our handyman at the embassy. Given a jeep, bolt cutters, rubber gloves, and a few miscellaneous items, this oddly assorted pair drove off into the night in the general direction of the antenna farm. Fifteen minutes later, the radio went dead.

The expedition to the commanding general was somewhat less conclusive. The general, obviously suspicious about U.S. motives in this whole exercise, was reluctant to move into the city in the dark. He did agree in principle, however, to a meeting with the rebellious colonel the following morning at the embassy, provided we would guarantee his personal safety. The government, in some numbers, was found surprisingly intact in the compound of the hospital adjoining the prime minister's residence. The coup had apparently occurred just as they were finishing a cabinet meeting and settling into a hearty lunch. In due course (presumably after they finished their lunch), they decided that the hospital compound was less vulnerable than the prime minister's residence and scuttled next door. I supposed they all climbed over the fence. They were quite pleased that the embassy was prepared to act to end the coup. They were reportedly ecstatic when the rebel radio broadcasts went off the air.

At this stage, we sent our assistant military attaché back to visit the colonel, sequestered in his silent radio studio. He was found there, tapping the microphones, kicking the consoles, and making other similar futile attempts to continue the broadcasts of his dramatic script. When he realized it was all to no avail, his bravado collapsed, and he understood that his escapade was over. He begged the attaché to stay the night with him and agreed to go with him in the morning to meet with the general at the embassy compound.

Since there seemed little else I could do that night, I set forth in my flag-decked official car from the embassy to the hospital, which also abutted the ambassador's residence on the opposite side from the prime minister's home. There, in the chief surgeon's residence, I found the cabinet just tucking into a large Lao dinner and agreed with alacrity to join them. They seemed in a jubilant mood and assumed that the coup attempt had failed.

The next morning, as arranged, the rebellious colonel was brought to the embassy and taken to our conference room. A few minutes later, the general arrived, accompanied by a rather large bodyguard, which stationed itself in our driveway. The city streets, incidentally, were void of any of the garrison forces that had controlled them the previous day. Traffic had returned more or less to normal. I met the general at the chancery door and took him up to the conference room. There, the young colonel saluted smartly and stood at rigid attention.

The general returned the salute rather glumly. I told them I would leave them alone and returned to my office, leaving the same rather tired assistant military attaché posted at the end of the corridor.

About forty minutes later, the door of the conference room opened, the two smiling Lao officers greeted the attaché, and he led them to my office. Both of them thanked us profusely for our good offices and assured us that all problems were settled. The colonel was to have another assignment in the south, the general's cousin would take over command of the garrison battalion, and no punitive action would result. The coup attempt was over.

There remained only the problem of getting the radio station back on the air. The Australian chargé produced his sober technician, our mechanic joined him in a jeep with his tools, and they set off once again in the direction of the antenna farm. Again, within fifteen minutes, the station was back on the air, just in time for the ramwong hour that had been interrupted by events of the day before. Vientiane enjoyed a restful siesta that day.

— 5 —

In the early spring of 1968, Lyndon Johnson decided to try serious negotiations with the North Vietnamese to terminate the war in Indochina. Although he made several overtures in this direction through the Soviets, the Poles, and others, he was unable to get a definitive response from Hanoi. He finally decided to go directly to the North Vietnamese themselves.

There were very few countries in the world outside the communist bloc where North Vietnamese and American diplomatic missions functioned simultaneously. Vientiane was one of these, and the only one in which the American representative was on speaking terms with his North Vietnamese counterpart, since Washington did not recognize Hanoi. In my case, because I had spent long months negotiating with North Vietnam on the neutrality of Laos, and because both countries had a special relationship to Laos, I continued to maintain civil social contact with the North Vietnamese representatives in Vientiane. This was rather anomalous because our respective combatants were at the same time fighting and killing each other on Laotian soil.

In any event, I received instructions to meet with the North Vietnamese and propose the convening of negotiations aimed at terminating hostilities. This action began a manic round of discussions over the selection of a city in which talks could take place. Because of the enormous attention concentrated on this subject, a horde of press and television reporters converged on Vientiane and turned the proceedings into something of a circus. Moreover, because Hanoi insisted that our meetings be considered secret, they took on aspects of a hide and seek game with the reporters. The matter was finally resolved when both sides agreed that Paris was an acceptable venue.

Johnson assembled a formidable negotiating team, headed by Averell Harriman, and including Cyrus Vance, General Andrew Goodpaster, Philip Habib, and others of stature. They flew off to Paris and prepared to meet with the North Vietnamese negotiators who were also assembling there. Two days before the negotiations were to begin, I received a cable from Harriman asking if I could join him for dinner at the Hotel Crillon at 8:00 p.m. the following evening. The message arrived in Vientiane about 5 in the afternoon. I called in my administrative officer and asked him to check airline schedules from Bangkok to Paris. Within short order, he was back to tell me that there were no flights to meet Harriman's proposed schedule. The best connections would put me in Paris after midnight. He proposed we send a cable to that effect.

I asked him to bring me the airline guide. I knew Harriman well and knew that he, as an old railroad man, had a thing about schedules. If he had asked me to be there at eight, I felt certain he had found an obscure route by which I could make it. After considerable search, I found it. There was a Scandinavian Airlines flight at eight in the morning from Bangkok via Tashkent to Copenhagen. In Copenhagen, there was a half hour to connect with an Air France flight to Paris, which would arrive at Orly at 7:15 p.m. With good luck and good traffic, I could be at the Crillon at eight.

I arranged for my air attaché to fly me to Bangkok at 5:30 a.m. in order to give myself time to get tickets and documentation. I asked the French embassy to request Air France to wait for me in Copenhagen if necessary. Then I sent a message to Harriman accepting his dinner invitation. As it turned out, all connections went well and I arrived at Orly on schedule. There I was met by Phil Habib and a young officer who undertook to retrieve my baggage. Phil and I headed for the hotel. When we arrived there and went briskly to Harriman's suite, we found all the other guests assembled. Harriman looked at his watch, and his greeting was "You're four minutes late."

The reason I had been brought across continents had to do with the way in which the American team felt the negotiations would proceed. They assumed the North Vietnamese would make a major propaganda play out of the formal sessions and stall any substantive progress. Therefore, they concluded that any real discussion would have to take place away from the glare of publicity. Harriman had spotted the name of one Vietnamese on the delegation with whom he knew I had previously had a civil working relationship. He thought it possible that I might be able to establish some sort of private liaison with that official to work toward some progress even while the formal talks were stalled. In the event, that official was never surfaced in any way I could get to him, and the unforeseen argumentation on the shape of the table surpassed even our most gloomy prognostications of dalliance.

Therefore, I had no real role to play in Paris. This was just as well, because I carried with me from Vientiane a severe intestinal infection and spent a good portion of my time bedridden. In my ambulatory hours, I acted primarily as a liaison between our delegation and the French, keeping the Quai D'Orsay informed of the various ploys we tried to get talks started.

While all this was going on, major civil disturbances broke out in Paris. Beginning with demonstrations at the universities on the Left Bank, and agitated by professional rabble-rousers, the young middle-class students tried to foment a social and political revolution in France. When *"les événements"* broke out, de Gaulle was in India and Pompidou procrastinated in his reaction. Within a few days, the situation had deteriorated. Whole sections of the Left Bank had been converted into an insurrectionary camp. Barricades had been thrown up, paving blocks stockpiled as weapons, and firearms brought into the impromptu garrisons. What began as a student protest began to take on serious proportions.

When de Gaulle returned to Paris, he ordered 50,000 police into the city, presumably to crush the revolt. These well-trained, tough-looking *flics* set up command posts and mounted garrison positions on the Right Bank. The Place de la Concorde and the areas around the Hotel Crillon swarmed with them. The assumption was that, at any minute, they would be given their marching orders and would charge across the river to tear down the student barricades. But, the orders never came.

As one who was crossing the river every day to carry out my briefings at the Quai D'Orsay, I could see the reasons for delay. The senior Foreign Office officials with whom I was dealing were in a frenzy of despair. Almost all of them had children on the barricades. And the same held true at the Ministry of the Interior, in the police, and at the Élysée Palace itself. Pledged as they were to preserving law and order and to repressing insurrection against the state, they were not prepared to call in the wrath of a blue-collar police force against their own offspring. Even if they ever entertained any stray thoughts in that direction during the crisis, they were imperiously directed away from such temptation by the constant jangling of their private line telephones, as their wives pressed connubial panic into their weary bureaucratic ears.

And so it dragged on and involved high Gallic drama, with de Gaulle flying to consult his troop commanders and communiqués hurtling across the Seine. In the midst of all this, an American cultural event arrived in Paris. It had been scheduled well in advance and involved a small ballet group that enjoyed a great reputation in Paris, the Paul Taylor Dance troupe. In the eneffable tradition of international culture, both French and American authorities decided that the show should go on, incipient revolution or not. They pressed ahead with the decision even when Taylor himself, as leader of the troupe, broke an ankle while rehearsing in a theater that was partly blacked out because of the disturbances.

Their decision was all the more bold because the presentation was scheduled for the lovely old Odéon theater, located on the Left Bank only a few blocks from the heart of the disturbances. But it did encouter one hitch that resulted from the confusion. That was the absence of an accredited ambassador in the American embassy. Sargeant Shriver, who had arrived to take the post and who should have been fully accredited when the ballet was scheduled, had been unable to present his credentials because of de Gaulle's preoccupation with *les événements*. Given the sensitivity of the French to matters of protocol, he decided not to make a public appearance at the opening of the ballet lest he be accused of overstepping the bounds of tradition.

Since the American organizers of the event desperately wanted a live ambassador in the box of honor, they prevailed on me to go there and to take Shriver's place. I had no particular tasks except to share the box with Jean-Louis Barrault,

Director of the Odéon, and with the American chargé d'affaires and his wife. At the end of the performance, I had also to present some roses and to congratulate the cast. Then, all the principals and the dancers repaired across the square for a late supper at the Atlantique.

As the evening grew later and the supper party continued, Barrault came to whisper in my ear and advise me to leave. He said that the students would be coming in about fifteen minutes to take over the Odéon, and he assumed they would block off the square. When I turned to sympathize with him on losing his theater, he shrugged and said, "Mais, je suis avec eux." We quickly disengaged from the party, and, gathering up the chargé and his wife, whose car we came in, we moved down into the square and had the car brought to the door of the restaurant. Just as Barrault was saying farewell, the students poured into the square. They surged all over the car and began to rock it back and forth. One of them managed to get a door open and lunged at the chargé's wife. Barrault climbed on the hood and was recognized. Through his intercession, the driver was able to extricate us and we sped out of the area and headed across the Seine.

I was in the front seat with the driver and got the full force of his reaction. In his barrack-room argot, he held forth all the way back to the Crillon about the so-called revolutionaries. He sputtered that his children didn't have the educational and other advantages that would permit them to get to universities. If those that did weren't willing to take advantage of the education the state was prepared to provide them, they should get out and let those like his children take their place. As far as he was concerned, the revolution these spoiled student brats wanted to lead was not for the likes of him or anybody else who had to work for a living. He was all for turning the police against them.

His outrage was an accurate reflection of the broader political situation in the country. When the students marched to an automobile factory and asked the workers to join in their revolt, they were met by a barrage of stones and chased back to their universities. Rebuffed, bewildered, and exhausted, they gave up their revolution and went back to their classrooms. *Les événements* were over.

In the meantime, the negotiations on Vietnam had made no progress—the shape of the table still hadn't been settled. My infection had gotten worse, and I had weakened considerably. French laboratories were closed by the labor strikes. So, I took a plane and flew back to Washington, where I spent the next two weeks in Bethesda Naval Hospital. By the time I was cured, I had lost a lot of weight, but was assured that I could safely return to Paris. Accordingly, I went around to make a call on Secretary Dean Rusk and tell him of my plans. He took one look at me and had his assistant book me a stateroom on the next crossing of the S.S. United States. In his sternest manner, he ordered me to take the ship and not to fly. It was a thoughtful order from a thoughtful and decent man, and its wisdom was proved by my discovery, on returning to Paris, that the negotiators had still not agreed on the shape of the table.

In view of the stalled negotiations, I decided to return to my embassy in Laos. I had been there for three-and-a-half years, engaged in the endless business of running a guerrilla war against the North Vietnamese. It was a demanding regimen, and I guess that Rusk, on seeing my bedraggled looks after emerging from the Naval Hospital, decided that I needed a change. In a few months, he brought me back again to Washington, told me that the embassy in Manila was going to be available, and asked if I would like to go there. Knowing his caution, I felt fairly confident he would not have offered it to me without having first cleared it with President Johnson. Hence, I accepted with pleasure, and Rusk made arrangements for me to visit with the president in order to get the official laying on of hands.

By this time, we were well into 1968, and Johnson had announced that he would not stand for reelection. He had therefore mellowed somewhat in his demeanor, but could never entirely shuck off the habit of wheeling and dealing that had become the mark of his political style. When I called on him this time, he came around the desk, draped his big arm around my shoulders and propelled me into the little room off the Oval Office where he had his reclining chair and three television sets. He sat me down on the couch and gave me "the treatment."

This was a practiced routine, which consisted of a lot of touching; hands on shoulders, hands on knee caps, hands clasped and wringing; fingers tugging on lapels, fingers tugging on his own ears; and all the while, the honey of his voice dripping from the large mouth fixed in a crooked smile. It would take a flinty heart and ice-cold belly to resist the appeal of a king-sized president operating in that mode. He talked of his decision to step down, of his need to finish off his days in the White House with a team he could count on, with people he "could go to the well with." He said he wanted me to stay in Laos through the rest of his term and asked me if I would be willing to make that sort of sacrifice for him. He never once mentioned the Philippines and never once suggested that he was ordering me to stay at my post. It was all done so effectively that I left him with the warm satisfaction that I had been able to do something to help ease the pain he must have felt in accepting the crushing frustration of his own resignation.

I had, of course, done him a favor of sorts. He was having all kinds of difficulties with the Congress about the policies being pursued by his Assistant Secretary of State for African Affairs, "Soapy" Williams. But, since Williams was one of the original Kennedy appointees, Johnson was not prepared to fire him. He was, however, prepared to exile him to Manila; and once my potential claim to the post was out of the way, that is exactly what he did. I learned the news of Williams' appointment shortly after I had returned to Vientiane, and the whole logic of the train of events in Washington became clear to me. Because, however, of the genius of the Johnson personality and his political prowess, I never felt embittered or held against him the subtle duplicity by which he had used the "treatment" on me for his own purposes. I could only shake my head in amused admiration for the filibustering finesse of that remarkable Texan.

Chapter Eight

The Indochina Peace Treaty
1969–1972

WHEN I LEFT LAOS in the spring of 1969 and returned to Washington, I was disappointed to be assigned to the same position I had left nearly five years earlier, in charge of our government's operations in Indochina. The disappointment was compounded of many facets. First, the assignment meant that I would have to extend the bone-wearying involvement in a crisis in which I had been immersed since 1961. Second, it meant that I would be taking over operations that had become increasingly militarized, and hence largely out of policy control. Third, it meant that I would be moving into a new administration with new personalities whom I didn't know and who didn't know me. (It was quite clear from the look President Nixon gave me when I was first introduced to him that he was not about to put much trust in someone who had worked as closely as I had with Presidents Kennedy and Johnson, and

The Indochina Peace Treaty

who had been Averell Harriman's assistant for three years.)

However, I was well received by the new Secretary of State, Bill Rogers, a very decent, sophisticated, and pleasant human being whom I came to respect greatly; and by the new Secretary of Defense, Melvin Laird, a canny, friendly, and self-confident politician who knew his way around Washington. On the basis of my previous experience in the same job with Dean Rusk and Robert McNamara, I assumed they would be the primary movers and shakers with whom I would work.

I soon discovered that arrangements on Indochina would be different in the Nixon administration than they had been in the Johnson years. Although the interdepartmental apparatus over which I presided was still largely responsible for the execution of policy in Indochina, it no longer made the policy decisions. That function had been taken over by another body, called the Washington Special Action Group (WASAG), which met in the White House Situation Room and was chaired by Henry Kissinger. I therefore found myself spending more and more of my time in the Situation Room and acting more and more as an executive arm for WASAG and for Kissinger.

The relationship with Kissinger was to pose problems for me. I was lodged in the Department of State and worked for Bill Rogers. However, Kissinger, with a fetish for secrecy, wished to bypass Rogers and the department. He did not trust the Foreign Service, and certainly not one of its members who had been so closely identified with two Democratic administrations. I was afflicted, therefore, not only with the problems of working effectively with Kissinger while maintaining loyalty to my boss, but also with the problem of being a credible instrument of the new administration. The first problem resolved itself when it became clear that neither of my two principals wished to move aggressively against the other and that both were prepared to use me as a buffer. I adopted the policy of listening without comment to whatever ire either vented to me and swallowing those comments without repetition to anyone else, including my wife and my close assistants. Ironically, the second problem did not resolve itself until a lengthy illegal telephone tap, both at my office and my home, convinced the new administration that I was a reliable member of its team. Then, the sudden transformation of my reception at the White House, especially from the president and his political acolytes such as Erlichman and Haldeman, bemused me. It was only later, when I learned about the tap, that I could account for the change.

One of my first assignments in my new job was to accompany the president to his first meeting with South Vietnamese President Nguyen van Thieu. It took place on the Godforsaken island of Midway, a tiny speck in the Pacific. Since this location had been chosen to assure absolute security against either terrorists or hostile demonstrators, the administration made a considerable effort to dress up the dismal locale into a spot for a hearty reception to an embattled ally. The small navy contingent on the island had all its buildings freshly painted, an impressive band and color guard were flown in, the few dependents were given banners and signs to wave. An enormous red carpet was laid out on the airport tarmac.

But, no one had found a way to control the gooney birds. These strange maritime birds use Midway as their home. They stay out at sea for months on end, but when their fertilized eggs are ready to be laid, the females return to the island and hatch their young. The males then act as food foragers, and the families remain together until the young are a few months old and able to forage on their own. Then, the parents go back to sea, while the young birds stay on Midway and learn to fly. Once they master the technique of long-distance soaring, they, also, take off to sea and leave the island in tranquility.

Unfortunately, the meeting of the two presidents happened to coincide with that period in the gooney bird cycle when the parents had gone back to sea and the fledgling young were learning to fly on the island. A four- or five-month-old gooney bird, making its first efforts to get airborne, is an awesome sight. The birds stand nearly three feet tall at that stage and have about a six-foot wingspread. Because their bodies are so heavy, they cannot spring into the air, but require a little headway on the ground to get airspeed. This means that they have to run along an open space, into the prevailing tradewind, to gain flight momentum. Their favorite place for practicing this maneuver had become, with the advent of modern man to Midway, the flat surface of the airport.

But the gooney bird is not a naturally graceful creature on the ground. Especially when the birds are young, their feet are large and awkward. When they begin their run, their feet often get entangled, and they trip and sprawl. The sprawl is usually quite ungainly, and they sometimes remain in particularly contorted positions for some time after their collapse, because the impact on the hard cement stuns them. In this brief season of the gooney birds' amateur aeronautics, the human population of Midway will often spend hours watching the stumbling, bumbling performance of the fledglings and roaring with laughter at the result. Gooney birds don't seem to mind. They are quite unfazed by human beings and strut among them without fear or favor.

And so it was, when Richard Nixon and Nguyen van Thieu stood at attention to salute the national anthems played with great pomp by the military band, that a young gooney bird felt it was an opportune moment to test his prowess at the takeoff maneuver. He managed to waddle out on the tarmac unseen by those designated to shoo the birds away. At the end of the long honor guard, standing rigidly with their rifles at attention, he began his clumsy runup, with wings flapping and feet churning. Although he was clearly visible by then, it was too late to stop him. Down the line of the honor guard he came, all his body in straining, uncoordinated motion, his head and neck bobbing up and down as he gathered momentum.

Suddenly, his feet became entangled and he splayed all ways for Sunday. He ended up on the red carpet right in front of the two presidents, his rump in the air, his wings crumpled, and his head, with its two stupid, beady eyes, twisted into stunned immobility looking up at the two men holding their salute. He stayed there until the anthems were over, and then, with the help of some flustered Navy men, was hustled away. It seemed to me, in retrospect, to have been an episode symbolic of the confusion of the times.

Back in Washington, we pursued the "two track" policy on Vietnam. This consisted of providing massive equipment and training to South Vietnamese forces while we gradually withdrew our own; and a concentrated effort in the Paris negotiations to reach agreements that would constitute an acceptable formula for peace. The process took far longer than had been expected, and it was not until 1972 that a real breakthrough emerged in the Paris talks. This did not come, it will be remembered, in the public forum of the negotiations, but in the secret talks that Henry Kissinger personally conducted with Le Duc Tho of the Lao Dong party.

By 1972, I had become a party to the Kissinger negotiating team. The element of secrecy was of Pimpernel proportions. We flew into a French military base in the middle of the night and taxied to the far end of the field. There, in total darkness, we disembarked and carried our baggage, files, and typewriters across the runway to a small French executive jet that was the personal aircraft of President Pompidou. In that plane, we flew to an airfield near Paris, while our U.S. aircraft, in accordance with its flight plan, went on to the Rhein-Main field in Germany. One night, in the rush of this mad scramble, a member of our small group left his suitcase by accident in the middle of that deserted runway. I don't know if he ever told Kissinger, but I have often thought of the bewilderment that must have afflicted the French Air Force man who presumably found it there.

The Indochina Peace Treaty

In any event, our negotiations inevitably became public, even though both parties, because of a rather ridiculous protocol that had grown up around the talks, insisted on holding them in awkward locations rather than at the Conference Center provided by the French government for the stylized, formal meetings that continued. We therefore had a complex relationship with the press, especially the television journalists, who seemed to relish recording on film whatever they could glimpse of the comings and goings, the musings and strollings, and the facial reflections of our ordeal. The French police kept the cameras at a significant distance from our locations so that their crews were out of earshot, but we didn't realize for some time how thoroughly their telephoto lenses compressed that distance for the viewers at home.

At the communist villa in Gif-sur-Yvette, for example, where the North Vietnamese were "hosts," we were aware that the French communist party had arranged to "bug" the entire room where we held our meetings and were recording the proceedings on elaborate taping machines located in one of the rooms upstairs in the house. Therefore, whenever we recessed for private consultations, there was nowhere in the villa where we felt we could talk among our own delegation without being overheard. We developed the practice of spending those recesses out in the large side yard of the villa. And there, day after day, as Kissinger and I, and when he was there, Al Haig, walked around and talked, our facial expressions were caught by the cameras, and the television viewing world could speculate on how the negotiations appeared to be going.

Someone in Washington told Kissinger that the stock market actually rose and fell on the basis of what speculators thought they saw reflected in our expressions. We doubted that was true but, at one point, decided on an experiment to test it. Over a period of several days, we consciously affected either gloom or elation whenever we knew the cameras were on us. To our astonishment, we discovered that we seemed to influence the market by about six points in either direction. Troubled by the implications of this frivolity, we began to try for as much deadpan lack of expression as we could muster as the negotiations dragged on.

That was not especially difficult to contrive, because the pace of our work began to drive us to fatigue. Kissinger's insistence on secrecy meant that we had to work with a very small delegation, about one-fourth the size of that of the North Vietnamese. It meant that those of us who did the negotiations also had to write the reports on them for Washington, prepare new texts and positions, handle the press, and consult with our allies. It became a regime that regularly consumed sixteen and occasionally eighteen hours a day. It was only with great difficulty that I was able to persuade Kissinger to let me bring over a State Department lawyer, George Aldrich, to help share the burden.

Another feature that contributed to our exhaustion was the constant need to travel. Either we had to go back to Washington for consultations or out to Saigon to argue with our recalcitrant allies in South Vietnam. On those long trips, I was always amazed by Kissinger's stamina and durability. That of his young White House staff was equally impressive. There were usually only two real sleeping berths on those presidential aircraft, and Kissinger and I used them. This meant that the staff had to do the best they could in the reclining seats and still be prepared for the volume of work Kissinger threw at them.

After one of those grinding trips from Paris to Saigon and back during the course of a weekend recess, the South Vietnamese delegation to the formal talks urgently asked for a briefing on the discussion we had held with their government. They came to the embassy residence late on Sunday evening when we were preparing for our Monday morning meeting. Those briefing sessions had become something of a routine.

The Indochina Peace Treaty 243

Although Kissinger sat through them, he insisted that I do the actual briefing because his patience with our Saigon allies and what he called their "Talmudic" questions was very limited. On this Sunday evening, that was the pattern we began. I sat on a couch with the South Vietnamese ambassador while Kissinger and three South Vietnamese sat in chairs facing us. About halfway through my own briefing, in the middle of a sentence, I fell asleep. The South Vietnamese, recognizing my fatigue, graciously withdrew. Kissinger never let me forget the event and enjoyed telling it at dinner parties for some days.

Le Duc Tho was by far the most impressive North Vietnamese we met. He was a man with limited formal education, but one who had read and studied rather widely. He used to laugh and say that the French gave him plenty of time to read in their jail cells. He had a certain dignity and exuded a sense of dedication and conviction. He might in some other setting have been considered a moralist. In practice, he was a revolutionary and wished to be considered as such. He had lived his entire mature life in struggle. He needed antagonism to survive.

And yet he had a sense of humor and enjoyed pulling Kissinger's leg. He could engage in repartee and could even, on occasion, appear solicitous. It then became somewhat difficult to remember that he was one of the small group of fanatic old men who had organized the brutal war to dominate all of Southeast Asia and who had caused so much carnage among his countrymen, their neighbors, and the youth of America.

When Kissinger and I went to Hanoi after the agreements were signed, we were able to observe Le Duc Tho moving among the Lao Dong leadership. He was so clearly superior in almost every way to Pham Van Dong, the North Vietnamese prime minister, that it brought home sharply the governing structure of that society. In Hanoi, the government was merely the administrative arm of the party. Pham Van Dong was rather like a professional city manager in a prosperous American midwest city, where the real power lay with the industrialists, the bankers, and the real estate people who controlled the town. As one of the real powers, Le Duc Tho could afford to be conspicuously contemptuous of Pham, who, after a few whiskies, became rather obnoxious.

Le Duc Tho took us on a visit to about the only cultural attraction that exists in Hanoi, a museum originally created by the French to celebrate the culture of Vietnam. It was clear that Le Duc Tho had never set foot inside the building before. He had always been too busy for that. As we moved around and a guide explained the archeological models and the artifacts, Le Duc Tho would interrupt with an amusing anecdote about some revolutionary action or other that had taken place near the archeological dig in question or in association with the region that produced the artifact. He seemed to have been either "in clandestinity" or in a French jail in every part of the country. He enjoyed the museum. It gave him an opportunity to be a raconteur. But, he didn't care a fig for the cultural treasures the museum director tried to point out during our tour.

By November, 1972, we felt we truly had an agreement in sight. There were only a few issues still in dispute and they appeared soluble. But, suddenly, after the outcome of the congressional elections in the United States became clear, the North Vietnamese began to stall. Not only did they balk at resolving the remaining issues, they began to reopen other matters that had already been resolved. It was clear that they felt they would have a better chance of getting things their way in January with the new Congress than they would in November. This opened up a serious dilemma for us.

President Nixon had declared a temporary suspension in our Rolling Thunder bombing campaign before the November elections, to remain in effect so long as reasonable progress was being made in our negotiations. Kissinger was required

The Indochina Peace Treaty 245

to report regularly, through Haldeman, that progress was indeed present. We had now reached the point when it became impossible to make such a report honestly. He and I both knew that, if we said progress had ceased, Nixon would feel obligated by the consistency of his strategy to resume the bombing. As November dragged on into early December, we began to face the moment of truth and to foresee a resumption of the bombing campaign in the middle of the Christmas season.

Kissinger discussed this prospect candidly and privately with Le Duc Tho. I did the same with my opposite number Nguyen Co Thach, who later became Hanoi's Foreign Minister. Tho was almost frivolous in his reaction, and Thach was steely cold. They both said they would take their chances rather than make any negotiated accommodations. Kissinger decided that he had better go back to Washington and discuss the situation directly with the president.

The afternoon before he left, he and I spent an agonizing two hours walking round and round the gravel path in the gardens of the embassy residence, in a damp, drizzling cold. We examined every possibility for some prospect of progress and rang the changes on all the consequences, both domestic and international, that would result from a major bombing campaign over the Christmas period. It appeared to be a no-win situation, but both of us gloomily knew what the facts of the situation would produce. Kissinger went off to Washington the next morning, and I savored the luxury of a good late sleep. The next day I received a message that the talks were being suspended and an instruction to return home myself. I reached Washington about the same time that the first bombers reached the outskirts of Hanoi.

Much misinformation has been spread about the results of our "carpet bombing" in that Christmas campaign. The impression has been left that it was an indiscriminate effort, aimed at terrorizing the population and government in Hanoi.

In actual practice, it was a carefully structured and effective move. It succeeded in destroying a number of military installations and economic targets with remarkably few civilian casualties. Most of all, it succeeded in using up all the North Vietnamese supply of antiaircraft missiles and leaving them truly defenseless against future air attack. Because the mining blockade of the ports was effective against Soviet resupply and because the Chinese refused to let anything in across their territory, the North Vietnamese realized that the jig was up. They came back to the table right after New Year's, we suspended bombing, and, in three weeks, we had an agreement.

However, it was that same bombing campaign, combined with Watergate, that made the agreement ultimately ineffective. The new Congress, in reaction to the campaign, passed laws that castrated the Nixon administration's ability to enforce the agreements and tempted Hanoi to violate them. The tragic irony, of course, is that, by violating them, the Lao Dong leadership, which fought at such great sacrifice to its people, to become independent of the French Empire, is now hopelessly entangled with the Soviet Empire. They are also bogged down in Cambodia and in an irretrievably lost war with their huge Chinese neighbors. If they had abided by the agreements, the Vietnamese might today be at peace and relatively prosperous. Instead, they continue to bleed and seem condemned to unending, irredeemable poverty.

As for the bombing campaign itself, the North Vietnamese showed its results to Kissinger, myself, and others who visited them in Hanoi shortly after the Paris agreements were signed. They were rather awed by the fact that our planes had, for example, destroyed the railroad workshops, but left unscathed the workers' dwellings, less than three hundred yards away. Their most grudging respect, however, was for what our Navy had done to the French embassy in Hanoi. A Navy divebomber, making a run at the Hanoi railroad terminal, had a "hung bomb" which had failed to release. As the pilot

The Indochina Peace Treaty 247

pulled up out of his dive, the bomb tumbled and destroyed the French embassy. Thach showed it to me and marvelled that the buildings on either side were untouched. He could appreciate the political subtlety of the gesture (which he refused to believe was an accident) and respect the professional precision of the pilot.

We, of course, had been mortified by the mistake. The French chargé in Hanoi at that time had been unabashedly anti-American, but there was patently no way in which we would have condoned his elimination by bombing. On the other hand, when our ambassador called on a senior French official to present our most abject apologies, the latter heard him out gravely and then said, "The building itself was a poor thing. It didn't do justice to the history of France in Indochina. But, there were some real losses. First, it contained a magnificent and irreplaceable Ming vase. Second, there was that lovely Egyptian girl from Alexandria who was the mistress of the chargé. And, then, of course, there was the chargé."

Chapter Nine

The Philippines
1973–1976

MY NOMINATION as ambassador to the Philippines in the spring of 1973 was not designed to mean a clean break with the tentacles of Vietnam. In fact, it was the intention that I should concurrently serve as the first American ambassador to Hanoi. After the Paris negotiations, my name had been informally proposed to the North Vietnamese and had been accepted. The concept had been based on the premise that the Paris agreements would be observed and that relations between Hanoi and Washington would be moved toward normalization. This would have meant the establishment of a small mission in Hanoi, to be permanently directed by a chargé. Because our Air Force had small executive jet transports located at Clark Field in the Philippines, I would be able quite literally to commute between Manila and Hanoi. In practice, however, it was presumed that I would spend a few days out of each month in Hanoi with my principal duties in Manila.

Due to the historical nature of the relations between the United States and the Philippines, those duties would be quite conspicuous. The Philippines had been the only colony of the United States, and Filipinos had been loyal allies of the Americans in the war against Japan. The transition from colony to commonwealth, and thence to independence, had left the United States with monumental buildings, a huge cemetery of war dead, a great many names on public places, and a very complex web of family, business, cultural, military, and political relationships to buttress our presence in the country.

All these features, as well as the interesting internal developments following the recent establishment of martial law by President Marcos, made the Manila assignment a fascinating one. However, I was not to obtain it without something of a struggle. By the spring of 1973, Nixon had been weakened by Watergate and his opponents took every opportunity to pounce on him. Senator Fulbright, the embittered chairman of the Senate Foreign Relations Committee, was among those in the forefront of the stiletto brigade. He decided to use his position to block a group of Nixon nominees from the constitutional "advice and consent" process in the Senate. I was one of those he chose to reject.

In the first instance, he used dilatory tactics, refusing to move my name to a committee vote even though my hearings had been completed. The effect of this, in my case, was nil, however, because I had been required to return to Paris for additional negotiatons with the Vietnamese even after my hearings had been held. By the time I returned from Paris, he shifted tactics to a more direct challenge. He waited until four members of the committee—two Democrats and two Republicans—were in Wuhan, China, before scheduling a snap vote on my name in the committee. He felt certain that, with those four absent, he could control enough votes to defeat my nomination.

When Sen. George Aiken of Vermont, who was the senior Republican on the committee, learned of this tactic, he was furious. He telephoned Secretary Rogers as soon as he learned of Fulbright's intention to say that the vote was scheduled for the next morning. He said that, if Rogers could arrange to get proxy votes from the four absent senators in my favor, it would be a great pleasure for him to vote them.

It was well before dawn in Peking, and our mission there had no private means of communicating with Wuhan. It would therefore be necessary for our people, on receipt of our urgent message, to get in touch with the Chinese authorities, have them convey the substance of the matter to their counterparts in Wuhan, and, through them, seek the four Senatorial proxy votes. The group was headed by Senators Humphrey and Javits, who could be counted on to swing the other two in my favor. Our message went out to China at about 6 p.m. Washington time. By 7:30 a.m. the next day, the duty officer called me to say that all four proxies had been received. We let Senator Aiken know before the committee met and he was happy to cast the favorable proxies. In the final tally, Fulbright had only two negative votes along with his own. It was a remarkable piece of assistance from the Chinese.

After I had been in Manila for a short time, it became apparent that the Vietnamese dimension of my duties would not materialize. The North Vietnamese were brazenly and systematically violating the Paris agreements as they had done with the Geneva agreement on Laos. As they came to sense how badly the Nixon administration was wounded by Watergate, they began to build up their military preparations for an all-out push to take over South Vietnam. In those circumstances, all thought of "normalizing" our relations with Hanoi through the establishment of an embassy evaporated.

However, the shadow of the Vietnamese war was never very far away from the Philippines. When our prisoners of war had been released, they came home through Clark Field. When we sent missions to Hanoi to attempt to arrest the deterioration, they went in by way of Clark. Much of the intelligence recording North Vietnamese aggression was confirmed through our military installations in the Philippines. We were keenly aware of the gathering catastrophe.

When, in 1975, the final assault was mounted from Hanoi, the Philippines was the first to feel the effects. The panicky evacuation of Americans from the path of the military onslaught was carried out in ships, planes, and helicopters that landed at American facilities in Philippine military bases. Indeed, as our officials arrived in Subic Bay aboard evacuation ships, they were then flown by helicopter literally into our front yard at the Embassy. We set up a processing center in our ballroom to document the evacuees in order to get an accurate count of those plucked from the chaos and to prepare them for onward transportation to their homes. We sheltered the ambassador and his immediate group at our home in Manila and, for a period of rest, at our summer place in the hills of Baguio. We accepted classified files, large sums of official cash, and all sorts of documents for safekeeping. We even, where necessary, provided clothing and other necessities to our temporary charges. All things considered, it was a remarkably efficient operation carried out without emotion or turmoil on the part of those involved.

On the first evening of this effort, after the last scheduled helicopter had arrived and its passengers had worked through our human assembly line, my deputy and I were standing on the terrace outside my office, watching the brilliant sunset over Manila Bay and discussing events of the hectic day. Suddenly, another large camouflaged helicopter loomed out of the sky and circled for an approach to our landing pad. Instead of making a normal landing, the big craft, which carried the insignia of the U.S. Marines, executed a "dust-off," with its nose in the air and its rotor blades turning, as a company of combat marines in full battle gear tumbled out its tail. We watched in astonishment as the big ship moved off again in the direction of Subic and the marines began to form up into a column of twos, their rifles at the ready. It appeared they were going to make a rapid march somewhere.

A telephone call to our embassy security officer succeeded in getting our own marine guard unit out in the garden to halt proceedings while we could ascertain intentions. A quick interview with the young captain commanding the company rapidly established the fact that he was going to march his troops out our front gate, down Roxas Boulevard to the port area, and out one of the piers where his transport ship was moored. His unit was the rear guard that had closed up the evacuation of the embassy in Saigon, and he was anxious to get his men back to their quarters. A little quiet explanation about Philippine sovereignty and the impropriety of forced marches on foreign boulevards convinced him to await other transportation. Our security officer soon procured a bus, and, with helmets in their laps and their rifles following in an Embassy station wagon, these slightly bewildered young men were returned to more familiar surroundings.

That incident, however, was the harbinger of more problems to follow. In the wake of the American evacuees came a flood of refugees. Almost as a matter of course, they headed for the U.S. installations. This presented both the Filipinos and ourselves with a dilemma. The Filipinos, worried now about a military power that seemed able to send the mighty American fighting force reeling back in defeat, were very cautious about appearing to offend Hanoi. Moreover, they did not want to end up with a horde of refugees on their hands. We, on the other hand, would require some time to prepare to receive this pitiful human flood in the United States. We therefore had to hold them for some period in the Philippine bases. The problem became compounded by the flat refusal of some jurisdictions, such as Hawaii, to have anything to do with the refugees, even on a temporary basis.

As this confusion endured, and as Washington was unable to come up with any concrete definition of our intentions, a certain degree of friction was introduced into relations between

The Philippines

our two countries. The Philippine press began to accuse us of disregarding their sovereignty over the bases and to suggest that we were using our military installations as "concentration camps." I had some sympathy for Filipino concern, but felt there was too much insistence on simple solutions and too little sympathy for the personal shock and suffering of the refugees themselves. I used the opportunity of a public speech to say so as gently as I could.

The occasion was the annual commemoration of the fall of Corregidor to the Japanese attacks in 1942. These rather solemn services had always been something of a Philippine-American family affair, with speeches marking the mutual sacrifice entailed and pledges towards undying friendship in the future. In 1974, President Marcos, after getting my agreement, invited the Japanese ambassador to join us in the ceremonies. This changed somewhat the tenor of the remarks, but preserved the general temper of peace. It was thus, in 1975, that I spoke about our common experience with the misery of defeat, and the need for compassion and a helping hand to those who had suffered the devastation of personal loss.

The speeches were delivered from a platform amid the ruins of the fortress of Corregidor and were carried on national television. The principal participants had travelled to the island by different means and we had had little opportunity to converse before we spoke. As we would all shortly leave in our own directions, I realized I would have to speak with Marcos there on the platform if there was any urgent matter I needed to raise. And, as of that morning, I did have an urgent problem.

The problem concerned the Vietnamese Navy. Although it was not large by world-class standards, it did consist of a fairly significant number of ships primarily designed to protect the long Vietnamese coastline against infiltration. Its major units were destroyer types and a half dozen former large weather station ships. All of these were of American origin, formerly used by our navy and coast guard. Smaller fleet units were minesweepers, patrol craft, and tenders. The whole lot of them, in the wake of the South Vietnamese defeat, were at that moment approaching the Philippines across the South China Sea. They were bulging, not only with their crews, but with the families of their crews, and, in some cases, with television sets, motorbikes, and refrigerators. Their destination was the U.S. naval facility in Subic Bay.

When I could detach President Marcos from others on the platform, I described this situation to him as quietly as I could and sought his reaction. As a very capable lawyer, with recent events at the bases very much in his mind, he pointed out that the provisions of our agreement permitted Subic to be used only by U.S. public vessels and that there was no sanction given to bringing Vietnamese naval units into the facility. He said he would have to stand by the terms of the agreement. I then told him that these ships had all previously been U.S. public vessels and that the terms of their transfer to Vietnam contained a clause specifying that their title would revert to the United States if they were no longer to be used for the purposes intended under the original transfer. This observation led to inquiries from Marcos about the possibility that title might subsequently be transferred to the Philippines. While such an eventuality was nothing I could promise, I assured him that there was a logical consistency to that outcome. After fifteen minutes of discussion we agreed that (a) all of the incoming vessels would be boarded on the high seas by U.S. naval officers, who would repossess them and run up the U.S. flag, so that they would have the character of U.S. public vessels when they entered Philippine territorial waters; (b) the crews and passengers would be a U.S. responsibility, and we would undertake to remove them from the Philippines; and (c) I would recommend to the U.S. government the transfer of most of the vessels to the Philippines.

On this basis, instructions soon went out to a small U.S. naval craft to stand out of Subic with a quota of junior officers and U.S. flags aboard, to rendezvous with the fleet in international waters, and to carry out the rest of the terms of our understanding. When I returned to the embassy to report all this to Washington, my deputy met me with great amusement. It seems that the instructions to the government-controlled television stations were to continue to run their telecast of the President so long as he was on the platform at Corregidor. And, hence, even after the speeches had finished, the nation's television screens had carried a live broadcast of their president and the American ambassador haggling over the terms of an agreement to permit the Vietnamese Navy to enter Subic Bay. Fortunately, the microphones had been cut off, and the viewing audience must have wondered with some interest what those two figures on the screen seemed to be hammering out with such intensity.

— 2 —

My relationship with Imelda Marcos was a rocky one. She insisted on being styled as the First Lady of the Philippines, and I could never bring myself to use that title. She resented this. Mrs. Marcos was an interesting woman, with a shrewd native intelligence, a certain physical charm, an earthy sense of humor, but a limited education. Because she was keenly aware of this last deficiency, she had a staff of young "experts" who could give her quick briefings on matters she was likely to encounter in her world travels. As they say in the theater, she was a "quick study" and could absorb this information rapidly, giving her the appearance of being informed on nearly everything.

In 1974, she undertook a major expedition to China. At that time, the Philippines still recognized the Republic of China on Taiwan, and most of the influential and wealthy Chinese community in the Philippines were refugees from the southern provinces of the mainland who had close ties with Taipei. Nevertheless, given the contacts the United States had already established with Peking, the Marcos government could see the trend of future events and believed Imelda's trip a prudent move.

Typically, however, Imelda managed to turn it into a dramatic performance. It was timed at a moment when the struggle between Mme. Chiang Ching with her "gang of four" and the forces led by Cho En-lai was reaching a climax. Unwittingly but inevitably, Imelda let herself be used by Chiang Ching. That formidable old schemer took over Imelda's trip lock, stock, and barrel and, "as one First Lady to another," became her sponsor at all events public and private. Naturally, this did not please Chou and his followers.

When Imelda returned, in what she regarded as triumph, she paused only briefly in Manila before flying on to her home province of Leyte. Her presence there was central to another of the great theatrical events around which she built her daily existence. She had to preside over the annual ceremonies marking the Allied landings on the beaches of that island in World War II, in fulfillment of MacArthur's promise that he would return to the Philippines. Those ceremonies always involved the participation of the American and Australian ambassadors, representing the Allies, as well as certain Philippine and American military units.

Since 1974 was the thirtieth anniversary of this event, a somewhat grander occasion than usual was planned. All the diplomatic corps was invited, some American and Australian veterans' groups were to be there, and I had arranged for the presence of a U.S. Navy landing ship with a contingent of marines, who would stage a mock landing while U.S. Air Force planes from Clark Field swooped overhead. It was certain to be a theatrical success.

In anticipation of all this, Imelda had constructed an elaborate stage setting for her role in the event. She had acquired a considerable stretch of beach-front land at the town of Olot, where she said she was born, and then built an "ancestral estate" there. This consisted of a large colonial-style house, with proper antique fixtures, a guest house, a swimming pool, a large coconut-log reception hall-cum-chapel and a number of bamboo and coconut wood cabanas all set among the palm trees. It was so new that the grass in front of the main house was literally painted green, but members of Imelda's entourage, with tongue in cheek, sententiously spoke of it as "The First Lady's birthplace."

It was here that she received the odd mixture of diplomats, senior government officials, and *demi-mondaine* jet-setters who always peopled her receptions. This affair was a catered luncheon for several hundred people, who swarmed over the Olot establishment in mild amazement at the stage set that had been created in a matter of a few months in this remote island in the center of the Philippine archipelago.

Imelda greeted me with rare warmth and asked if my wife and I could join her for a "private" lunch. This meant that we sat with her at a small table for four, joined by a Jesuit priest who was her confessor, while the huge polyglot swarm were seated at various tables at the "ancestral" home, the guest house, and in the reception hall. She began by conveying greetings to me from several people she had met in China, including a number of Chiang Ching's entourage whom I had encountered over the years in negotiations with China.

She then moved immediately into the urgent business at hand. She felt she owed it to the United States as an ally to prevent us from making a serious mistake as we pursued our new relations with China. She was disturbed to realize that we had misperceived the situation there and was pleased to offer her "Asian eyes" to set us on the right track.

She said that our actions indicated we thought Cho En-lai and "his small clique" would inherit power when Mao Tsetung died. She wanted us to know that Chou controlled only a few bureaucrats in Peking and that "all the rest of the country" was securely in the hands of Mme. Chiang Ching. She was acutely aware of this because she had travelled "all over China" outside of Peking in company with Chiang Ching and had personally seen the enormous enthusiastic support the First Lady of China enjoyed. There was no question that, when Mao died, she would be the new ruler of China. Imelda coyly said that she had established an excellent working relationship and personal friendship with Chiang Ching as "Asian woman to Asian woman" and that, because she thought it was important to the peace of the world, she would be glad "to serve as a bridge" between the U.S. Government and Mme. Chiang Ching. Anything she could do to ease that transition would be done discreetly, she assured me, and with full respect for the close ties between the United States and the Philippines.

I should probably have just thanked her very much for this kind and generous offer and said that I would relay it faithfully to my government. In that way, we could have gone on with our very pleasant meal and completed the afternoon ceremonies in good spirits. Instead, I guess the devil made me do an unchivalrous thing. I proceeded, in gentle tones, to tell Imelda that she, rather than we, had misperceived the situation in China. I characterized Chiang Ching as one in a long sequence of "left-lining deviants" from the mainstream of the communist party who, like Li-li-san and others before her, would be "wiped out." I predicted that she and her group would disappear within three months after Mao's death and that, therefore, we would continue to do our business with Chou En-lai.

Imelda heard me out painfully, and, finally, her chin trembling, she burst into tears and left the table. My wife chastised me for my brutality, and I was, indeed, duly abashed by the scene I had created. I urged the Jesuit to go quietly in pursuit of her and ask how I could make amends. He returned solemnly in a few minutes to say that she was recovering her composure and resting. He then offered as his personal view that she had interpreted my remarks in a very subjective context as indicative of the attitude the United States would take toward her if President Marcos should die in office. I assured the priest I had meant no such inference, but it was clear that the luncheon was over, our conversation had been a disaster, and it was only with great difficulty that Imelda could be persuaded to participate in the remaining ceremonies that after noon.

My relations with her never recovered from that luncheon. After that, our encounters were always polite but aloof. She obviously considered me unsympathetic to the aspirations of "Asian women." Nevertheless, two years later, when the 1976 Leyte landings events were scheduled, I was, as tradition demanded, still scheduled as the principal speaker and we were still Imelda's guests at the estate in Olot. In the meantime, a few weeks prior to the event, Mao Tse-tung had died, and, within one month (not three, as I had predicted), Chiang Ching and the Gang of Four had been arrested. Our assessment of her position in the power struggle had been affirmed.

I went to Leyte determined to avoid at all costs any mention of the developments in China. My wife, who had more sympathy and affection for Imelda than I, reinforced that determination by some very solid advice of her own. I was therefore somewhat relieved when I learned that luncheon arrangements were considerably less intimate than they had been two years before. Instead of lunching at the "ancestral," we were all to be fed in the huge reception hall. A large round table, set to accommodate about twenty-four, was the head table, and there I was seated on Imelda's right. It seemed an assured arrangement for jocular, generalized, and insubstantial conversation.

However, to my chagrin, my Australian colleague soon broke the spell. He leaned over and, in a loud voice that drowned all other conversation, asked Imelda what she thought about what had happened to her "mate" Chiang Ching. My instinct was to slide quietly out of sight under the table. But Imelda moved before my instinct could assert itself. She didn't even look at the Australian when she answered. Instead, she swung directly toward me and, in remarks she had obviously prepared in anticipation of anything I might have said on the subject, she made her views known. They were, in simple terms, that Chiang Ching had not moved quickly enough. When Mao died, she should have seized the center of attention and the role of authority. She should have placed herself in charge of the funeral and issued all instructions and invitations as the inheritor of her late husband's mantle. She should never, for instance, have permitted herself to be photographed as part of the official mourning group, occupying not the first, but the *fourth* place of honor. That, observed Imelda, was a very serious mistake.

No one at the table said a thing, presumably expecting me to reply to what sounded like a prepared, peremptory challenge. This time I had the good sense to change the subject, and cantered off trivially about the construction of the reception hall, with its abundant use of coconut product. Imelda apparently appreciated my gambit, since it gave her a chance to recite a small soliloquy on the many economic uses of the coconut, committed to her facile mind from some modest briefing paper and produced on this occasion before a genuinely appreciative audience. This was particularly true of those Philippine officials at the table who were aware that their President was not immortal and did not choose to dwell publicly on the probable manner of his succession.

Chapter Ten

The Iranian Revolution
1977–1979

THERE HAVE BEEN only three revolutions in my lifetime worth experiencing. The first, in China, was a long, rolling epic, involving enormous armies moving back and forth across a continental landscape. The second, in Cuba, was so short and sharp that it caught much of the world by surprise. The third, in Iran, took about a year to unfold. Although the industralized world watched it vicariously through the medium of television, I was among the few foreigners who had the opportunity to live through all its sights, sounds, smells, and emotions in an intimate way.

When I moved from the American ambassador's residence in Manila to its counterpart in Tehran, I was transported from a society with an impish sense of levity to one which took itself very seriously. The gentle, self-mocking smile of the average Filipino was replaced by the stern, rather dour frown of the Iranian. The male dominance of Iranian society, the drab clothes of its people, the dun color of its countryside, all contrasted sharply with the light, frivolous colors of the cities and the brilliant green of the forests and fields in Southeast Asia. There seemed to me to be a heavy, oppressive patina on Persian culture.

This sense was accentuated by the practices of the Shi'a religion. The only days that seemed to be commemorated were those observed for martyrs, and the most popular form of celebration was flagellation or a keening, lugubrious wail of prayer. The whole atmosphere, in comparison with the ebullient, spontaneous, and bubbling good humor we had known, even in the midst of war, was sullen and uncomfortable. The few westernized Persians who sought to recapture some of the lively spirit that characterized their nation's early history were a welcome exception to the general rule.

The Shah's Imperial Court was an even more leaden institution than the society it surveilled. The solemnity of its formal occasions, the intricate weight of gold braid on its members' uniforms, the massive, rather tasteless chambers in which it deployed its ceremonies were all part of the pattern. As the representative of a democracy, I was required to wear white tie and tails in command performances. The Italian ambassador, similarly condemned by his democratic origins, puckishly mocked his Persian hosts by acquiring an old naval uniform, complete with a fore and aft headpiece of the variety worn by Lord Nelson and, getting a tailor to adorn his chest and cuffs with as much gold braid as they would carry. Nobody seemed to share his whimsy.

Many observers of the Iranian revolution have characterized it as a religious upheaval and have suggested that it implied a renascence of Islam. While it is true that secular power in the country has passed from the monarchy to the religious

The Iranian Revolution

hierarchy, it cannot be inferred from this fact that religion alone was the inspiration for this political and social upheaval. It was, as most revolutions are, a complex event. The revolutionaries came from a broad range of social, political, economic, and regional groups. They each reflected their own particular grievances with the Pahlavi system and their own plans for change. For example, the old representatives of the dynasty displaced by the Shah's father and the old tribal chieftians whom he defeated in battle wanted an unrealistic return to a nostalgic past. The old landowners whose properties had been expropriated in the Pahlavi land reforms and distributed among their tenants wanted their villages back, despite the fact that most of them had become city-dwelling industrialists.

The more prominent leaders of the revolt had more realistic goals. Those best known to the western world were the members of the National Front. These men were primarily social democrats, who had achieved a brief hold on power during the ascendancy of Mohammed Mossadeq, the charismatic prime minister overthrown in 1953 with American and British assistance. They were largely educated in France or the United Kingdom, believed in the European parliamentary tradition, and were mostly middle-class professionals. Although they played a prominent role in the revolution against the Shah, they would have preferred an evolutionary process of change that prevented political power from slipping into the hands of the great unwashed mobs in the streets.

Those mobs, of course, had long been the center of interest and attention among the politicians of the left. Most prominent among these were the Moscow-trained and Moscow-controlled adherents to the Tudeh Party. Tudeh had been created by the Soviets in their zone of occupation of Iran during World War II and continued under Soviet domination in the period of parliamentary politics that came to an end in

1953. Tudeh, however, had never truly caught on in Iran because of its close identification in the popular mind with the Soviet—and, indeed, the Russian—tradition of aggression. Iran's northern neighbor had always been the country's most ruthless predator. This fact alone was enough to contaminate Tudeh and make it ineffective as an instrument of revolution among the urban proletariat.

A possibly more effective political unit on the left was the mujahadin, especially that element which took its inspiration from the writings of Ali Shariati. Shariati, writing in the 1960s, attempted to reconcile socialism with Islam, and thereby introduced the basic tenets of Marxist thought into a vernacular that would be acceptable to the urban poor. His works attracted many followers especially among the young intellectuals, and found particular favor among university youth who came to higher education from the lower income groups. Tehran University was an extraordinary center of influence for these young revolutionaries. However, there is no evidence that urban poor themselves had great sympathy with the ingenious efforts of Shariati. Although they accepted many of his slogans and a number of firebrand young leaders from among his followers, they did not seem to have any deep-seated attachment to his social and economic theories. In the aftermath of the revolution, the mujahadin were largely exterminated.

Finally, there were the religious leaders of Shi'a Islam. These ayatollahs, mullahs, and other members of Islam's only hierarchic *ulema*, had been largely discredited over the years. Many of them were personally corrupt, their lives were anything but exemplary, and their political ideas seemed archaic. Moreover, the Shah had for many years successfully manipulated them one against the other through a complex system of bribes, blackmail, and intrigue. Although they clamored for the Shah's overthrow and had organized terrorist groups

The Iranian Revolution 265

that used assassination as a political technique, no observers gave them very much chance for success. What made it possible for them to take the leadership in the revolution and ultimately to exploit it by eliminating all the other competitors was the nature of the urban proletariat to whom they addressed their appeals. These same uneducated and unsophisticated workers who rejected Marxism in either its Tudeh or mujahadin embodiment were prepared to accept fundamentalist Islam as expounded by the Ayatollah Khomeini. The reason for this phenomenon had largely to do with the rather unique nature of the proletariat in Iran's larger urban centers.

They were not a class or an institution of any antiquity. The members of the bazaar and of the urban service groups that had given cities such as Tehran, Shiraz, Tabriz, and Isfahan their flavor were small scale artisans, porters, and such who had long since learned to live with the class distinctions and other inconveniences associated with city life. However, in the 1960s and 1970s, with the new era of petroleum wealth, they were overwhelmed and outnumbered by a new group, which came into the cities from the more egalitarian countryside. These newcomers were the product of the Shah's impulsive drive for industrialization. By and large, they were the spillover of agrarian neglect, or, as some would say, of the Pahlavi land reforms. Those reforms were only in part motivated by enlightened concern for the serfs who were their nominal beneficiaries. Far more important to their inspiration was Pahlavi pique against the political resistance of the landowners, as typified by the obstreperous Mossadegh. Hence, the reforms took the land away from the landowners and transferred it to the peasants. But they did nothing to replace the services formerly supplied by the landowners in the way of irrigation, seeds, fertilizer, and credit.

My first visits to the Iranian countryside appalled me. I

had been used to primitive conditions in Southeast Asia and India, but I had never encountered anything quite as squalid as I found in the villages of Iran. The people lived in crude mud huts with crumbling walls, without sewage, paved streets, or sanitation. The old tunnel systems of irrigation, called *ghanats*, which were formerly maintained by the landlords, had been allowed to collapse. They had no electricity and scarcely any transportation.

When I told the Shah about the rural electrification programs on which I had spent most of our AID money in the Philippines and suggested to him that small turbo-generators could be installed in these villages, he reacted as if I were a retarded child. He leaned over and said, "Mr. Ambassador, don't you understand? I don't want those villages to survive. I want them to disappear. We can buy the food cheaper than they can produce it. I need the people from those villages in our industrial labor force. They must come into the cities and work in industry. Then we can send all those Afghans, and Pakistanis, and Koreans back home."

And come into the cities they did. In ever-increasing numbers. But no provisions had been made to accommodate them. They earned larger wages than they had ever anticipated. They learned new crafts and trades. But they never felt at home in an urban setting. All those western ways and all those obvious class distinctions disturbed them. They saw the luxury in which the urban elite lived, and although they envied it, it never occurred to them to seek to emulate it. They did not aspire to cosmopolitan wealth. Home to them was still their neglected villages where, more often than not, their families continued to live. They wanted to go back to their land and make it bloom.

They were people who had grown up in the rustic vernacular of Islam. Their daily lives were described in the verses of the Koran. Even if Tehran might teem with jet-set sophisticates in tight blue jeans, the proletarian terms of reference were much closer to those known by the Prophet Mohammed, or by Ali and Hossein. They felt there was something violently wrong with the system in which they had come to live, and they were prepared to resort to violence to make it right. They had been raised in a rural life style which placed great stress on the role of the mullah. His homilies had more influence in their thoughts than the slick syllogisms of Shariati or the crude alarums of the Tudeh.

For them the most appealing voice was that of Ayatollah Khomeini, who spoke in their dialect, and who captured their frustration. He had been a leader in the clerical opposition to the Shah in the 1960s and had been sent into exile. By the miscalculated manipulation of the Shah's own ministers, he had been moved from that exile to Paris, where he enjoyed a televised pulpit, and he began to broadcast regularly into Iran. It was his weekly sermon, regularly repeated in every Iranian mosque, that brought the mobs into the streets. They came in overwhelming numbers, on some occasions as many as two million in Tehran alone. They were surly, brutal, and persistent. There was nothing charismatic or attractive to the western eye in their demeanor as they marched along, shouting their slogans, clenching their fists, followed by their quiet, black-shrouded women, shuffling along in a sullen phalanx.

For this reason, it was very difficult for a foreigner who was present in Iran during the revolution to get caught up in its spirit. There were no romantic followers such as those of the Great March or adventurers such as those of the Sierra Madre among the outsiders who watched the eclipse of the Shah. My memories of the revolution do not have the piquant flavor of those earlier Foreign Service officers who lived with Mao in the caves of Yenan or of the journalists who picked their way through the rain forests with Castro. While I recall with considerable sympathy many conversations I had with members of the National Front and others in opposition to the Shah, the real force of the revolution was not any intellectual element, but rather the frenzied, mindless mobs who dominated the streets and eventually engulfed the nation.

I saw the revolution from two perspectives. The first vantage point was one shared with the country's elites, who were the first victims of the revolution's success. The second vantage point was one shared with those who took part in the uprising, but who ultimately suffered the same victimization.

To most people, of course, the elites began with the Pahlavi family, and with the Shah, who was its titular head. He was a man considerably different than the public myth attached to his name. Instead of being a harsh, vain, unreasonable tyrant as his liberal critics claimed, he was a rather timid, insecure, and indecisive man. His vanity was carefully cultivated by the sycophants who surrounded him, but he ruled by manipulative indirection rather than by blunt confrontation. He would, for example, deliberately place material and financial temptations within the reach of government officials in order to hook them into the occasion of a scandal. Then, he would let these officials know that their peculations were a matter of record, which he would suppress only so long as they were loyal to him. Such tactics did not breed endearment.

As the revolution confronted this man, I got to know him well, and met with him in a whole spectrum of circumstances. On large, formal occasions, resplendent in one of his gaudy uniforms, with his handsome Shabanou by his side, and surrounded by his courtiers, he could radiate imperial grandeur and magisterial charm in four or five different languages. In those surroundings, he looked equal to his myth as the master of his fate and to his title as the Shadow of the Almighty. However, sitting in a straight-backed chair in the small office of his private palace, running his fingers through his thinning hair, shrinking his neck down between his shoulders, and

The Iranian Revolution

looking vacantly off into space, he seemed once again the 21-year-old youth who had the weight of empire thrust upon him when his father was removed from the throne by the British and the Russians in 1941. As the revolution closed in on him, his initiative was paralyzed and his self-confidence dissipated.

Mostly, of course, I met him in his large official quarters with its ornate desk and sumptuous furnishings. There, he liked to rehearse his admirable knowledge of world affairs for visitors and display his impressive technical comprehension of scientific, military, and industrial developments. It was his best pose, the posture of an enlightened statesman, and the one which most official visitors carried away with them. But I recall him also, in beach clothes, in a small study at his island home in Kish, sitting with half a dozen dogs ranging from a small black poodle to a Great Dane. And I remember how he laughed when all the dogs heard the Shabanou's footsteps on the stairs and raced to greet her. The Great Dane, whom the Shah had been stroking, put one foot on my lap and bounded over my head in order to be the first out the door. As soon as the Shah realized the laugh might have been offensive, he put one hand over his mouth like a teenager and apologized. Not exactly the sort of gesture one would expect from the Light of the Aryans.

In short, he was a complex man whose private humanity belied the stern, rigid public figure he affected. It is, I suppose, hard to reconcile the fact of this somewhat tender, insecure, but intelligent private person with the starchy monarch whose secret police killed, tortured, and brutalized his subjects. But, when the revolution came, it was the former character that asserted itself and shied away from the use of military force to confront his subjects in the streets. This was something that President Carter and his adviser, Zbignieu Brzezinski, who had known only the refulgent imperial image of the man, could not understand. Carter, who had so much invested in the appearance of his concern for human rights, would never officially convey the suggestion that military force be used, no matter how desperately he might have wished that consummation. Brzezinski, with less concern for the potential charges of hypocrisy, could never believe that the Shah would reject such an option.

The others among the elite were equally torn by the nature of their characters. Many of those who were closest to the Shah in terms of political power were among that group which had succumbed to the temptation of financial corruption and resented the hold of blackmail that the Shah exercised over them. Their zeal to support him and his system was mitigated by the care with which they sequestered their funds in Switzerland, or London, or New York, and bought "summer houses" on the Riviera. Their willingness to sacrifice their well-being for the defense of the Pahlavi dynasty was limited.

This same attitude extended to many of the senior military, who hedged against the success of the revolution either by establishing clandestine contact with "the other side" or by sending their families and their liquid funds abroad. In the business community, it was even more common, although perhaps more comprehensible. By the time the full force of the revolution gathered for the final blow, very few of the Shah's "supporters" were visible in the capital.

And, then, of course, there was the "old regime," the Qajars, descended from the dynasty the Shah's father had overthrown. They could hardly contain their glee as they watched the Shah beset by the forces of violence. For them, he and his family had always been upstarts, unworthy of the Peacock Throne. It was useless to try to reason with them about the chaos which would follow in the wake of the Shah's defeat. I tried in vain to understand the logic that impelled my social secretary, who came from one of the "old families," to sup-

The Iranian Revolution

port the revolution. She was a liberated woman, educated in England, who liked the modern, westernized society and realized that after the victory of the mob she despised, she would be forced to wear the traditional shroudlike garmet called the chador. Nevertheless, she was passionately convinced that the Shah should be toppled.

And so it came about, with only limited resistance and nowhere near the hundreds of thousands of casualties now claimed by the victorious mullahs. Iran was, as De Gaulle said of Vietnam, "un pays pourri"—a rotten country—that fell apart.

My acquaintance with those who made the revolution was less extensive than it was with those who lost it. However, I did know a number of the intellectuals who played an active role in the opposition to the Shah. Most of them were French-educated professionals in the law or medicine, who considered themselves mildly socialist and who were loosely grouped in the National Front. Only a few of them had any direct association with the religious leaders or groups who were the militant activists. Those who did, such as Mehdi Bazargan, Amir Abbas Entezam, and Nasser Minatchi, called their organization the Liberation Movement. They, and others such as former Prime Minister Ali Amini, conformed to the general western conception of a loyal political opposition. They wished to change the regime radically and to convert it into a parliamentary democracy, but they didn't necessarily wish to overthrow the monarchy in a violent revolution. Because they were forced by the regime's paranoia to operate in a clandestine mode, they were often, nevertheless, perceived as revolutionaries.

The real protagonists of the revolution, and, ultimately, the real wielders of political power in Iran, were the street mobs. These mobs were made up of angry young men who resented the system, not for any political or ideological reasons, but simply because they were frustrated by it. Their anger was always voluble and often violent. It was a habit that seemed to be with them instinctively. I first felt it in the streets of Tehran shortly after we arrived there. Much to the annoyance of my security people, I tried to walk on the crowded sidewalks in the more interesting parts of town just to get a feel for the pulse of the capital. It usually proved a thoroughly negative experience. The jostling that occurred as I tried to walk among pedestrians was more often than not accompanied by bad humor and malevolence. Young men deliberately elbowed or shoved as part of their method of walking. They particularly seemed to resent women in their way and usually edged them perilously close to the *jubes,* or open sewers that bordered every Tehran sidewalk.

At first, I thought this rudeness might have been directed only at me as a foreigner or at women who wore western dress. But, in observing the patterns of pedestrian mores from an automobile, I could see that it was more universal. Iranian men in more traditional clothes and women in chadors received the same treatment. There was some inner fury in these men that appeared to need physical release.

There was, for example, an occasion when we were skiing in the mountains above Tehran. A German woman, who had been patiently waiting for a tow bar lift, was just about to reach for it when a young Iranian cut in front of her and beat her arm away. She resisted and he also missed his grab for the bar. He thereupon turned and raised his arm to beat her. Fortunately, she was accompanied by her strapping teenaged son, who stepped around her and dropped the molester with one good stiff punch to the jaw. The young Iranian then picked himself up and scuttled off, shouting curses.

Another time, we were on an official visit to Isfahan and had been put up at the opulent Shah Abbas Tourist hotel. The swimming pool had a small snack bar, and we decided to have lunch there. However, my wife was delayed in arriving

The Iranian Revolution 273

at poolside because she was making some telephone calls in the room. When she came down, I was already eating, and so she approached the man at the bar to order. He refused to take her order even though he was not closed for business. When I saw what was going on, I left my table and went to help place the order. The attendant came around the bar yelling at the top of his voice and wielding a knife. One of my police bodyguards intervened, and a shouting and scuffling match ensued. When it was all over, the man closed his snack bar and left, but apparently was not arrested. I never could discover whether his outrage had been touched off by the fact that my wife was dressed in a bathing suit, or whether some other violence just erupted within him.

After observing these incidents for some months, I concluded that most of these angry young men were suffering from traumatic frustration. They were, for the most part, country and village people, who had come into the big city partly because the Shah's policies had deliberately dried up any promise in agriculture and partly because of the large wages being offered in urban industry. However, even though they were earning more than they could ever have expected in the villages, they were not content. Everything in the cities cost so much more than they had anticipated. Even though they saw large luxury apartments standing empty, they ended up crowded into dark rooms in the city slums. They watched the heavy limousines glide through the streets and saw women dressed opulently in western clothes shopping in boutiques and acting as if they were equal to men. They were ready for revolt, any kind of revolt.

They were the ones who made up the mob in the fall and winter of 1978. They roared through the streets, throwing bricks, breaking windows with stones, beating automobiles with iron bars, and spreading arson in their wake. They probably would have rioted against anyone or any organization that seemed to represent authority. But, since the Shah apparently represented the whole system and since they blamed the system, rather than themselves, for their inadequacies, he became their target. When the Ayatollah Khomeini came to lead them, they found an articulation for their hatred. And when our president and his national security advisor sought to confront and defeat the Ayatollah, he turned their fury against us.

On February 14, 1979, after the Shah had left and after the revolution had succeeded, but while Washington was still refusing to accept it, part of the mob attacked our embassy compound. It was a well-coordinated action, with machine guns and automatic weapons mounted on all the tall buildings surrounding our three story chancery and my three story residence. It was a murderous barrage, lasting about three hours, and culminating when all one hundred of us Americans had been captured. Miraculously, no Americans were killed, and most injuries were superficial. Moreover, at the end of the assault, we were rescued from our attackers by a mujahadin force sent by Mehdi Bazargan and his new government.

I had experienced physical fear many times before, but always in the secure conviction that I would survive the immediate danger. That convinction always gave me the courage to face the risks, make logical decisions, and prevail over the chaos that accompanies violence. In this instance, however, I came to the conclusion, after the first hour of the incessant barrage, that I would not survive. I considered this prospect while crouched under a table, delivering random commands into a walkie-talkie radio and hearing the rounds thudding into the wall above my head. I did a quick balance of my life, decided that it had been satisfactory, that my widow and children would be quite well placed, and that it would be a relatively timely end. This set of conclusions gave me a relatively equable perspective on our immediate circumstances, and made

The Iranian Revolution

it possible for me to go about the business of saving peoples' lives with a rather detached sense of good humor towards all involved in the trauma. It was almost as if I were a disinterested outsider.

It may have been this mood which caused me, after our rescue, to make an unorthodox decision about our immediate future. I had long since realized that the embassy compound was indefensible, but had not realized what a tempting target it must have been to the recently armed revolutionaries, if they could squat safely on top of apartment buildings and shoot at us like fish in a barrel. I therefore decided I wanted some Iranians inside our compound to mitigate our danger. Consequently, I asked Foreign Minister Yazdi, who headed the rescue effort, to provide us with eighty guards, forty of whom would be stationed inside our compound, in contravention of all normal diplomatic practice. Not only would they act as a deterrent to a recurrent shooting, but they might also serve as a reassurance to suspicious revolutionaries that we were not engaged in some nefarious practices. It was with the assignment of these people that I got a better look at those who had toppled the Shah.

They came in different packages. One small unit of about twelve was assigned by Yazdi as my personal bodyguard and detailed to protect my residence. It consisted of university graduates, most of whom spoke English and had traveled abroad. Several had close relatives in the United States. They were members of a left-wing mujahadin, but proclaimed a vigorous religious fervor. Their leader, a young man who had recently returned from the United States, said his ritual prayers with great ostentation. He was a dedicated follower of Ayatollah Khomeini.

This group set up a command post in a small cloak room off the main foyer in my residence. The room was equipped with a telephone and had lavatories and toilets. It had previously been used as a guard post for U.S. Marines during my predecessor's tenure. In its new capacity, it served as a place for the young men to meet for endless political discussions, to organize their defense of the residence against the nightly hit-and-run raids that came from the streets; and, eventually, to conduct a shakedown business against departing Iranians.

This last entrepreneurial pursuit, which ultimately landed most of this group in the Ayatollah's jails, came about because of an extension of the group's activities into the supervision of outgoing air freight. This function developed as we sought some way to ship out the household possessions of our departing staff without subjecting them to pilferage. For some informal considerations, we engaged the group to "ride shotgun" on our shipments from the embassy compound to the airport and through the mujahadin guards that controlled airport departures. This soon led them to a share in airport departure controls, and, in due course, to a shakedown racket in which they "rescued" a number of expensive carpets from departing baggage and reclaimed them as "national treasures." In traditional Persian fashion, they appointed themselves as the custodians of these treasures. When some of their rivals in this business denounced them, after my departure, most of them were arrested.

I met from time to time with the leader of this "bodyguard" group and discussed his political observations. Although he pretended a deep piety, it was hard for me to assess its sincerity. Some of our younger Farsi-speaking officers who spent more time with the group gave them somewhat more credit as genuine political moralists. If so, it appears that their morality did not extend to business ethics.

The other group assigned to our compound was of different origin. It also called itself mujahadin, but made no pretense to the political sophistication of my bodyguard unit. It was the nucleus of our rescue force and was headed by a huge, hairy butcher named Marshallah, who was armed to the teeth and who occasionally administered discipline to his unit through a sharp cuff to a young man's head. This group had a somewhat vague relationship with Ayatollah Taleghani, who was an associate of Khomeini but considerably more enlightened.

By agreement with Yazdi, we gave this group primary responsibility for protecting the perimeter of our compound and access to the chancery. They functioned under the general supervision of our military attaché, who developed a close working relationship with them. They also developed a close interest in the warehouse we maintained on the compound to stock our commissary and convenience store. This warehouse contained a large supply of liquor, as well as luxury items such as watches, television sets, and cameras. It was a temptation our protectors could not resist.

For this group, ideology was secondary to personal relationships. In due course, whatever their original attitudes towards Americans had been, these young men came to identify with us. They developed friendships with our marines, with some of our employees, and great respect for our military attaché. I became "their" ambassador. Hence, when I went out to travel around the city, they accompanied me in "chase cars" just as the Iranian police bodyguards used to do. I recall one Saturday when I went for brunch at the residence of my Dutch colleague and arrived accompanied by two carloads of these bearded, thuggish-looking characters armed with G-3 rifles and strung with bandoliers. They swarmed over the compound and took up guard positions in strategic points, their weapons pointed at nearby apartments.

This scene sent something of a shiver through the other guests, all of whom were ambassadors and their wives. When I finally assured them that the group was friendly, their curiosity got the better of them, and the day finished with photo sessions, in which the fashionably dressed diplomatic ladies posed with the guerrilleros for the albums of their future progeny.

But, this group also came to a sad end. Their pilferage from our warehouse engaged them in black marketeering and conflicts with local *komitehs* of the revolution. Their identification with Americans led them to sharp anti-Soviet positions, which eventually resulted in a raid conducted personally by Marshallah in which he arrested a Soviet KGB representative meeting with a senior member of the revolutionary leadership. Although the Soviet was expelled and the leader arrested, this action sowed the seeds for Marshallah's own arrest and his incarceration in the infamous Evin prison.

This sort of behavior and the constant friction between the two guard units eventually led to a decision taken in Washington long after my departure to have the guards withdrawn from the embassy compound. I was, by that time, out of the government and cannot assess the wisdom of that move. I have, however, often wondered whether our people would have been taken as hostages had some tolerable Iranian presence still been there on November 4, 1979.

I was no longer there at that time because the Carter administration and I had come to a parting of the ways. I had recommended that we accept the fact that a revolution was in progress and seek to use our not inconsiderable influence to steer its success toward its more moderate protagonists. Washington chose instead to confront the revolution head on, banking on the assumption that an armed force of 400,000 men equipped with the world's latest weaponry could crush an unarmed mob in the streets and restore discipline to a nation so badly vent.

It was a decision and a policy so alien to the experience of my past forty years that I rebelled against it, and eventually resigned. When I did, I was among the last and among the

The Iranian Revolution

most senior of our shrinking cohort of centurions. Secretary of State Cyrus Vance, who was indeed our most senior, did not last much longer. Now, just about all of us have left the public service.

For most of us, the period from 1939 to 1979 was a time of turmoil, but also a time of many satisfactions. The Chinese have an ancient curse: "May you live in interesting times." We lived in interesting times, and most of us did not feel accursed. I think we left a better world than we found. But that is for the historians to say.